P9-CJW-202

DATE DUE

DE 6 '91	DE 19 '08		
JA 8 '93			
JE 11 '93			
JY 2 '93			
MY 13 '94			
DE 22 '95			
AP 19 '96			
MY 10 '96			
RENEW			
JY 15 '96			
DE 17 '96			
JY 17 '97			
MR 12 '98			
AP 20 '99			
NV 13 '99			

DEMCO 38-296

THE COMPLETE
WORK-AT-HOME
COMPANION

HOW TO ORDER:

Quantity discounts are available from the publisher, Prima Publishing & Communications, P.O. Box 1260WH, Rocklin, CA 95677; telephone (916) 624-5718. On your letterhead include information concerning the intended use of the books and the number of books you wish to purchase.

U.S. Bookstores and Libraries: Please submit all orders to St. Martin's Press, 175 Fifth Avenue, New York, NY 10010; telephone (212) 674-5151.

THE

COMPLETE

WORK-AT-HOME

COMPANION

Herman Holtz

Prima Publishing & Communications
P.O. Box 1260WH
Rocklin, CA 95677
(916) 624-5718

Editing by Victoria Nelson
Typography by TBH/Typecast
Production by Rosaleen Bertolino, Bookman Productions
Jacket Design by The Dunlavey Studio

Prima Publishing & Communications
Rocklin, CA

Library of Congress Cataloging-in-Publication Data

Holtz, Herman.
    The complete work-at-home companion / Herman Holtz.
      p. cm.
    Includes bibliographical references and index.
    ISBN 1-55958-010-0
    1. Home-based businesses. I. Title.
HD2333.H65 1990   89-10849
658'.041--dc20   CIP

90 91 92 93 RRD 10 9 8 7 6 5 4 3 2 1

Printed in the United States of America

PREFACE

The editors of *U.S. News & World Report* reported, "All of a sudden, it's becoming, well, fashionable."* They are talking about an office in your home. They and many others suddenly appear to have discovered (where have they been?) that many people find it more comfortable to work at home than to make the daily trek to a distant office, weaving their way across miles of traffic jams, overturned tractor-trailers, major and minor fender-benders, and irate fellow motorists goaded by the frustrations and irritation of early morning traffic into risky and infuriating highway gymnastics.

Perhaps they also hate the obligatory lunches in pricy restaurants, the office bores and cretins, the inevitable and maddening bureaucratic absurdities that exist in most large organizations, and other assaults on their human dignity, not to mention the need to feel useful and have a sense of achievement and career growth. In any case, the articles—there are several, counting the sidebar stories—note the growing popularity of offices at home, which, they estimate, number 14 million, counting both part-time and full-time ventures and employment in home offices. (They find this an 18 percent increase over the previous year, 1987.) In short, there appears to be an increasing number of individuals who have, in what is probably characteristic of the American society and our traditions, a burning desire to be free and independent in more than an abstract political sense.

Peter H. Lewis, writing in the *New York Times,*† quotes research firm Link Resources as stating that about 9.5 million of the home workers are self-employed and about 15.5 million who work at home are employees of others. On the other hand, Barbara Brabec, publisher of *National Home Business Report*, estimates 13 million full-time home-based businesses in the United States, and an additional 14 million part-time entrepreneurs and corporate employees working at home.

---

* "Your Home, the Office," September 26, 1988.
† "Electronic Cottages Take Root," October 16, 1988.

Nor are *U.S. News & World Report* and the *New York Times*
the only publishers to take note of this trend. *Home Office Computing*,* which took note of what was happening by shortening
its name from the original *Family & Home Office Computing*,
listed current books and periodicals bearing directly and
indirectly on the subject. Moreover, these sources cite others,
such as the regular "Office at Home" section of the trade journal
Consumer Electronics Monthly, as further evidence of the
growing importance of home-based business as a significant
market segment. The movement has also been noted by many
other writers. Articles on the office at home, especially when it
is the office of a home-based entrepreneur, have also appeared
in *PC Computing, Family Circle,* the *New York Times,* the
Washington Post, and many other publications.

There is also the *Working from Home Forum* of CompuServe,
a general-interest database to which computer owners may subscribe, and a growing number of periodicals, including *Home
Business News, National Home Business Report,* and *The
Worksteader News,* have sprung up to serve the information
needs of these home workers.

A related phenomenon is the inevitable development of
associations of homeworkers, including American Home Business Association, Mothers' Home Business Network, National
Association of Home Businesses, and National Association for
the Self-Employed.

Another barometer indicating the trend is the increasing
focus of many advertisers of computers and other office equipment, fixtures, furniture, and supplies, whose advertisements
are increasingly addressed to the home office market. Some
even publish special catalogs, such as a recent one bearing
the title *Crutchfield Personal Office,* featuring computers, FAX
machines, and a variety of other office equipment and related
supplies. And, unlike most catalogs, this relatively slender publication does more than list and describe items for sale. Many
of the item descriptions are quite lengthy, obviously intended to
help the individual choose wisely, but the catalog also contains

* "Upfront," September 1988.

detailed narrative information on certain subjects obviously addressed to the individual, such as how to upgrade an older computer and what one ought to know about copiers and FAX machines. Moreover, the home office focus is emphasized in many pages generously illustrated by color photos of individuals working in their home offices with equipment presumably bought from Crutchfield.

The desktop computer is obviously partly responsible for, and has played a key part in, the surge of home-based offices from which professionals, consultants, craft workers, and entrepreneurs of many kinds telecommute to their jobs daily or operate their independent ventures. But, contrary to many predictions of only a few years ago—notably that of futurist Alvin Toffler (*Future Shock* and *The Third Wave*)—and despite the impressively large numbers of people now working in their homes, at this time the majority of workers employed by others spend their business days on the employer's premises, although admittedly this situation appears to be changing, at least for those kinds of work that can reasonably be done in one's home. A significant movement is taking place in the latter direction, although there also appears to be an even more rapid increase in the numbers of self-employed—that is, those whose offices at home are the headquarters of independent business ventures.

The computer, in effect, conferred on the small business entrepreneur and beginning professional a great deal more business self-sufficiency than was ever before possible. The desktop computer has thus functioned as a leveler in the business world: As one of the editors cited earlier pointed out, the smallest business today enjoys some of the advantages that were formerly available to only the larger organizations, such as computer capabilities for automated mailing, accounting, inventory control, and many other important business functions. And quite possibly the desktop computer or, more likely, its almost immediate success on perhaps an unprecedented scale, inspired other developments, such as the rapidly developing desktop publishing software and hardware technologies. And the latest success story, almost paralleling that of the desktop computer, is the breathtakingly swift acceptance and growth of the FAX—facsimile machines—for rapid and convenient communication: We now expect to see a FAX number on all business cards and advertising.

Many factors, including some already noted, have inspired and encouraged the movement to home-based offices and ventures: high rents in office buildings, daily business luncheons in expensive restaurants, and other burdens of doing business in downtown business districts such as parking, insurance, utilities, and other costs. But it is also partly due to the sheer desire to avoid that daily deadly struggle to reach the downtown office. For many beginning professionals and small business owners, basing their ventures at home is the only practicable way to get started. (And many prefer never to outgrow their at-home facilities.)

This new trend has inspired the development of a special segment of office suppliers, furniture manufacturers, and other industrialists designed especially to accommodate the needs of those with offices and related facilities in their homes. Many such suppliers have created special divisions to serve the needs of work-at-home entrepreneurs.

Of course, the pages that follow will be about far more than an office at home per se; they will be about all the elements of establishing a venture at home—the technical, physical, moral, psychological, legal, and business considerations, with all the pros and cons, and with suggestions for turning those cons into pros or, at least, solving and neutralizing the problems.

—Herman Holtz

CONTENTS

PART ONE

Is HOME-BASING YOUR WORK A PRACTICABLE IDEA FOR YOU?

Working at home is not a new idea. It was the dominant industrial method of an age past, reaching its peak as an industrial and economic factor in the era of cottage industries. Minor vestiges survived into the twentieth century, however. During the Great Depression of the thirties, many who could not find steady employment worked at home. One revival of the cottage industries was in the garment industry, as workers brought home piece work from the factories and the whole family pitched in to turning belts and ties, pinning and folding shirts, and doing many other low-skill, labor intensive chores of the garment industry. And many skilled seamstresses and tailors who had sewing machines at home did more important tasks, also on a piece work basis. Much of this practice was later outlawed because it involved child labor and unfair labor practices, for some manufacturers took advantage of desperate economic conditions and exploited home workers mercilessly. More recently, with such exploitation increasingly rare and with much of the cottage industry consisting of independent business ventures run by entrepreneurs, many of these laws have been moderated and even repealed as unsuited to the conditions of today.

Recent years have brought a renaissance of the office/business at home and of the home-based employees, due at least partly to the rapidly changing nature of our economy from that of a major industrial nation, producing an abundance of the world's goods, to that of a nation deeply engaged in information- and service-related activities. Many credit this movement to technology, particularly to the emergence of the inexpensive desktop computer now available to truly small business. ("Small" is a relative term, of course, and by "truly small," I deliberately exclude the $8–10 million, 500-employee organizations that are defined as small business by the U.S. Small Business Administration.) More recently, the FAX machine has had a major impact in influencing the migration to at-home offices.

There are two aspects to the office at home: independent small business ventures based in the home and home-based employees of organizations. There are situations as well in which the individual is not truly an independent entrepreneur nor yet an employee. (Today the IRS takes the position that an "independent consultant" is not truly independent if he or she is retained exclusively by a single client but is actually an employee of that client, a somewhat analogous situation.)

Despite the abundance of jobs and generally prosperous economic conditions that have prevailed during most of the years since the end of the Second World War, piece work, working at home, and home-based ventures, both part- and full-time, have never disappeared completely. The entrepreneurial spirit and the tradition of free enterprise in America still persist and are virtually unquenchable. Many observers of this sudden growth in offices at home—in both home-based businesses and in home-based employees of business organizations—tend to treat this recent trend as a new development. But there are ample historic antecedents in certain types of enterprise that have long been practiced as home-based ventures. One of the oldest and most popular such businesses is the mail-order and direct-mail businesses. It is estimated that some 2 million individuals enter that field each year, although figures on the survival rate—a low one, admittedly—are not readily available. And many insurance agents, brokers of various kinds, manufacturer's representatives, public accountants, freelance writers, artists, craft workers, newsletter publishers, consultants, lawyers, and other professionals and paraprofessionals have long found it easy and convenient to work at home because their businesses are essentially one-person enterprises.

How practicable is it for you to work at home—that is, to shift your center of income-producing work, whether you are salaried or self-employed—to your own home? Will it work for you? (It does not work for everybody.) *Should* you work at home—or even consider it? (Certainly, you should consider it—honestly and objectively.) Are you well suited to working at home? (Not everyone is.) Or, if you are an employer, how practicable is it for you to send your employees home to work? Can you control them? Assure yourself of getting a fair day's work each day? Comply with all laws?

There are a lot of questions to answer, and the answers do not come easily. We'll begin to explore those questions in Part 1, for that is one basic purpose of this book—to help you identify and answer the right questions so that you can make the right decisions. A bit later, we will probe more deeply into this question of home-basing an independent business venture. First, though, let us address the more difficult question of working at home as a full-fledged employee of some organization. That is a new trend and is still largely in a somewhat cautious, experimental stage.

Chapter One

Work-at-Home Employment

The idea that a great many employers will soon be sending their employees home to work has been gaining some currency, with mounting evidence that it is coming to pass, to at least some extent. But to what extent?

TELECOMMUTING

Until recently, working at home usually meant working in an independent venture of some sort or, at the least, as an independent contractor or broker—that is, being paid fees, commissions, or piece rates rather than a regular wage or salary. To some extent, the personal computer, probably more accurately referred to now as a *desktop computer*, has changed this definition. A new trend, one that appears to be gaining strength almost daily, is growing out of the immense popularity of desktop computers and related activities: An increasing number of employers now have regular salaried employees working in their homes, usually in touch with their employers' offices by telephone and modem (computer-to-computer) connection and, more recently, increasingly via FAX (facsimile) machines. This new way of working has come to be called *telecommuting*.

What Is Needed to Telecommute

The "language" a computer speaks is a primitive one, expressed as a stream of electrical impulses. The telephone is a voice device designed to respond to audible signals. For one computer to "talk" to another via dial-up telephone lines, it must "speak" in audible tones. That's the job of the modem, to convert the inaudible impulses that represent the information into audible signals that can be carried over the telephone lines and then to reconvert those audible signals to the pulses the computer can understand. So a modem is required at each end, and this modem must be able to do both conversions: sending and receiving information.

The computer, with its modem, does not represent the only way to telecommute. FAX machines are proliferating with amazing speed, sending data back and forth between more and more offices every day. A FAX machine is considerably simpler to operate than a computer and modem (although the FAX does have a modem of its own), and you need only give it something printed on paper to scan and transmit. It converts the printed information to signals that it sends over a telephone line to another FAX at the other end, which reconverts the signal to a printed image. A full FAX machine is a standalone unit that needs nothing but a telephone connection and has nothing to do with a computer. It is possible, however, to install a device known as a *FAX board* in a computer, permitting the computer to act as its own FAX machine, but with somewhat different characteristics and, in some respects, more limited capabilities. (More details about this device will appear later.) These two communications devices, particularly the computer and modem, are basic to the rationale and justification for establishment of work-at-home employees.

The Pros and Cons of Telecommuting

Telecommuting sounds like an attractive proposition for both the employee and the employer. The employee has the advantage of working in the comfort of his or her own home, avoiding the time, expense, stress, and a number of other disadvantages of daily commuting and working in an office with a large number of others. The employer benefits by being spared a great deal of expense—rent, furniture, fixtures, and other business costs—because he or she does not have to furnish nearly as much in the way of facilities. The employee can work a full day and yet set his or her own hours, within limits, allowing a little time and opportunity to look after personal needs, such as seeing the kids off to school and being there when they get home, or even driving them back and forth to and from school. The employer, competing with others for employees in this time of severe labor shortages, gets a full-time employee whom he could not have gotten otherwise.

Of course, there is a downside, too, for both. (Is there not always?) Working at home is lonely. Many people need to be in the company of others and thus have great difficulty in working alone. Home conditions are not always conducive to work: A household with small children, for example, can be a most difficult work environment even for a worker with a spouse or someone else to look after the children during the day. And of course it is often especially difficult for a single mother with small children to work at home.

There is the problem of self-discipline, too. Not everyone is able to discipline him- or herself to work energetically and conscientiously at home, as he or she would in an office on the employer's premises. To work at home, alone, one must be able to resist the temptations to distraction, which are many—a TV show, a magazine article, and a personal telephone call or two, to name just a few common items that try to lure one from the desk.

There are the problems of labor laws and other legal implications: Do OSHA—occupational safety and health—laws apply? If so, is the condition of the workplace the employer's problem or the employee's problem when the employee works at home? If someone is injured while visiting the employee in his or her office at home, is the employer or the employee liable?

There is the matter of insurance. Can or should the employer pay for insurance to cover the employee working at home? And not just health and hospital coverage, but also life insurance and liability coverage that covers possible liability for mishaps in the workplace?

There is the matter of organized labor. How do labor unions feel about their members being assigned to work in their own homes? Does this somehow interfere with their rights as unions of organized labor? Does it make the role of a minor union official known as a "shop steward" insignificant and unnecessary? And does it affect how employees feel about belonging to labor unions—that is, does it tend to discourage joining a union and paying dues, a tendency that would ensure the union's hostility to the idea of so decentralizing employees, as might other considerations also?

And there is, of course, the matter of the employer's control of the employee. How can the employer feel assured of getting a full and honest day's work for the employee working at home, unobserved? How can he or she control the number of hours worked and charged? Paid time off? The validity of claimed illness? Of claimed overtime?

Obviously, many questions need to be answered, many changes in attitudes and laws will have to change before salaried people will be working at home on anything approaching a grand scale, and that may never come to pass. Some kinds of work and kinds of conditions lend themselves to the idea of telecommuting, and some do not at all.

A FEW EXAMPLES

Among companies cited as examples of those who have hired people to work at home or sent employees home to work are J. C. Penney, Control Data Corporation, Blue Shield, American Express, McDonald's, Prudential Insurance, Amtrak, Pacific Bell, U.S. West, and IBM. Metropolitan Life of New York occasionally authorizes individual employees to work at home, although the company does not have an organized work-at-home program and will not permit an employee to work permanently on this basis.

The California state government initiated a pilot program in working at home as a possible approach to reducing physical commuting and thus combating traffic congestion and air pollution while conserving energy. Reportedly, about fourteen California state agencies and some 300 employees are currently in the program.

A 1988 survey by LINK Resources Corporation, a marketing research firm in New York, reported 15.4 million corporate employees working at home at least some part of the work week, and estimated an 8.5 percent increase in home-based workers over the year 1987–1988.

Among the benefits to employers are the incentives telecommuting offers individuals. This may prove an increasingly important benefit in a time of severe labor shortages in many occupations. Travel to downtown offices or to any location requiring physical commuting is becoming more and more distasteful. Avoiding that, plus the benefits of flextime inherent in working at home and the boon of being judged purely on results—productivity—instead of the appearance of busyness and hours expended is a great incentive for many workers today. (Of course, managers and supervisors are now being compelled to devise means for judging employees on this basis.)

Some of the companies cited have made a commitment to having some employees working at home on a regular basis, and others have pilot programs or are experimenting gingerly. Not many employers are willing to make a total commitment to such a drastic change in their basic business philosophies without ample justification, which can be realized only through testing and evaluation. There are many claimed benefits of greater efficiency, happier employees, reduced operating costs, and other payoffs resulting from this modern idea, but there is not yet a great deal of firm data on which to base conclusions, despite many optimistic projections of improved employee morale and increased productivity. Buck Benham, reporting on Denver-based U.S. West's pilot program,* states that two years

* Jill Kirschenbaum, "Home Base Workplace for the 90's," *Incentive*, May 1989.

of records on the program show a range from zero productivity increase to 30–40 percent increase.

The change, if and when it comes in significant scope and breadth of acceptance, is going to come slowly, as a growing conviction of the benefits to be gained and, even then, only if the attendant problems can be overcome.

Who Works at Home?

Obviously, not every job is suitable for a work-at-home application. An employee whose job is automobile repair or supervising construction cannot do his or her job at home. On the other hand, many occupations lend themselves readily to working at home.

For those in the academic world, working at home part of the time evidently poses fewer problems than it does for those in the business and industrial world. As Richard Chused, professor of law at the Georgetown Law Center, observes, "working at home is routinely possible" for academics, usually on an informal basis and when they do not have classes in session. Only once, in his own case, was working at home a formalized arrangement, when he arranged to meet his classes on Tuesday and Thursday and worked at home the other days. On the days he had to teach, his wife, a lawyer practicing independently, worked at home. That solved their babysitting problems nicely without interfering with their careers. Others on the staff have made similar arrangements, as necessary, he says, often without formal arrangements. They are, of course, expected to use good judgment in this and be fully available as needed.

David Chessler is an independent telecommunications consultant, working from his own home office in the Washington, D.C. area most of the time. Earlier he was a research faculty member at Ohio State University for three years and worked at home for approximately half the work week. He points out some problems, however, such as the difficulty of persuading family, friends, and neighbors to accept the reality that he cannot babysit children or handle other personal tasks during his normal working hours. And he also finds the problems of conducting his business venture at home considerably more complex than working at home as someone's employee.

Of course, many other jobs can be done at home, such as:

Computer programmer
Production typist (i.e., word processor operator)
Clerk, various kinds
Researcher
Telephone order taker
Reservation agent
Securities analyst
Transcriber
Marketing analyst
Technical writer
Design engineer
Copywriter
Actuary
Personnel specialist
Executive

The last-named position, *executive*, may give you some pause, but it is surprising how often the executive, even the chief executive, works at home much of the time. Studied objectively, this practice makes sense for many, if not most, executives. Their jobs do not require their full-time attendance at the office every day—in fact, they normally spend much of their time outside the office on various missions—and so they can spend many days or parts of days in their comfortable, quiet offices at home.

Sam Redman, codirector of Personal Computer Support Group, works almost entirely at home.* When Redman and his partner started their firm (forty employees today), they employed secretaries who worked at home and were impressed

* Jill Kirschenbaum, "This Boss Spends 95 Percent of His Time at Home," *Home Office Computing,* September 1988.

with the efficiency they achieved. The partners have several employees—programmers and one assembler—working at home, in touch with the office via computers and modems to send files and FAX machines to transmit documents.

MAKING THE COMMITMENT

Working at home and telecommuting do not mean that you never go to the office. It means that you do not have to be there all of the time, probably not most of the time, and that your office at home is your main place of work, with your employer's offices a place to visit now and then, as necessary. (But it may also be the case that you work in both locations, although spending most of your working time in your home office.) G. Alan Hunter, an executive with the California Franchise Tax Board who manages four home-based workers himself, believes that home-based employees ought to be brought into the central office at least once a week for discussions with supervisors.

No one has yet postulated a set of rules or procedures to pursue in deciding whether to authorize home-based employment, but it is reasonable to assume that an employer wants *bona fides* of some sort, sound evidence of an employee's serious intent to make a firm commitment to conscientious, if remotely located, employment, and of that employee's ability to handle such employment.

Telecommuting is not for everyone, regardless of whether the job is one that can be done at home. Managers agree generally that self-starters and other motivated people should be selected for working at home, and only those with ample experience and capability for working without supervision.

There is also the question of whether the employee has or is willing to establish suitable facilities at home—that is, the adequacy of the home-office facilities for handling the work capably and efficiently. For David Chessler, "the main problem is lack of space." But for others, the problem is the need to invest in a computer, modem, printer, and FAX machine as the probable minimum equipment requirement, plus the probable need for such software as a word processor, communications program (although this may come with the word processor), database manager, and spreadsheet.

In authorizing an employee to work at home under the direct control of only the employee's own sense of duty, an employer is overcoming entrenched and traditional prejudice against the idea of unsupervised workers. (It's hard enough to persuade some employers to do away with time clocks!) The employer regards this as a risk. Even those corporations that have made a commitment to trying out the idea are likely to have a cautious attitude about who they hire for such remote employment. The burden of proof will fall on you, if you are the one requesting approval.

Accepting this as a premise, the employee must then make a full commitment to the idea in advance of applying for approval, establishing a true office, a proper place of work, at home. That does not mean an itinerant or part-time office, set up on a kitchen or dining room table after breakfast and getting the tots off to school, and cleared off in time for dinner every night. Nor does it work to stick a computer bench in a corner of your bedroom and call that an office. These represent improvisation, not commitment. Working, whether for oneself or for someone else, is a serious undertaking, or should be, and one can hardly expect an employer or prospective employer to take the idea of telecommmuting seriously if the employee does not make what appears to be a truly serious commitment. (It is even possible that an employer will want to inspect the home office to verify its suitability, as government agencies often do before approving a contract.)

The computer must be adequate for serious work, not one of those early machines that were little more than toys. An inexpensive dot matrix printer may be suitable, especially if copy can be transmitted to the employer's office for printing, but if laser-quality printing is needed and must be done in the at-home office, a laser printer must be installed there. (Many of the latest 24-pin dot matrix printers deliver excellent results, however, and at least one ink-jet printer is reported to have true laser-printer quality of output.)

David Chessler, the independent telecommunications consultant mentioned earlier and interviewed via electronic mail, has a few words to say on the subject of the physical facilities required, including these:

> Apart from obvious hassles about the IRS (if your garage is separate from the house, convert it and save a *lot* of problems with deductibility), the main problem is lack of space. A computer installation with wide-carriage daisy wheel and small dot matrix, a system unit, and a monitor takes space, especially if you need a sound on the daisywheel so you don't waken the whole household when you have to do a 300 page print job. (At an honest 29.5 characters per second, it's still going to run all night.)
>
> The other big problem is supplies. Where do you put them? I use 500 sheets of paper a month, when working. (It's getting to be less, as I make fewer interim printouts.) So, where do you store a full box of cut paper, plus a full box of fanfold, plus a box of wide paper, plus a cut paper, plus a few reams of letterhead and second sheets, plus envelopes, labels, etc?

Space can be a real problem and we'll discuss some possible solutions in Chapter 16.

Favorable and Unfavorable Basic Conditions

There are several possible situations or conditions surrounding the prospect of salaried employment at home that affect the probability of approval for remote (work-at-home) salaried employment. First is the situation in which the organization is receptive or even already committed to the idea of having some employees work at home, whether permanently or on an experimental basis. The question here is who is to be so authorized and assigned. The alternative situation is the one in which the organization is not committed to the idea—may or may not have even considered it yet—and must be persuaded to try it. Obviously, the first situation is the more favorable one.

There is also the matter of whether one is already an employee of the organization or is applying for employment with the stipulated place of employment an at-home office. Some businesses that are experimenting with the idea will not hire anyone specifically to work at home but want first to observe the worker in the office and assess the employee's suitability for working alone at home. They tend to consider only those already employed by the organization and there long enough to be a valued and trusted employee, perhaps one in a senior position.

POSSIBLE CONTINGENCIES

Some possible circumstances will greatly affect the question, too. One quite important influence is current economic conditions, especially labor supply, as these conditions affect the employer's needs. Frequently, there are severe shortages of certain classes of labor, especially skilled classes such as computer programmers, engineers, and other technical categories. (These shortages are, in fact, becoming steadily more severe as we progress further into the high-tech era.)

Sometimes an organization experiences a work overload that may or may not prove ultimately to represent a permanent expansion, so the employer does not wish to enlarge or add to the existing physical facilities to accommodate the additional staff that must be hired.

There are variants to these conditions. An organization may know that, given enough time, they can hire the people they want, but the demands of their operations require immediate staffing. Or an organization may be expanding physically by building a new facility but has a problem housing everyone in the meanwhile, which is often quite a long interim period.

Such problems have led and do lead employers to resort to many methods that they would not consider if they had a choice. Because of the need to solve such problems, employers have hired consultant specialists as long-term technical/professional temporaries. They have hired people as part-timers or on reduced hours of work, such as 6 hours a day instead of 8 hours. They have hired people on a temporary basis. And they have otherwise broken with traditional practices and tried new approaches. (It is not unheard of for sales organizations to hire sales representatives who visit the employer's offices only once or twice a week, or to hire telephone solicitors to work from their own homes and telephones. But these are isolated cases; never before has there been a trend to work-at-home employment on anything approaching a sizable or general basis such as we are now beginning to experience.)

For any of these or similar conditions, an employer whose work requirements permit application of this modern idea of having employees work at home may welcome the idea or, at least, consider it. But even then the employer may have to be sold. We all have difficulty accepting radically new ideas, especially those that require us to abandon long-cherished notions of right and wrong. What this means is that you have to *market*—that is, *sell*—the idea to the employer.

MARKETING THE IDEA

At some later point—in Part 3 of this book—we will be discussing marketing, an exceedingly important subject, so we will not devote a great deal of time and space to it here. (You may refer to that part of the book now, if you wish.) Marketing and selling pursue the same principles, no matter where, what, how, or to whom you are selling. And, as a highly successful manager of marketing pointed out to me many years ago, whenever two individuals have an exchange, marketing is taking place: One party sells something, even a simple idea, to the other. To persuade anyone to accept your viewpoint—to agree with you, and especially to persuade someone to actually *do* what you wish him or her to do—is marketing indeed. And so, if you are the employee or prospective employee trying to win approval to work at home, you must market or sell your idea to the decision maker in the organization.

The principles of selling are not complex. They are, in fact, quite simple and can be summed up in a single, simple statement: To sell something to the other party, show him or her how to benefit by buying what you wish to sell. But having said that, I must hasten to qualify it in a few ways:

- The prospective buyer must perceive the result you promise as a true benefit. Your perception of what constitutes a benefit does not count if your prospect does not agree with it.
- The benefit must be important enough to the prospect to be worth the trade—what the prospect must give up to get the benefit.
- The prospect must agree that you can and will deliver the benefit in exchange for what you ask. This means that you must focus entirely on what the other party wants and will get—what you can and will deliver—not on what you want. You must think that way, namely: What great things do I do for this organization when I work at home? And here are a few of the basic benefits that should result:
- The employer's immediate problems of shortages in labor and/or office space are solved by this move.
- Labor turnover—keeping your good employees on board—is reduced by this modern approach to accommodating the employee's needs.
- Many employees become much more productive when working in their own homes.
- The employer's costs for doing business are greatly reduced, putting the organization into a more competitive position. This opens the door to a labor pool not otherwise available—individuals who can work 8 hours a day only by working at home or who are not available for even part-time work if they can't work primarily at home. Ergo, this approach makes the employer far more competitive in the labor market, seeking help.

The same sales arguments can be turned around and expressed in another orientation, essentially a fear orientation, which is more effective with some prospects:

- Labor and space shortages are becoming more severe, and the longer employers put off turning to this solution, the more difficult it will become for them.

- Labor turnover is steadily increasing in the growing competition for good help, and this is one method that helps you reduce that turnover.
- Productivity is declining, but having some of your workers working at home helps greatly to combat this trend.
- Costs for doing business are mounting rapidly, and other employers are turning to this as one method for reducing those costs.
- Other employers are turning to work-at-home employees, so it is important to do so to remain competitive in the labor market.

Of course, any application or appeal you make for work-at-home employee status must also provide the assurance of suitable personal credentials attesting to competence and skills, an adequate work space, and appropriate facilities in that work space. In fact, an appeal of this nature is more like a contract proposal than a job application, and it is probably helpful to think of it in this orientation, in spite of the fact that you are really seeking to be placed on the payroll as a regular employee, albeit under the special conditions of providing your own work space and related facilities.

DO'S AND DON'T'S

It is easy to make mistakes in pursuing such a matter as this. Where you and I, as individuals, might be highly motivated by finding something we want at a significant percentage of dollars under the regular market, that is not always a business organization's prime concern. What is likely to be of greatest appeal to a prospective employer will vary with circumstances. But it is safe to make this general rule: The business executive, like all of us, is motivated by what appears to be the most worrisome problem of the moment. When gasoline is plentiful, many of us go in quest of the service station offering the lowest price. But when it is in short supply and hard to find, what gasoline costs is no longer important; only getting it, at any price, is important. And so, in times of labor shortages, point to the boon of getting good help by permitting key staff members to work at home as the benefit of the new wave in personnel policies.

You therefore need a special résumé. In addition to the usual information that you would ordinarily include in a résumé, list your office equipment and facilities, your proposed method of operation and staying in touch with the employer's organization, your proposed schedules, and whatever else you deem appropriate. Offer to meet and discuss details of the working arrangement, indicating flexibility on your part and explaining why you propose this working arrangement, tactfully pointing out all the benefits to the employer, but focusing primarily on that or those you believe to be most significant and asking specifically for a face-to-face interview. Be tactful, but aggressive and persistent, until you succeed in sitting down, face to face, and discussing your proposal with the decision maker.

Chapter Two

Home-Basing an Independent Venture

There have always been many home-based ventures in this traditionally entrepreneurial, free-enterprise society. It is the unprecedented sudden and great increase in such new business start-ups that is a remarkable phenomenon of the new high-tech era.

WHY AN OFFICE AT HOME?

Some significant movement has definitely taken place toward decentralizing certain kinds of employment, permitting employees to set up their own workplaces—offices—in their own homes. The forecasts of such futurists as Alvin Toffler reflect careful studies and must be taken seriously. A number of factors are involved: Labor shortages, traffic gridlock, steadily rising costs, and excessive labor turnover—we have become a most mobile society—are just a few that make that the trend an increasing probability, wherever it is a feasible alternative to employment in the traditional workplaces. Despite this reality, by far the majority of offices at home today represent home-based independent business ventures by entrepreneurial individuals and couples. It is this home-basing of new small business ventures, both part-time and full-time, that accounts for the bulk of the new and rapidly burgeoning offices and other workplaces in large numbers of enterprising individuals' homes.

This is not itself a new idea, of course. People have always maintained offices in their homes, sometimes as adjuncts to their main workplaces in office buildings and sometimes as their home-based headquarters for the practice of their professions and business ventures. But we have not experienced home work-places in the great numbers that we are now finding, and we are not sure just what this unprecedented increase signifies. Whether it marks the ushering in of a new era — of change having global significance and long-term permanence — is moot, al-though many believe that our economic system is undergoing or about to undergo massive, even revolutionary, change, due to effects and impact of modern electronics, computers, communi-cations, and the high-tech era in general.

What we are interested in here, however, is simply whether an office at home is a practicable idea for you, especially as the basis of an independent business venture, either part-time or full-time. And there are a number of things to consider in reach-ing a conclusion about that.

First, let us discuss what kinds of ventures can be con-ducted in or from your home.

WHAT KINDS OF VENTURES ARE SUITABLE?

People who write about business conducted via mail order are fond of saying that anything can be sold by mail, knowing that this is not a literal truth except if we define what "sold" means in rather loose and liberal terms. Very much the same thing may be said for the kinds of businesses that can be conducted in or from an office at home. Theoretically, any business can be run in or from your home, but in a practical sense, as in the case of mail order, the range has many limitations. Obviously, you can-not have a steel mill or an automobile showroom in your home, and to maintain an office at home as headquarters for a business that is really housed elsewhere does not make a great deal of sense. So let us concentrate on ventures that can be conducted from your home—*completely* from your home—in a practical sense.

Certain kinds of ventures have been almost traditionally well suited to housing in your own home, at least if or while they remain ventures run by a single individual or a couple. (Many ventures that start in the home do grow to a point where employees and more space are required and must be ultimately moved to typical commercial locations, but that does not bear on this discussion.) It has been commonplace to find real estate and insurance brokers, manufacturer's representatives, lawyers, accountants, mail-order dealers, writers, artists, composers, agents, and others—even various kinds of medical practitioners—working in or from offices in their homes. These kinds of quiet ventures, principally ventures that you can operate all by yourself or with only a spouse, for which you require only a simple office with typical modern office equipment and furnishings, and in which you contact your customers or clients almost entirely by telephone, mail, FAX, and personal visits, are "naturals" for home basing. It takes little imagination to see that. Many kinds of ventures, however, are not so obviously suited to such a workplace, although they are also not of the steel mill or automobile showroom variety. In many cases, such ventures, apparently not suitable for running from your home, can be made suitable—with a little imagination and some special business knowledge. Let's look first at a few ideas for ventures that are well suited by their nature to being operated from or in an office at home. Later, we will look at some ideas for methods of successfully adapting the apparently unsuitable ventures to the home-office environment.

Independent Consultants

There is a quite extensive array of independent consultants—specialists in computers, marketing, publishing, editorial functions, health, fringe benefits, economics, stocks and bonds, plant security, construction, electronics, weapons systems, engineering of all kinds, public services, proposal writing, office management, manufacturing control, inventory management, taxes, training, and hundreds of other subjects. And most of these fields are far too broadly designed, so there are consultant specialists in many specific areas of each. For example, the electronics field alone has dozens of subdivisions in many areas: A consultant here may specialize in a type of equipment (radar, TV, mobile radio, and satellites, to name only a few), in function (manufacturing methods, test methods, documentation, or training), or in somewhat arcane areas such as EMP (nuclear effects, creating electromagnetic pulse or EMP) or Tempest (security against unwanted broadcasting of signals, permitting eavesdropping).

In fact, independent consulting comprises so many fields that almost anyone with a better than average knowledge or skill in some given area may well be able to hang out a shingle as a consultant and operate such a service successfully. Are you an expert in office procedures or office arrangement? In employee benefit packages? In insurance programs? In taxes? In government regulations in some field, such as environmental control or occupational safety and health? In writing and editing or publications practices? In inventory management? In training? If you can answer *yes* to one or more of these, you may wish to begin considering the possibility of offering your services as an independent consultant, with an office at home!

In fact, consulting is not truly a profession or trade as much as it is a way of practicing a profession or trade. For example, let us suppose that you are an expert locksmith of many years' experience. Perhaps you do not wish to, or perhaps it is not feasible to set up a shop in your home, but you can become a security consultant, specializing in security devices and systems — that is, the security hardware — safes and locks for homes, offices, and plants. But there are other devices connected with security, such as intrusion detectors and burglar alarms. And there is security against fire, including escape devices, fire alarms, and fire-fighting equipment.

There are consulting specialties within specialties, and security is one such, for it has even more specialties: for example, military-industrial security, such as must be observed and practiced in defense plants, and security against terrorists, kidnapers, and industrial espionage.

That principle of turning a craft or skill to employment as a basis for consulting services works for a great many professions, trades, and crafts. Many can be the basis for a consulting practice in which you advise others, design systems for them, help them order and install what they need, and otherwise support them as necessary. There have been and are consulting opportunities for writers, engineers, real estate appraisers, moviemakers, stock brokers, computer programmers, and just about everyone who has a well-developed knowledge of some special field or a special skill of some kind.

Craft Workers and Small-Scale Manufacturing

It is possible to do small-scale manufacturing at home as long as you meet two conditions: (1) You do not commercialize your property in any way—no outside signs or placards, no streams of cars and customers visiting all day, or otherwise doing violence to the customary zoning ordinances that prohibit commercial or industrial use of a private residence, and (2) you do not employ others than yourself and family—those who live in the residence.

That means that you can sell your output only via other means than using your residence as a retail store open to the public. You must either wholesale your products or retail them via mail order and/or via retail outlets away from your residence, such as trade shows and fairs, and booths or concessions in malls and markets. Wholesaling your product means either selling it to distributors who will resell it to retailers or selling it directly to such large retailers as department stores, supermarkets, and chain stores. For example, one couple in Philadelphia stencils designs on towels and sells them to a large department store there. (The store takes all the product these two can produce, so they focus entirely on production and don't have to worry about marketing at all.)

Another entrepreneur manufactures lead sinkers for fishing enthusiasts, including a very large one that is called a "cannon ball" in that trade. He does all of this in the basement of his home, assisted by his wife and children, and wholesales the product to stores. But his business has grown so that he must now hire help and move it out of his home, although he can still keep his office at home and avoid that expense.

A sheet metal craftsman in Upper Darby, Pennsylvania (a Philadelphia suburb) is employed by the Philadelphia Navy Yard and uses his skills to manufacture stainless steel sinks and bars in his garage, where he has the sheet-metal brakes and other necessary equipment. When printed circuits became the latest technique in electronics manufacture a few years ago, more than one entrepreneur began to manufacture pc boards (at that time, "pc" referred to printed circuits, not to personal computers) in basements and garages because pc board manufacture does not require a great deal of space, equipment, or special skills. In short, a great deal more small-scale manufacturing is going on in private homes, on both a part-time and full-time basis, than is generally known.

Many entrepreneurs spend most of every working day away from any facility — home, office, or plant — conducting their businesses "on the street," figuratively. This kind of work encompasses quite a wide variety of ventures. Most maintain an office at home to take care of the paperwork and other administration.

Freelance Construction Contractors and Subcontractors

Independent contractors install windows, shower enclosures, doors, and other such construction subcontracting, working entirely from well-equipped vans. Others who also work out of vans do "handyman" repairs, renovations, and additions to people's homes. Their customer contact is almost invariably at the customer's home, although they sometimes meet prospects and make customers of them at other places and via telephone first contacts.

Real Estate Appraisers

Professional real estate appraisers are freelance experts who do nothing else but inspect properties all day and render official estimates of the market value of each property. Most concentrate on private homes, for that is by far the largest and busiest market for their service, which is required by banks and mortgage companies.

Manufacturer's Representatives

Manufacturer's representatives work on the street all day, visiting prospective customers. They usually handle several lines that are not competitive with each other, and they work on a commission or discount basis.

Printing Brokers

Printing brokers handle only large printing jobs. They know and are well known by a great many organizations who vend large printing jobs frequently as well as by major printing plants that handle large printing jobs. The broker bids printing jobs every day, sometimes spontaneously, estimating what it will cost to get the printing done, although sometimes only after checking with some of the printers to get their prices. When the broker wins the job, he or she places the work, arranges for delivery, and bills the customer, acting in all respects in the place of the actual printer.

Many printing brokers handle small printing orders, at the retail level, primarily by mail. They work primarily in their own offices at home and have the actual printer drop-ship the order to the customer.

Some of these entrepreneurs specialize in printing—one I know specialized for a time in business cards—but even then customers begin to ask for other work such as stationery, brochures, booklets, note pads, and other printed items. Often the entrepreneur finds it necessary to either turn the work away or diversify. Of course, most choose to diversify.

In fact, some individuals sell printing by mail but do the actual printing in their own homes. It is possible to do this because efficient small presses, even table-top models, can turn out professional work up to letter size—on paper and card stock that is up to 9 × 12 inches or 10 × 15 inches in size, which covers the bulk of the printing work ordered by small businesses.

Mail-Order Merchants

Large numbers of small mail-order merchants sell a wide variety of goods by mail, including office supplies, books, vitamins, advertising services, rubber stamps, typesetting, business plans, food supplements, novelties, and merchandise of many kinds.

Book Dealers

Many people operate retail book dealerships from their homes. Obviously, there are two obstacles to running a retail bookstore in your home: (1) You probably do not have the space to maintain a typical bookstore inventory and display spaces—a showroom of sorts, in fact—and (2) you cannot have streams of customers and prospective customers in and out of your home all day long.

Home-based book dealers solve these two problems by avoiding them. First, they sell books by mail. Customers do not visit them personally. The dealer mails out catalogs—you may have received one or more of these yourself—and customers browse through the catalogs in the ease of their own homes. Second, these dealers may or may not carry an inventory in their own homes. In most cases, it is possible to have books *drop-shipped*—that is, you can take orders for books and send the orders on to the publisher, with payment at the wholesale price, and the publisher will ship the book to the customer. You are really more a broker than a dealer, in fact. You take a little less gross profit on each sale than you would if you carried an inventory and did your own shipping, but you have no investment in inventory, no shipping costs, and little or no risk.

There are a number of variants on this method of operation, and we will discuss it again, in much greater detail, in later chapters. You should also know, however, that drop-shipping is not peculiar to the book business. A great many things are sold in this manner, and that reflects one approach to conducting a business in a way that enables you to confine yourself to "the paperwork"—marketing, mailing, billing, recording, corresponding, and similar office chores—while you avoid the physical labor and attendant problems of inventory, packing, and shipping. But there are other approaches to this problem, and one is to make use of services for all the tasks that are unsuitable for handling in your at-home office/workplace.

Contracting Out Some Functions

In some ventures, the most important or leading roles may be conducted in a small office, but many other important necessary functions require more space, equipment, and help. Take that mail-order book dealership, or any other venture in which the leading functions are marketing and order processing. It's easy enough to decide where to advertise, order your advertising, and send out drop-ship orders for *fulfillment* (the term used in the trade to refer to the filling of orders received) by the "prime sources" for whatever you are selling; you don't need a lot of space for any of that. But let's take the case of a direct-mail (dm) venture, which differs from mail order, strictly speaking, in that you solicit orders by mailing out literature to a list of names rather than running advertisements in various media. In this mode of operation, you must maintain an inventory of printed sales literature and supplies for mailing in substantial quantity; dm requires a number of pieces of literature stuffed into an envelope, as you learn when you receive in your own home what some refer to as "junk mail." You begin to need a little more space. Your little office begins to shrink as you start piling cartons in corners and trying to find more desk or table surfaces on which to lay out the literature and stuff envelopes. Still, even if the work occasionally spills over on the kitchen or dining room tables and you have to work many hours, you can manage the preparation of mailings to 1,000, 2,000, and even 5,000 names.

But then come the effects of necessary expansion: You discover that to make your venture even minimally successful, you must mail out several times the amounts you have been mailing—perhaps you must increase your mailings to 25,000 dm packages at a time or even more. You have reached the point where you lack not only the physical space for the material and the work, but the time or the capability to deal with them adequately. Mailing in large quantity requires either a great deal of labor or large equipment, neither one of which is a feasible alternative for you. It's time for another solution, one that is entirely feasible: You can turn to a mailing house, of which there are many waiting to handle this end of the dm business. Even the largest mail-order firms use such services to handle that end of the work.

This common practice makes it feasible to operate a home business, even when large rations of space, labor, and equipment are necessary to handle important functions. You cannot very well contract out the management of your business—the marketing, accounting, and general administration—but you can often contract out all the tasks and functions you cannot handle in an office at home. Even order fulfillment can be handled in this manner and is done so by many business owners. The publisher of a newsletter, for example, may have a single mailing house handle all printing, mailing, and fulfillment of orders. Many mailers offer such a complete set of services, even mailing list management.

There are middle-road approaches, too, where you decide to arrange for services for some, but not all, the functions. For example, many printers will store your printed materials, delivering to you only the quantities you want as you want them, thereby helping you with your inventory and space problem (and enabling you to achieve the economies of printing in large quantities). Also, many printers will sort and collate your literature, making the envelope-stuffing task much simpler.

How Much Independence Do You Want?

Independence is a variable, not an absolute. Manufacturing is a more independent venture than retailing and dealership are. It gives you control of the product and its price, for one thing. But it also is the least structured of these activities; there is no supplier to offer help—suggestions, literature, advertising copy, and other aids. More significant, perhaps, is the sense of security involved here. Right or wrong, in the least structured and most independent venture environment, you are likely to feel least secure and believe that the risk is greatest. For that reason alone, many are hesitant to venture into manufacturing, and they may turn to an alternative:

There are many "opportunity" periodicals. Some of those on the newsstands are *Entrepreneur, Income Opportunities,* and *In Business.* But there are more, many more, and many other periodicals carry "opportunity" advertising. The philosophy behind all this literature is to offer ideas to "opportunity seekers"—those who want to start new ventures and/or find ways to make more money and supplement their incomes—in response to those desires. Many are entirely legitimate and practical ideas and plans. Many are scams, although within the law. And a few are out-and-out frauds. The appeal of these ideas is based on the notion and the promise or clearly implied promise that risk is zero, and the advertiser will all but hold your hand and guide you to success. (We will have more to say on this later.)

Is It for You?

There are some other factors to consider before you come to a firm conclusion about whether you want to set up a workplace at home, and we will discuss those matters as we proceed, especially in the next chapter. We have already examined a few basic factors, such as the benefits of working at home as well as those of having an independent venture of your own. That was the "good news." But there is a downside, and it would be unwise to even attempt to make a decision before looking at the "bad news." Let us do that now.

Chapter Three

Some Common and Basic Problems

The typical problems in working at home fall into more than one category. There are, in fact, psychological, legal, and practical problems. But most are problems only if you permit them to be problems—i.e., there are solutions for all of them.

A FEW TYPICAL OFFICE-AT-HOME PROBLEMS

Most of us who have an office at home and work there full time are envied by those who must travel to their own places of work every morning and have never tried to cope with the problems of an office at home. They seem not to understand that there are problems with an office at home, too. There is, for example, usually not as much space as you would like to have, nor is there as much privacy, either. Family members find it difficult to understand that your office door is closed, figuratively if not literally, during business hours, and you are not to be disturbed or distracted during those hours. Merely keeping regular hours can become a problem.

KEEPING OFFICE HOURS IN YOUR HOME

One of the most common obstacles to working at home is a psychological one. If you have the fear that you will be unable to work at home because of distraction by the intrusions of your family as well as the normal difficulties of disciplining yourself to keep office hours in your own home, you are not alone: It is a most common fear, one I have heard expressed many times and one I experienced myself in the days before I first tried working in my own home.

Many people are conditioned by long practice to believe that they must have someplace to *go* every morning, that it is a psychological need, if they are to have a suitable attitude—be conditioned to work—for the day. They believe that they must be surrounded by what they have learned to regard as a business or working environment and that they cannot discipline themselves to attending strictly to business all day long in what is to them not a working environment.

It is a real enough problem, but it can be and is being solved by an increasing number of people obviously, since the number of work-at-homes is growing steadily and rapidly. The solutions, however, are many and varied according to individual circumstances, which are themselves highly variable. You may have to solve both psychological and practical problems to be able to discipline yourself and concentrate on work in the informal and relaxed atmosphere of your own home. Solutions vary as widely as individual characteristics and needs. There is a related problem of productivity, which we will shortly consider.

THE NEED FOR A WORKING ENVIRONMENT

Some people can work at the kitchen table or set up two orange crates as a desk and chair in a musty basement and work cheerfully all day there, completely shutting out shouting children, tradespeople knocking at the door, clattering garbage cans being emptied, and all the other normal noises and distractions

of everyday life. (One of my own former employers, today the owner of a multimillion-dollar business, actually did launch that enterprise thirty-eight years ago at his mother's kitchen table!) These are exceptional individuals; most of us cannot attain quite that degree of self-sufficient concentration and discipline. But even accepting our shortcomings in that respect, some of us go to extremes in our negative approach to the potential problem, working overtime at conditioning ourselves to make our fears a reality.

Your own attitude can be a cause or a cure. If you firmly expect to have trouble disciplining yourself to work at home all day, it may easily become a self-fulfilling prophecy. You can persuade yourself to make the prophecy or fear a reality. But you can also take the opposite approach: Condition yourself to believe that you can and will work comfortably and steadily in your office at home. That alone will be helpful. There are other things you can do, however, that will help you learn to regard an office at home as a workplace just as much as you do an office in an employer's facilities many miles away: You can create a working environment in your home.

Most of us need to have our own special space, comfortable furnishings, and a reasonable measure of privacy or isolation. To work at home, you probably need to establish a *working atmosphere*, such as a room that is furnished as an office is normally furnished, with a conventional desk and chair, telephone, typewriter, computer, and whatever else is needed for the everyday conduct of your business.

That is the first step in solving the problem of working at home: Create a separate world that is not part of your residence, despite being located physically within it, setting it up in a manner that is appropriate to whatever your needs are so that you can feel that you are truly "at work." Whether you bundle up on a cold day and get your automobile out to drive off to somewhere, or stroll a few steps down the hall to your office, should make no difference. Once there, you are "at work." Close the door, if necessary, and even post a *Busy: Do Not Disturb* sign on your door, if that helps, but do condition your thinking to accept that this is your place of work. Your home and your personal affairs are *outside* this room, and they should be kept outside, as your work is kept inside. (In Chapter 16 we will discuss some of the practical matters of furnishing and equipping this separate business world in your home.)

Keep regular hours. If possible, adjust your hours to your conditions. If you are an early riser, early morning hours may be your most productive time. (I usually have several hours of work done before I shower and dress every morning!) Or you may find it advantageous to put in a few hours late at night, when things have settled down and it is, indeed, quiet both in your residence and outside. But do make it your business to establish some kind of working regimen and stick to it as faithfully as possible. It is quite important for most of us to have the firm commitment to a routine and a regular schedule.

Sometimes your family—children, spouse, or others, if you are not married and still living in your parents' home—can be a problem of a different kind: Family members may have trouble understanding your need to keep regular hours, undisturbed and uninterrupted, that you are at work just as much as when you go off to an employer's offices. They tend to feel free to burst in on you at any time without ceremony or warning to ask a question or demand that you fix a leaky faucet, prepare lunch, join them in watching a TV show, or drive them to a friend's house.

This is a problem a bit more difficult to solve, but it too is amenable to solution. If your spouse or others go off to a job every morning and/or your children are in school every day, you have at least several hours a day when you have the house or apartment all to yourself. But if you have a spouse at home, you may have the kind of problem cited and will need to look for a solution. And one direct way to solve the problem of interruptions by a spouse is sometimes fairly easy to solve by the simple expedient of making your spouse your business-partner! Make sure that he or she has as much stake in the business and as much to say about the conduct of the business as you do. You may soon find yourself driven harder by your spouse/business-partner than you ever were by the most demanding employer!

WORKAHOLISM

A frequent complaint by work-at-homes is "burnout." They complain that they are weary of so many hours and so much hard work. But that is because they are driving themselves excessively. They have become workaholics, hardly having a life outside their offices and businesses. And it is true that they are burning themselves out by failing to take enough time off for the rest of their lives—for weekends, holidays, and vacations.

There are two common reasons for this kind of lapse into excessive dedication to the home business: In many cases, the individual is not turning enough gross profit to draw a decent salary because he or she is charging excessively low prices. You must guard against the temptation to deceive yourself that you are "just doing this to get started" and you will raise your prices later. Unfortunately, you may never last until "later," and so never get to raise your prices! But this is not all of it, and in fact this dilemma is related to a much larger and more common problem that leads to workaholism and consequent business difficulties: Many fledgling entrepreneurs who are under-financed to begin with (a most common situation!) become so conditioned to the desperate need for sales and money that they are unable to say no to any business offered and to any demand made by a customer. And so they undertake many impossible tasks and accept many sales that they should have refused.

That is a major problem of entrepreneurship. To be a successful entrepreneur, you must learn how to say no to some business, to business that is not worth having—that is, to business that is really outside the normal bounds of whatever you sell or do. You must learn to say no to all business that you must make special price cuts to get. You must learn to say no to all business that is conditional on your meeting unreasonable demands, such as impossible delivery dates. (There are exceptions, but they ought to be most definitely exceptions.)

Strangely enough, when you begin to start saying no to customers who demand impossible prices and performance, they usually become far more tractable and reasonable! That has been my experience, and many others have verified that it is a truism. It takes a bit of fortitude to say no to business, but then no one says success comes easily.

IT CAN BE A LONELY JOB

Some people are loners by choice, actually preferring solitude as a steady diet, whereas most of us probably choose the solitary environment only occasionally, as a relief; we normally prefer to be in the company of others during business hours. But there are also those who absolutely require the comfort and reassurance of being with others, having face-to-face contact. They find working alone, with only occasional contact with others, intolerable. If that is the case with you, and your business is essentially a lonely one—one that keeps you working alone in your office all day, for example—you will have to seek a solution. One way to relieve the silence and solitude is to make frequent use of the telephone; for some, that is an acceptable substitute for face-to-face contact. (I use a modem and dedicated telephone line with my computer, and through that I maintain a steady correspondence with others, taking breaks occasionally to read and respond to the message traffic on the electronic bulletin boards to which I subscribe. I find that a welcome relief from the typical solitude of full-time writing, but I also am able to turn this channel of communication into a useful business asset.) Another approach is to make it your business to get out of the office and the house at least once or twice a day, even if it is just running an errand to buy a new typewriter ribbon or a trip to a favorite local restaurant for lunch. Better yet, meet a friend or business acquaintance for lunch occasionally.

Some people require absolute silence when they work, finding it difficult to concentrate otherwise. Others prefer soft music in the background and find it helpful. And anyone who has ever worked in the city room of a large newspaper has probably observed that there are individuals who actually enjoy working in a bedlam. If you are one of those, you might enjoy playing an office-sounds tape all day, providing a soft background of typing, chatter, and other typical sounds of a busy office. (Such a tape is now available commercially, although the intended use of it is as "window dressing"– that is, to provide the illusion of a busy office when the work-at-home entrepreneur is talking to customers and prospective customers on the telephone.)

PRODUCTIVITY

Aside from the psychological and practical problems of working at home in "solitary confinement," that problem of self-discipline and the psychological problems of self-employment in your own home, there is the corollary problem of productivity. Will you be more or less productive working in your office at home than you were working for someone else?

Many people working in large organizations are convinced that much of their time is wasted every day. They waste time traveling to and from their places of work every day. They waste time with innumerable distractions, most of them unnecessary, every day. They waste time with inefficient standard processes and procedures dictated by the bureaucracies for which they work. They would be far more productive if they worked away from all of this commotion and in an environment where they were in complete control. So they believe. But is it so?

The temptation to be the most lenient employer in the world is sometimes overpowering when you are your own boss. Typical accounts by freelance writers, whose work is inherently solitary and self-imposed, illustrate the point. They recount the incessant pencil sharpening, straightening papers on the desk, repeated trips to the kitchen for another cup of coffee, cleaning out unused and unwanted junk from disorderly desk drawers, staring out the window, and innumerable other evasions every morning to avoid facing the day's work tasks.

Some of that is peculiar to the nature of freelance writing. For many of us, the mental pump must be primed every morning, and many writers have no convenient and reliable way of doing it: Each morning is a struggle to somehow trigger the beginning of the day's flow of thoughts. But much of it simply reflects difficulty in imposing the sentence of work on oneself every morning. It is not peculiar to freelance writers, but a problem or potential problem for every self-employed individual to some extent, but especially the work-at-home, with so many temptations.

Motivation

Until and unless you can enforce a discipline on yourself that is at least the equal of that normally imposed on you by an employer, your productivity may actually decline when working at home. But why should you now work even harder for yourself than you ever did for an employer?

The answer lies in motivation, for motivation in one situation is quite different from that in the other situation. Most of us working for an employer have two basic motivating forces driving us: We want to "get ahead"—win promotions and salary increases—and we feel peer pressure.

The drive to win promotions is not entirely a drive for more money, although we usually want that, too. But we want even more the recognition of worth and achievement that is reflected by promotion, especially when promotion brings with it desirable new job titles. According to the well-known Robert Half job-placement and recruiting firm,* 47 percent of those who voluntarily leave their jobs, some to start their own ventures, do so because they believe that their jobs offer limited opportunity for advancement; 26 percent leave because they believe that they suffered a lack of recognition; and the remainder leave for other causes, not entirely unrelated to these complaints, including dissatisfaction with their salaries and benefit packages.

We need to do as well as our peers also, and we need their respect to inspire and support our self-esteem, as we need to avoid any slightest suggestion that we are not holding up our end of things. In that respect, the two motivations are identical:

---

* As reported in "Business Beat," *Entrepreneur*, February 1989.

Pride and self-esteem are important factors everywhere, but especially so in the typical workplace and environment of the organization, among fellow workers. The sheer power of these drives probably explains the phenomenon of the workaholic.

Those factors are nonexistent or, at best, remotely sensed in you office at home. Here the chief motivation is gain and the need to vindicate your venture by succeeding at it. (Conversely, the fear of failure is often a powerful motivator.) But there is no daily, ever-present peer pressure, the sense of competition with fellow workers, and so the pressure is indirect—not immediate—and largely self-imposed. For at least some of us who work at home, it is necessary to substitute something else to motivate ourselves. But that is a quite different factor for one individual than it is for another.

For some work-at-homes, the chief motivator is sheer pleasure in the process itself. (I believe that this is the case for me and for many other writers, although some are reported to have said that they hate writing but love having written.) You are fortunate, or perhaps wise in your choice of venture, if you get immediate and enduring pleasure out of the work itself. But not everyone does. For many, the motivator is success per se, the feeling of winning in a competitive world and, perhaps, in an exceptionally competitive business. And for still others, the drive is for money itself, prestige and recognition within the business world, perhaps in a trade association or in a community, the power that comes with business success, or any of many other possible rewards. (Why else does an individual who is already a millionaire many times over, with thousands of employees and a huge corporate staff, continue to work late every night and take a personal interest in the tiniest details of the business?)

The Power of Persistence

One element that must be present for you is faith in your venture, an unshakably firm belief in what you are doing, that it is right and that you will succeed. Succeeding without that faith is rare; it is the dogged determination to keep on in spite of all problems and obstacles that characterizes most, if not all, successes, and that kind of persistence — that ability to withstand and endure the disappointments and setbacks that are common to business starts — arises only out of firm conviction and complete confidence in what you are doing. And you will probably meet with setbacks and disappointments along the way; you must regard them as mere detours on the road to wherever you are planning to go.

The "positive thinking" of Norman Vincent Peale and the many who have since been his echoes state the case as clearly as it can be stated: Believe earnestly enough and enthusiastically enough that it is so and it becomes so, for there is no power like the power of an idea, if you keep faith with it and with yourself. Calvin Coolidge, thirtieth president of the United States, is credited with the following words:

> Nothing in the world can take the place of persistence. Talent will not; nothing is more common than unsuccessful men with talent. Genius will not; unrewarded genius is almost a proverb. Education will not; the world is full of educated derelicts. Persistence and determination alone are omnipotent.

Make no mistake about it: These are important words. They explain success as clearly as or perhaps more clearly than does anything else that has been said by anyone. Thomas Edison, seeking out and testing a reported 10,000 materials to find one that would serve as a filament for his electric light bulb, never doubted that he would find a material that would work; he was absolutely sure that his basic concept was right, that there *had* to be a right material somewhere. In fact, he is widely quoted for his explanation of just the point being made here by observing that "genius is 1 percent inspiration and 99 percent perspiration," which has since become conventional wisdom.

Writers who have verified for themselves the power of positive thinking have devised methods for putting the concept to work, for applying it to your own life and aspirations. The basic method is autosuggestion, called colloquially "psyching yourself up," by writing and verbalizing "positive" statements to yourself designed to help you visualize yourself already having achieved the goal you have set. If you are by nature a highly optimistic, "upbeat" individual, you may not need much of this kind of assistance in internalizing the philosophy, but if you are by nature fearful or pessimistic –"negative"– such measures help by reminding you. (I am usually optimistic and self-assured, but I still find it helpful to remind myself by keeping the Calvin Coolidge message posted on my bulletin board, where I see it constantly from my desk.)

OTHER KINDS OF PROBLEMS

All of the foregoing does not mean that there are no practical problems, often formidable practical problems that you must solve by highly practical means. There is, for example, the legal aspect of conducting a business in your home. The zoning laws of most communities, laws that dictate what uses may be made of various kinds of properties in various areas or zones, prohibit all business operations in private residences, except as specifically exempted. The theory that underpins zoning law is, of course, that business, industrial, and residential zones should be separated so that quiet residential neighborhoods are kept that way. The basic idea is that people living in residential zones should be protected from the "nuisance" that an industry or business would create, that they have a right to quiet and peaceful conditions in their residential zones, and that they have a right to the protection of their property values, which would presumably be compromised or damaged if businesses were permitted to operate there. Theory and practice are not always the same thing, however.

What Is a "Business"?

My "business" is freelance writing, although I also consult and lecture occasionally. I consult on my client's premises, and I lecture there – or, sometimes, in a college classroom or auditorium. Am I in violation of the zoning laws in my community?

Frankly, I do not know, and I suspect that it would be difficult to get a legal opinion. Logically, it would seem not (is writing as a freelance contributor a business?), and practically no one will complain because I have no signs, no visiting customers, no noises louder than the click of my keyboard, and no other evidence of business activity. And there is certainly ample precedent for writers working quietly in the comfort of their own homes. Their right to do so has never been challenged, to the best of my knowledge.

Rarely, if ever, does any local authority go out looking for zoning-law violators. Almost without exception, authorities take action in zoning cases only when a complaint has been made. On the one occasion that I was, in fact, guilty of a zoning-law violation, I was the victim of a complaint made as an act of spite by a neighbor after a quarrel with my wife. I had used my garage occasionally for business purposes, but totally without signs, visitors, or other outward evidence of business activities. It's doubtful if anyone other than my immediate neighbor, with whom I shared a driveway leading to my garage, even knew that I spent perhaps six or eight hours a week working in my garage. The city attorney and the magistrate who heard the case were genuinely regretful to create a difficulty for a small business-man who was trying to earn a living and not creating a nuisance, they said, but they were forced to act when a complaint was made. I was required to cease and desist and pay the grand sum of $9 in court costs. There was no fine or penalty imposed.

There are other examples. An associate called me from Michigan recently to ask my advice on a matter concerning his alleged violation of zoning laws. He is a consultant, and he has a desk at home, of course, but he uses a post office box for his business address — a wise move, if you anticipate trouble with zoning laws. A spiteful neighbor, disgruntled by something she believed an offense directed at her, had complained that he was running a business in his home.

In fact, Steve's is probably a borderline case. As a consultant, Steve works on his clients' premises, although perhaps he prepares invoices at home and talks to clients from his home.

The fact that his business address is a box number helps: He does not even get business mail at home, and he does not use his home address as a business address. It will be difficult to make a case that his is a business run in his home, and that is the sole criterion here — not that he is quiet and does not create or consititute a public nuisance, for that is irrelevant; the criterion is the letter of the law. Steve must demonstrate that he does not have a business in his home. He really does not, since he is in essence a professional temporary, as many consultants are. If your own work is of that nature, where you visit clients and work on their premises, you might do well to consider using a post office box as your business address. The fact that you do not receive business correspondence in your home, do not receive clients in your home, and do your work on the clients' premises should give you a defense, if necessary. (In fact, the complaint against Steve was dismissed as unjustified.)

That is about the size of zoning laws generally. First, most zoning laws are archaic and do not relate logically to modern conditions, but legislatures are always reluctant to repeal old laws. Even so, many of the zoning laws are ambiguous and unclear. It is not always easy to even determine what constitutes a business, let alone what constitutes a violation.

You have several possible courses of action. You can make inquiry at City Hall and/or the public library and try to determine just what the zoning laws are, as they apply to you and to the venture you plan. It is unlikely that you will have a much better idea of how the law applies to you after such research than before it, unless you have a lawyer investigate it for you. Even then, the result may be inconclusive.

You can try to get a "variance," gaining official sanction to do what you want to do. It will take a long time for resolution and, frankly, what few precedents there are for such efforts are not encouraging.

You can go ahead and start your business at home, keeping peace with your neighbors, operating as quietly and as unobtrusively as possible, and keeping your fingers crossed. If you have no signs, no constant stream of visitors, and no clear evidence of conducting a business at home, the probability is that no one will ever bother you—but it is a possibility that someone will. You must be aware of that.

A hairsplitting legal definition of a business would probably hold that any venture conducted regularly to sell anything for a profit is a business, and that might serve to define the borderline or gray-area cases, such as that of a freelance writer, insurance broker, or tiny mail-order business; these are income-earning ventures that are home based almost by longstanding tradition. However, a practical, working definition of a business that is a clear no-no from a zoning viewpoint would identify a venture that creates a nuisance for neighbors and/or clearly attracts attention to itself as a business by drawing a continual stream of customers, posting signs, generating noise, and other such clear commercialization of a residential structure and locality.

Despite the reluctance of authorities to invoke zoning laws when no one makes a formal complaint, evidenced by several million small full- and part-time ventures conducted in people's homes, some businesses simply cannot be conducted in your home without serious possibility—perhaps probability—of bringing complaints from neighbors and unwelcome visits from the local authorities. If you make prominent your personal name and your street address by advertising in various media, you increase the risk of complaints immediately, for example. If you place commercial signs on your house, inviting trade, you raise it still further. (In some cases, such as in a relatively new and upscale residential neighborhood, signs will usually raise the odds from a distinct possibility to a high degree of probability.) There are some things you can do to lessen the problem, however, especially if you do not depend on people visiting you to do business.

For one thing, do not advertise your personal name and street address. Use a trade name and a post office box, if you need a mailing address. (If you check the daily newspapers and even some other periodicals, you will find some businesses supplying only a telephone number.) You may find it advantageous to also install a special line for a FAX machine and advertise that number, especially if you will do business with other firms; business firms are using FAX transmission increasingly.

TELEPHONE USAGE

Perhaps the thought that zoning laws may be a problem has not entered your mind. For example, you may be breaking the law, technically, by using a private telephone for business. Most, perhaps all, utility commissions make it clear that answering your telephone with a business name, soliciting business over the telephone or making any of many other clearly business uses of the telephone, or even listing the telephone number on business cards and letterheads is a clear admission that the telephone is being used for business purposes. That, they say, is illegal if the telephone is a private line, rather than a business line. The telephone company can compel you to convert your line to business or add a business line.

Using a "DBA" Name

Perhaps you have seen a notice that refers to "John Smith, dba Hercules Tool Company." "Dba" means *doing business as*, and in most jurisdictions you are required by law to publish your own name as the true proprietor of a business if you operate it under any name but your own personal one. Many people retain a lawyer to handle this matter for them, but it is usually simple enough to do for yourself, if you wish to. You can get guidance at your local city or town hall and, possibly, your county seat also, since you may have to register your business name with both the county and city or town. Usually, the city clerk or county clerk can advise you and may very well have a printed form or instruction sheet to help. You must usually fill out such a form or forms and advertise your personal name and business name in the *Legal Intelligencer* or a local general newspaper.

Post Office Boxes

Post office boxes come in several sizes, the largest actually a drawer and sometimes referred to as such. But it does not matter whether your mailing address is Post Office Box, P.O. Box, POB, Box, or Drawer; as long as you have the number correct, you will get your mail. And if something too large to fit in the box is sent to your box number, you will get a notice asking you to come to the counter and pick up the item. You can rent the box by the year or pay for it in six-month periods, as you choose. I have used a post office box for years to receive my business correspondence (recently supplemented by a FAX machine), and found it a wise investment in more than one way.

In many post offices today there are no vacant boxes, and you must have your name put on a waiting list to get one. That has led to the development of private post office boxes, a service in which a private firm, operating a storefront establishment, sets up boxes and rents them to customers. You use the address of that establishment, plus your box number, as your mailing address, and you pick up your mail there, very much as you would at a regular United States post office. Usually, such establishments offer a variety of other, often related, services, such as express shipping (they are often agents for major express shipping firms) and packing, and they may sell shipping and office supplies, too. If there is such an establishment near you, you may find it advantageous to investigate it as a possible asset or at least a great convenience in general.

So much for the practical problems of the home office. In Part 2 we will examine how businesses work and what sort of business structure and support services are appropriate for your home-based venture.

PART TWO

THE VERITIES OF BUSINESS (NO MATTER WHERE/ HOW BASED)

We are always ready to admire and extol the genius of outstandingly successful entrepreneurs. But their success is always due, in part at least, to certain truths and principles of business that are as readily available to contribute to your own success as to theirs. Whether you work at home, in a rundown industrial building of a dreary factory district, or in a plush office in a modern high-rise office building; whether you sell goods, services, or both; whether your sales are big tag, medium tag, or small tag; whether you do business on your premises, on the customer's premises, or in cocktail lounges; whether you refer to the people who buy your goods or services as *customers*, *buyers*, or *clients*; whether you sell retail, wholesale, or both; and whether you sell to individual consumers, business organizations, or both, the facts of business life do not change materially. Fact remains fact, and myth remains myth. The principles and practices by which the ventures of major corporations and major industries survive, prosper, or perish will be the same ones by which your venture will survive, prosper, or perish.

This is inescapable truth and will not change, despite the many sociological and technical changes that have and will continue to come about.

Chapter Four

Incorporation, Partnerships, and Related Myths and Misunderstandings

Many forms of business organization are possible and available, but no single one is universally most suitable or most beneficial. You must choose the form that best suits your own needs.

A PREFATORY NOTE

In discussing the many basic types of business organizations, it is inevitable that many questions of legal considerations and tax implications will be raised. That is what makes these prefatory notes necessary, for I am neither a lawyer nor an accountant, and I make no pretensions to professional expertise in either of these fields. I am, instead, an experienced businessman who is reporting what I have personally experienced and observed over a number of decades as relevant and applicable to the general case. If you need competent legal opinions on your own special circumstances, please consult a licensed, practicing attorney. If you want specific tax information on your own situation, consult a tax or financial specialist, who will probably be also an accountant. Indeed, the tax laws change almost every year, and even the specialists have difficulty keeping up with the changes.

In that spirit and on that basis, then, here are my observations on how to organize to do business.

SHOULD YOU INCORPORATE?

One of the most common questions asked by the new or prospective entrepreneur is, "Shall I incorporate?" In a great many cases, the question is prompted by common misunderstanding or myth, notably the myth that a business that can add "Inc." or use the word "Corporation" in its name is immediately much more prestigious, impressive, and credible to bankers, investors, and prospective customers than those underprivileged business organizations not so blessed with the cloak of incorporation.

That is not to derogate the worth of incorporation, but only to place it in proper perspective as a business maneuver. In fact, much of this chapter will be devoted to the various subjects of incorporation, for it is not only a most important subject, it is a diverse one as well and should not be brushed lightly aside. But first let us survey the several basic ways of organizing a business—any business—and we will return to the subject of incorporation later.

Of course, you need not make an immediate decision on the type of business organization you want; you can always start as a sole proprietorship, or even as a partnership, if you are not alone in the venture, and incorporate at some later date, if you decide to. The sole proprietorship is the most basic and popular form of small business organization, and unless you believe that there is a serious danger arising out of personal liability early in the history of your venture, you may decide to begin as a sole proprietorship, with time enough later to reconsider your position.

THE MANY FORMS OF BUSINESS ORGANIZATION

By far the simplest kind of business organization is the *sole proprietorship*. Organizing your venture as a sole proprietorship means, in as simple a set of terms as possible, that you and you alone own everything—all assets—and are personally responsible for everything—all liabilities and potential liabilities of the venture. You pay taxes as a self-employed person, although if you employ others you are obligated for all taxes normally exacted from employers, and you need no special permits or documents other than whatever licensing fees are normally imposed by your state and/or local government on enterprises such as yours.

If you are not alone in your venture but have one or more partners, and you choose not to incorporate your venture, you will be wise to draw up a formal partnership agreement. That means an agreement on paper, duly signed and witnessed. Do not depend on verbal agreements, no matter how close you are with and trust your partner. Many partnerships founded on a handshake and verbal pledge have been successful, but many more have not—have not, in many cases, survived even formal, written agreements, let alone informal, verbal ones. Nor are possible difficulties arising out of partnership entirely a matter of getting your fair share of all income and assets; there is also the quite serious matter of being responsible for only your fair share of all liabilities, for you are all personally liable under a partnership.

But that is getting ahead of ourselves a bit: Other considerations precede even that of making formal agreements. And they are not only the many legal implications that a lawyer would point out to you; they are the many practical considerations of a working partnership, for I assume that both or all of you would be actively engaged in conducting the venture.

The question of entering into a contract—an agreement is a contract—at all, with anyone and under any circumstances, merits serious consideration always. No written instrument protects you against an insincere customer, supplier, or partner. The purpose of the agreement is not to keep the other honest, but to make a record of what you have agreed to. If you do not have confidence in the other's honest and sincere intent before you start, you would be ill advised to enter into an agreement of any kind. That is a first consideration.

Even then, there is the consideration of whether the proposed partnership is a completely practicable one. Two acquaintances or friends who get along well with each other socially may or may not make good business partners, where you usually operate under some degree of stress, and where each of you must make your own contributions and handle your own duties and responsibilities. Is each of you properly equipped to make an equal contribution of money, labor, and talent to the venture—that is, to "carry your own weight"? Do you respect each other in a professional or business sense? Are you each prepared to make equal sacrifices? (It will probably be necessary to do so.)

I base this on personal experience. On more than one occasion I have found that someone I liked, trusted, and got along with well made a completely unsatisfactory business partner. The characteristics needed for one of those roles are quite different from those needed for the other role.

Unlike a corporation, a partnership does not require the payment of a separate income tax, for the partnership is not an entity, as a corporation is. The partners are each liable for individual income taxes, however, as they would be in any case.

It would probably be a wise move to have an attorney draw up your partnership agreement. Should you decide to do it yourself, however, be sure that the agreement contains all the following kinds of information stated unequivocally:

Date of the agreement

Full identification of the two or more parties entering into agreement

Name of the partnership or business

Intended term of the partnership (until death of one, until some date, or until termination as provided in the agreement)

Place of business

Nature or objective of business
Role of each partner
Capital investments by each partner
Compensation of each partner
Regular meetings
Authority of each partner
How partner may dispose of his/her partnership
Who signs checks
Special provisions

This may serve as a checklist of sorts. A lawyer might suggest a number of other clauses as being wise to include, however, depending on the nature of the business and the working arrangements.

A partnership can assume a number of special forms. First, it can be entirely informal, sealed with nothing more than the exhange of vows and a handshake, it can be entered into with an informal or formal written agreement, and it can be a limited or unlimited partnership. In a *limited partnership*, for example, a partner may invest a certain sum in the enterprise and then limit his liabilities for losses to that amount. Too, for income tax purposes, the very term *partnership* may be synonymous with *group, pool, syndicate, joint venture,* or similar terms. There is also such a thing as a *family partnership*, which is one whose members are related by blood or marriage. These can offer certain tax benefits in some cases.

With so many complications possible and all the implications for tax purposes, it is probably wise to consult an experienced attorney before entering into a partnership.

These have been general notes on partnership and partnership agreements. Let us now turn to a more complicated form of business organization, the corporation.

INCORPORATION

The simple fact is that in most, if not all states, incorporation costs about $40 to $50, can be accomplished easily by an individual—yourself—and usually requires nothing more than completing a simple one- or two-page form. (The practical consideration in whether you should do your own incorporation or retain a lawyer to do it for you is, probably, whether you will or will not have other principals—business partners, in fact, although technically shareholders in the corporation.)

If it is your idea that incorporating your venture lends you prestige, consider the fact that you or anyone else can be incorporated in most states for a few dollars and with a simple form. How much prestige accrues to an organization as a result of such a simple and inexpensive procedure? Obviously, not a great deal; there are more valid and worthy reasons for incorporating if, indeed, you ought to do so.

The Pros and Cons of Incorporating

Because various forms of incorporation are available to you, each with its own characteristics, any listing of pros and cons must either be highly specific to a given corporation or else phrased in the most general terms. The following few basic pros and cons of incorporating your business are therefore stated only generally, with more detailed discussions to follow.

Pro: As a separate legal entity, the corporation is responsible and liable for its own actions and debts, so your personal assets are sheltered generally, although there are some exceptions.

Pro: As a corporation, you may be able to find tax benefits and reward yourself with generous, nontaxable fringe benefits.

Pro: Incorporating is an excellent way to work with others as coventurers, in many ways preferable to a partnership.

Con: A great deal of extra paperwork is involved in operating a corporation.

Con: You are liable to certain taxes imposed on corporations that you would not have to incur under other forms of organization.

These points are stated as they apply to the beginning of a small business, for there are numerous potential or nominal advantages to incorporating, such as the capability for raising capital by issuing stock, that are usually not practical benefits for the newly formed small corporation.

Corporate Models

The most common model for the small beginning venture is, probably, the *close corporation*, sometimes also referred to as a "family" corporation because the number of stockholders is limited and is often confined to the members of a small family engaged in a small business, with certain obligations to enable the stockholders to keep ownership within the family. It is also possible to include clauses in the Certificate of Incorporation that provide for the shareholders to have the powers normally assigned to directors, so that there is no need for directors and directors' meetings. In fact, you can even hold all the offices yourself, although most individuals make friends or family members officers and directors.

On the other hand, a *close* or *closely held* corporation may not make a public offering of stock shares, but that is entirely in keeping with the philosophy of the *closely held* business organization.

Gerre Jones, an Albuquerque marketing consultant (Gerre Jones Associates, Inc.) and publisher (*Professional Marketing Report*, a widely read newsletter), would incorporate as a *Subchapter S corporation*, if he had it to do over, he says. This option is available to the small corporation (less than ten shareholders and little or no investment income) and has the advantage that the corporation is not required to pay corporate income tax, as the close corporation is required to do.

But even that apparently desirable feature is not necessarily significant; it has no meaning if the corporation has no profits to tax. If, for example, your salary is $40,000 and that consumes all the gross profits of the corporation, it has no net profit on which to pay taxes anyway! And many small businesses have little or no net profit left after all expenses are paid and the principals—you, especially—take salaries. So the Subchapter S corporation may or may not have practical value for you.

Domestic and Foreign Corporations

The word *foreign*, as applied to corporations, has a special meaning here. It is a name applied to any corporation doing business in a state other than the one in which it is incorporated. If you do business in Missouri but choose to incorporate in Delaware (as so many have in years past), you are a foreign corporation in Missouri. And a corporation doing business in many states is a foreign corporation in each of those states other than the one in which it is incorporated.

As a foreign corporation, you must register with the local authorities, pay certain fees and taxes there, and maintain a registered agent in the state where you are incorporated.

Places to Incorporate

For many years, Delaware was the favorite state for incorporation, even of companies that made their headquarters in other states, because it offered favorable conditions, such as low costs. So many corporations, large and small (over 75,000), opted for Delaware incorporation that it became something of a local industry! Other states began to liberalize their own conditions and fees for incorporation, and today you can incorporate in your own state, in most cases, under conditions as liberal as those of Delaware or, at least, competitive with Delaware's conditions for incorporating.

Kinds of Corporations

There are many kinds of corporations, aside from being a *close* or *closed* one that is the favorite choice of those incorporating one-person or family businesses, including public, private, profit, and nonprofit, as well as foreign and domestic. For our purposes, I will assume that you might be interested in incorporating as a private, profit, close corporation.

Requirements for Incorporating

Each state has its own set of requirements, forms, and procedures for registering a corporation, but these are the five basic steps:

1. Choose a name.
2. Fill out the official form (articles of incorporation).
3. File the form, with the required fee.
4. Get a corporate kit.
5. Hold the organizational meeting.

The name you choose must be unique, and the state office with which you file your papers will make a search to be sure that it is unique before they will approve and register your corporation.

The form used to register the articles of incorporation is usually quite simple. In Maryland, where I registered HRH Communications, Inc., it consisted of a one-page form, and other states usually offer equally simple forms, based generally on the Model Business Corporation Act of the American Bar Association's Committee on Corporate Laws. The form may vary widely, from state to state, but the differences are not likely to be greatly significant. An example of a simple form is offered as Figure 4-1. It assumes one incorporator, but incorporation can be done by more than one person. A few comments on the form represented by this figure may be helpful:

Unless you are forming a corporation for some special and temporary purpose, the word *perpetual* is appropriate for the second item.

You can, if you wish to, add an appendix or attachment of some sort to explain the purposes of the corporation in more detail, but it is usually not necessary to say more than is suggested in the figure.

You may issue some small amount of stock—perhaps 100 or 1,000 shares—and give it a par or no par value, neither of which has any great significance at this point, unless the corporation is to be heavily capitalized initially.

The filing fee, which must accompany your certificate of incorporation, will probably run on the order of $25 to $50. In my own case, it was $40 plus an optional $6 if I wanted a certified copy of the approved form returned to me for my own files.

You need a set of bylaws, forms for recording corporate resolutions (you need a resolution, for example, to open a cor-

Articles of Incorporation

The undersigned, being of age _____ or more, acting as incorporators for a corporation under the laws of the State of _____, hereby adopts the following Articles of Incorporation for such corporation.

First: The name of the corporation is _____.

Second: The period of its duration is _____.

Third: The purpose for which the corporation is organized is to engage in any lawful act or activity for which corporations may be organized in the State of _____.

Fourth: The total amount of authorized capital stock which the corporation shall have the authority to issue is _____ shares of _____ value.

Fifth: The name and mailing address of the incorporator are

_____

(*name*)

_____

(*address*)

_____

(*city, state, zip*)

Sixth: The names and addresses of directors are as follows:

_____   _____

(*name*)   (*name*)

_____   _____

(*address*)   (*address*)

_____   _____

(*city, state, zip*)   (*city, state, zip*)

Seventh: The address of the initial registered office is

_____

and the name of the initial registered agent at that address is

_____

Dated at: _____

State of: _____

County of: _____

_____

(*signed*)

Figure 4-1 *Typical Form for Incorporation*

porate bank account, but the bank will probably furnish its own form to execute), and you should have a corporate seal, although it is not a legal requirement. (A rubber stamp will serve the purpose, too.) You can buy a complete corporate kit, including all these and other items you need, in a well-stocked office supplies emporium or in any of the corporate specialties suppliers found in most metropolitan areas. (Check the phone book's yellow pages for these.)

A corporation needs officers—a president, secretary, and treasurer, at least, although many small corporations combine the latter two—and directors. For the typical family corporation, it is common practice to appoint members of the family to these posts, but it is also possible to hold all the positions yourself!

Technically, you should have an organization meeting to elect permanent officers and conduct other beginning business, such as adoption of bylaws and approving issuance or distribution of stock. If you are a one-person corporation and wear all the hats yourself, however, a simple corporate resolution or two should satisfy the requirements.

Where to File

In many states the office of the secretary of state handles the creation of the corporation. Other states have created special offices for the purpose. The list that follows contains the best known addresses of the responsible authorities in the various states. An inquiry to the office listed for your own state will bring you the necessary details and forms.

Secretary of State
Montgomery, AL 36100

Commissioner of Commerce
Juneau, AK 99801

Secretary of State
Little Rock, AR 72200

Secretary of State
Phoenix, AZ 85007

Secretary of State
Sacramento, CA 95801

Secretary of State
Denver, CO 90202

Secretary of State
Hartford, CT 06100

Secretary of State
Dover, DE 19901

Office of Superintendent of Corporations
Washington, DC 20000

Secretary of State
Tallahassee, FL 32301

Secretary of State
Atlanta, GA 30300

Director of Regulatory Agencies
P.O. Box 40
Honolulu, HI 96800

Secretary of State
Boise, ID 83700

Secretary of State
Springfield, IL 62700

Secretary of State
Indianapolis, IN 46200

Secretary of State
Des Moines, IA 50300

Secretary of State
Topeka, KS 66600

Secretary of State
Frankfort, KY 40601

Secretary of State
Baton Rouge, LA 70800

Secretary of State
Augusta, ME 04301

State Department of Assessment & Taxation
301 West Preston
Baltimore, MD 21201

Secretary of Commonwealth
Boston, MA 02100

Department of Commerce
Corporation Division
P.O. Drawer C
Lansing, MI 48904

Secretary of State
St. Paul, MN 55100

Secretary of State
Jackson, MS 39200

Secretary of State
Jefferson City, MO 65101

Secretary of State
Helena, MT 59601

Secretary of State
Lincoln, NE 68500

Secretary of State
Carson City, NV 89701

Secretary of State
Concord, NH 03300

Secretary of State
Trenton, NJ 08600

State Corporation Commission
Santa Fe, NM 87501

Secretary of State
Albany, NY 12200

Secretary of State
Raleigh, NC 27600

Secretary of State
Bismark, ND 58501

Secretary of State
Columbus, OH 43200

Secretary of State
Oklahoma, OK 73100

Corporation Commissioner
Salem, OR 97301

Department of State
Harrisburg, PA 17101

Secretary of State
Providence, RI 02900

Secretary of State
Columbia, SC 29200

Secretary of State
Pierre, SD 57501

Secretary of State
Nashville, TN 37200

Secretary of State
Austin, TX 78700

Secretary of State
Salt Lake City, UT 84100

Secretary of State
Montpelier, VT 05601

State Corporation Commission
Richmond, VA 23200

Secretary of State
Olympia, WA 98501

Secretary of State
Charleston, WV 25300

Secretary of State
Madison, WI 53700

Secretary of State
Cheyenne, WY 82001

A FEW RELATED MATTERS

Among the areas that have accumulated an abundance of myth and misunderstanding are patents, logos, trademarks, registered trademarks, and copyrights. A little knowledge of these matters can save you a great deal of grief in the future.

Contracts

Lawyers have written tomes of information and opinions about contracts, and the courts are kept busy hearing cases revolving about contract disputes. So there is no doubt that contracts are an important subject, not only to those in the legal profession, but also to those in business and in private life. They are thus unavoidably a subject to which I will be compelled to return, from time to time. For now, let us deal with only the basic facts and common myths.

First of all, stripped to its essentials, a *contract* is an agreement between two parties, either individuals or organizations, although an agreement may exist among several parties, in some cases. In the agreement, the parties commit themselves to certain promises, usually an exchange of money for goods or services. This is the simple definition. Lawyers, especially law professors, will talk about "valid considerations" and other contract elements, but those are the finer points that do not ordinarily concern businesspeople and lay people, as far as legal matters are concerned.

The most common misunderstanding, probably, is the mistaken notion that a contract is a piece of paper or that it must be recorded on paper and signed by the parties to be valid. In fact, verbal or oral contracts are as binding as are written contracts. When a dispute arises over a verbal contract, however, there is usually a problem in establishing just what the contract provided. It is primarily to avoid the necessity for relying on human memory (and, perhaps, human honesty!) that it is wise to have contracts in writing and in as much detail as possible, for even then disputes may easily arise and often do.

There is also the myth that once someone signs a contract, he or she is "sunk," even if the contract proves patently unfair or the signer changes his or her mind. In fact, contracts entered into in good faith and with complete understanding and agreement by both parties are considered to be binding, but contracts lacking these qualifications may be considered by a court to be invalid. For example, an individual who was persuaded to sign a contract in which false promises were made and whose wording only a lawyer or equivalent expert could fully understand may challenge the contract and may well be successful in that challenge. Contracts are often overturned because they are defective in some respect.

Despite this, right and wrong vis-à-vis contracts and contract law are by no means crystal clear, and caution in writing and signing contracts is always well advised, as is writing them in the clearest language possible. Today, in the interest of clarity, even many lawyers are abandoning Latin terms and legal jargon in writing contracts.

Copyright

Authors, composers, artists, and other creative artists—for example, computer programmers—can secure and protect title to their creations by simply claiming copyright, although it is wise to place a notice on the product immediately, even under today's much liberalized copyright law. A copyright is now effective for the lifetime of the copyright owner plus fifty years, and failure to post the claim to copyright immediately does not necessarily cause immediate loss of copyright, as it did under the older law. Copyright owners may sell copies of their property directly to consumers, but more often they sell publishers the rights to distribute—that is, sell—their work and are paid royalties on all copies sold.

Contrary to popular notion, a copyright need not be registered with the Copyright Office, a division of the Library of Congress, to be afforded copyright protection, although it must be so registered in the event of litigation. Posting the notice of copyright on the property is enough to provide a common law copyright. Registration with the Copyright Office can be done at any time, even much later.

An interesting sidelight: Titles cannot be copyrighted, so it is not illegal to use the same title as another work does, nor need you therefore worry about whether you have inadvertently chosen a title that is already in use, unknown to you.

You should also understand that you cannot copyright a name or slogan. If you wish to reserve to yourself rights to a name, slogan, or title, you must seek to do so by registering it with the Patent Office as a trademark. (See also the discussion of trademarks.)

Implied Contract

As you may have surmised when you read that verbal contracts are binding, there is such a thing as an *implied contract*. That is one in which the agreement of an exchange – some act for which a consideration is promised – appears to have been clearly intended. If you hire a house painter and agree to pay the price he quotes, a contract is clearly implied here, and should a legal dispute wind up in court, the judge is likely to infer that a contract was entered into by implication.

Judgment

In the legal sense, a *judgment* is what the judge grants the victor in a suit in which the victor has demanded money and been awarded it by the judge or jury. But an award – a judgment – does not guarantee payment. There may be a problem in collecting. The judge does not collect for you; he merely gives you the legal right to go after your opponent's assets – bank accounts, property, jewelry, or other negotiable items. It's up to you to find the assets and seize them, if the opponent does not willingly pay the amount of the judgment. Individuals who declare themselves to be "judgment proof" often are those who have hidden their assets and defy creditors to find them.

Trademark

A trademark is some distinctive name, slogan, logo, design, or other mark that someone uses to identify and distinguish his or her company, goods, or service. *Xerox, IBM,* and *WordStar* are all trademarks, for example. Trademarks are registered with the U.S. Patent Office (part of the Department of Commerce) and, when approved, become registered trademarks and are so identified. While the registration is pending, the trademarks are identified with a superscript ™; after registration they are identified with a superscript ®.

Chapter Five

Lawyers, Accountants, and Other Specialists

You will need the help of many technical and professional specialists, but you need also to know when and how to use their services wisely and in such a way that they serve your best interests; you must never give up ultimate control over your business.

THE AGE OF THE SPECIALIST

We live in an era of specialization, probably the inevitable consequence of the growing expansion of knowledge in most areas; it has simply become impossible for the average practitioner in any field to be the master of the entire field. For example, today the word *engineer* must be prefixed by one of a large number of adjectives: we have mechanical engineers, electrical engineers, electronics engineers, rocket engineers, stress engineers, computer engineers, civil engineers, aeronautical engineers, and many other engineering breeds; the list goes on. But it does not stop there; even within each special field there are subspecialties that develop as the field grows, and the trend is fated to continue, steadily creating even newer specialties.

Lawyers specialize—criminal lawyers, corporate lawyers,

trial lawyers, divorce lawyers, medical-malpractice lawyers, and others. Physicians have long specialized, and even the general practitioner is now a specialist, engaging in the "specialty" known as family practice, much of which is concerned with preliminary diagnosis and knowing what kinds of specialists to refer the patient to or call on for consultation. Even accountants specialize, as the variety of needs expands.

Inculcated as we are with the philosophy of specialization and our need for specialists' services, it is not surprising that we turn to specialists for guidance, nor is there anything wrong in doing so. But a great deal is wrong, quite often, in the ways we seek out such help and even more so in the ways we use that help.

Do You Need a Lawyer?

We all have legal problems, from time to time, and sometimes they are serious enough problems to require the services of a lawyer. In some cases, a letter on a lawyer's letterhead works wonders. When I could get no response from a former employer who owed me several months' salary, a letter from my attorney brought a prompt response, indicating a willingness to negotiate. And when I needed to know what the law was and how it would probably apply in a specific situation, I consulted my lawyer for his opinion and advice. But sometimes I had a problem that was "out of his field" and I had to seek out another lawyer, one whose specialty covered my need of the moment.

Aside from this, and regardless of which specialized legal eagle I consulted, I always understood that what my own lawyer advised was his opinion, based on his knowledge of the law, his experience as a lawyer, and the information I had provided. I understood, too, that what my lawyer offered was *opinion*—his opinion—not final judgment from on high.

That is not an insignificant observation. Quite the contrary, it is the very point of this entire chapter: The experts you consult—lawyers, accountants, engineers, computer specialists, and consultants of various stamps and breeds—offer their judgments and opinions, and we hope that they offer reasoned, objective, and wise recommendations. But these are, at best, only recommendations, not the *decisions* that must be made; only you can make those final decisions. Do not expect or permit those specialists to make your decisions for you. Despite their education and experience, they can be wrong. In any case, decision making about your venture is your responsibility — always. You cannot escape it, and no one can usurp it.

Take the simple case of your question about whether you ought to incorporate. You put the question to your lawyer. Can he or she give you a truly objective answer? It is difficult to do so because arranging your incorporation probably means a fee of $1,000 or more for a relatively simple and routine set of services.

You need to know what to ask for when you seek expert help. Properly, you should not ask your lawyer whether incorporation is a good idea for you. How does he or she know? Your lawyer is a legal advisor, not a business or management advisor, and does not understand your business and your business needs (presumably). What a lawyer can and should tell you — should be asked — is what incorporation costs and what it means:

- What is the initial cost?
- What new taxes and other costs will you have to support as a corporation?
- What are the secondary costs — e.g., additional accounting and other reports and paperwork?
- What are the benefits (if any)?
- What are the alternatives — e.g., less costly and less difficult ways of accomplishing the same purposes?

Only armed with answers to these and perhaps other, related questions are you in a position to ponder the advisability of incorporating. It is easy enough and cheap enough to become incorporated, but perhaps you only become committed in doing so — open a Pandora's box of resulting problems and costs that force you to throw money at problems resulting from the act of incorporating.

Most experienced lawyers understand these principles quite well and will not attempt to force their judgments on you or make your decisions for you. They will usually try to present a balanced view—the alternatives available to you and the pros and cons of each—and ask you to express an opinion or, at most, will offer a recommendation even if it is not specifically asked for. But there are others who, in their eagerness to serve, will attempt to force their opinion on you to invoke a decision they champion. It is up to you not to permit this to happen.

IS IT ALL OVER YOUR HEAD?

We all get a little confused, awed, and even intimidated by the special jargon of lawyers, accountants, engineers, and others, and we suspect that perhaps they deliberately use that jargon as a defensive measure to perpetuate their mastery and dominance. We sense, sometimes, that they seem to be saying to us, "You wouldn't understand, so take my word for it."

I reject that, and so should you. It is my opinion that every specialist you retain to help you in some way is obligated to make verbal or written reports justifying his or her actions and bills but, most important, explaining what he or she has done. I believe that I am capable of understanding every situation, in principle at least, and that it is the obligation of any specialist I hire to explain matters to me in language I can understand. I insist on that, and you should also; understanding is what you are paying for, and recommendations are of little value to you if you do not fully understand the basis—the rationale—for them so that you can judge them for yourself.

The Case of the Accountant

Perhaps the most difficult professional for us ordinary people to understand is the accountant. Consider only the kinds of minds—accounting minds, if the IRS—that have developed the forms, manipulations, and instructions necessary to prepare even a simple tax return!

The tax laws grow more and more complex even as we are assured that they are being simplified, and we grow more and more reliant on accountants to keep our books and prepare our tax returns, especially when we are in a business venture and must cope with such added complications as assets, liabilities, depreciation, amortization, and other mysterious terms that trip so easily from the accountant's lips. But let us first get a better understanding of why we must keep accounts and what we ought to do with the record—what, in fact, accounting is. (It is true that a great many people in business, small and large, do not understand what accounting is.)

Many people believe that we are required to maintain accounting systems for the convenience of the Internal Revenue Service. It is easy to understand how such a notion has gained currency: We *do* have to have records to substantiate our tax returns and claims made therein. And our accounting systems ought to be designed to maximize the tax benefits possible. The prime purpose of the accounting system, however, is to help us manage our business successfully. Specifically, it is to provide feedback—information—on which to base our management decisions, detect unwarranted expenses, determine which operations are profitable and which are not, and otherwise guide us. The system ought to generate reports for that purpose, and in large systems they do, today usually in the form of thick computer printouts distributed to the managers. In the small system, such as you and I normally use, we usually get our information directly from the books by scanning them frequently. And that is one of the problems in turning your books over to a public accountant—at least to some public accountants I have met: They either have your books in their offices most of the time or they visit you to make postings only once a week or once every two weeks. The information you get is history, not current events, and so is therefore not very useful directly in managing your venture. (More on this in the next chapter.)

The Communication Difficulty

I think it quite possible that accountants and other specialists are so accustomed to thinking only in terms of their own jargon that they become quite incapable of thinking of what they do in plain English; much less can they translate it for others. Take the simple term *cost of sales*, for example; what does it mean?

You or I might ordinarily assume that *cost of sales* refers to the cost of marketing, the cost of winning the orders. That is a reasonable inference, and it is a figure that is of considerable use to a manager. But that is not what the term means to an accountant. The accountant regards cost of sales as including all costs incurred for or by an item before it is sold. Beware of applying everyday language definitions to accounting terms; they are not reliable indicators of meaning in this special world. Take the apparently simple distinction of running your business on a *cash basis*. To us lay people, that means cash "up front," on delivery, and in some businesses it even means currency only accepted; no checks or charges. But that is not what the accountant means by a cash system. He means you post a receipt, a record of income, when the check arrives, and you post a debit when you pay a bill. The alternative system is to post a receipt as income when you send out an invoice to customer and to post a debit when you receive a bill.

In light of all this, it is easy to understand the difficulty of communicating with an accountant. So you must learn the language of accounting, at least at a beginner's level, compel the accountant to explain himself or herself in simple English, or abandon all efforts to probe the mysteries and simply accept what your accountant does and says.

Certainly, you ought to reject that last option. It represents too many hazards; you almost surely underestimate the importance of accounting to the success of your venture if you are willing to do that. The second option may be little more than hope; many accountants, I have found, have great difficulty making the translations. The first option is probably the best bet, although you must still press your accountant for precise explanations, and do apply some of that ordinary wisdom we refer to as *common sense*. For example, pressed by my accountant for a decision on the cost estimates in a proposal, I demurred because I was skeptical of the costs presented; I thought the risk of loss rather excessive. But the accountant, working with the executive who had worked up the proposal, offered me a rather elaborate presentation of his cost analysis, showing a favorable bottom line, or so he alleged.

Innocent as I am of financial and accounting expertise, I was unable to understand and appreciate this sophisticated presentation, so I was forced to either accept it or find a means to analyze it. I therefore resorted to a simple expedient to study the figures offered: I drew a line down the center of a blank sheet and headed the two columns thus created, as shown in Figure 5-1. Then I asked that each of the numbers in the presentation be transferred to the appropriate column, after which I added each column and compared the totals. The accountant in question was no longer able to support an argument for profitability of the contract in question.

OUTGO	INCOME

Figure 5-1   Simple Method for Analyzing Costs and Profits

I am sure that the accountant was sincere in offering me his cost and profit analysis, and that is perhaps the danger in abandoning our basic human judgment and replacing it with elaborate methodology: It is easy to practice an unconscious self-deceit.

BEWARE OF READY-MADE SOLUTIONS AND CONVENTIONAL WISDOM

Experts you turn to may attempt to impose their favorite, preconceived ideas on you, basing their urgent recommendations on their authority as experts. Beware of experts with favorite formulas for success, ready-made solutions to your problems, and other patent or improvised ideas about how to conduct your business. Well-intentioned though many of these experts are, they often tend to try to force-fit you to their own notions of how your business ought to be run. (My own accountant periodically attempts to interpose himself as my business manager, suggesting how much I ought to charge clients, what services I should sell, and otherwise advising me in matters about a business with which he is not at all familiar.)

One of the hazards presented by consultation with many experts is their advocacy of conventional wisdom, for there is a body of conventional wisdom surrounding every business and profession. For example, some of those advising me on the mail-order business years ago explained the conventional wisdom of that field, as they understood it, including the following, among other choice morsels of knowledge all but guaranteed to keep me out of trouble and bring me to early success:

- Summer months, June through August, are dreadfully "slow," and it is a waste of money to do much advertising in those months.
- Business will pick up briskly after Labor Day and will remain good until spring.
- To be successful, a mailing must produce a 4- or 5-percent response — percentage of orders, that is.
- A mail-order item must sell for at least three times its cost to you, to be profitable, and even that is a bit too close for comfort.
- Sales literature printed in several colors produces better results than literature printed in one color ink only.
- Sales literature printed on a better grade of paper will increase the number of orders returned.
- A postage-paid return envelope enclosed with the sales literature will greatly increase the number of orders returning.

Are these all myths? No, they are not myths. But they are not reliable rules, either. They are partial truths, true under certain circumstances or true occasionally and untrue at other times. There were years in which business was good all summer and not so good in the autumn and winter. I have run profitable campaigns with a 1 percent or even smaller response, and it is impossible, under certain conditions (e.g., with a $2 or $3 item) to make profits even with a 10 percent response. The improvement in response due to multicolor printing and/or postage-paid response envelopes is so slight, in percentage terms, that a significant increase in income (if any) is apparent only when the mailing is very large. Postage-paid response envelopes help some when you are mailing to individuals but are of negligible influence when you mail to businesses, I have found. And I could find no evidence that spending more money for a better grade of paper improved results.

And yet, despite this, I do not discount the advice, for something prompted those beliefs. And that something was probably that these bits of wisdom appeared to make a difference in some cases. The problem is that it is not possible to predict, with any certainty, in which cases they will prove to be helpful, but only that they will be valid for certain situations. And later, when we discuss mail order, we will raise the question again and suggest a course of action that is reasonably reliable.

THE INHERENT PARADOX OF CONVENTIONAL WISDOM

But of course mail order is not the only area where those with experience present themselves as experts and offer advice and pat answers that are not total untruths, yet are often highly misleading. Every field has its burden of conventional wisdom. But in our dynamic era, conventional wisdom has an inherent paradox: It tends to be obsolete by the time it becomes conventional wisdom! That is, it is often a collection of yesterday's truths in today's changing world.

The best use of conventional wisdom is to accept it as a working premise before committing your resources to it. Do not reject it totally, for it does represent someone's successful experience and knowledge, but do not accept it as instantly applicable to your situation and use. In fact, treat all expert advice with that kind of caution, for even the general truth is valid only for an assumed set of circumstances and conditions and is rarely if ever universally true. When I was advised by someone that an advertising piece I had designed was dreadful and inevitably destined for failure, I was dismayed because I had already had a large quantity printed. Reluctant to discard them and waste the money spent on printing, I invested enough additional money to make a test mailing. To my delight, the mailing was highly successful, and I mailed the rest of the new literature in a successful follow-up campaign. That does not mean that my adviser of that moment was incompetent, but only that he was too sure that his assessment was correct for me and my situation of the moment. Another time, that sales piece might well have been a complete loser.

The lesson is really that there are no sure things. Even an exact duplicate of a prior success does not ensure another success; there are imponderables in most situations, factors and influences—some of them pure chance. Just consider some of the fads and the businesses built on them to see how unpredictable many of these situations are.

Twenty-five years ago, someone introduced a novelty called the hula hoop. Some manufacturers acted quickly enough made a great deal of money; those who were a bit slower to tool up and produce hula hoops lost a great deal of money, for this wild fad lasted just about six weeks, after which enthusiasm faded swiftly.

Gary Dahl is reported to have made a million dollars in ninety days with his "pet rock" novelty. He is fortunate if he did, for the enthusiasm for that item lasted just about that length of time.

There have been many such fads that roar aloft suddenly, soar wildly, and fall back to earth just as suddenly, after an indeterminate but usually short time in the spotlight. The family of such items includes yo-yos, miniskirts, and Rubik's Cube, among others. Cautious testing of the market would never pay out here, for the whole market for such items is usually short lived; marketing is an out-and-out gamble in these cases. Your own judgment or "gut feeling" is as dependable as anyone's, expert or not. No one can tell you what the next yo-yo or hula hoop will be or how long there will be a viable market for it. This is not to say that there are not cases where a home-based entrepreneur has created a hot item, as in the case of Joe Cossman and his ant farms. Cossman learned of the existence of this item as a hobby and arranged to promote it, making a profitable venture of it. But that is his style, selling a single item at a time, typically one for which there is or can be created a short-term demand, and then getting out of it to begin seeking the next item, when the demand begins to fall off.

A FEW HAZARDS

There are many hazards for the new and even for the experienced entrepreneur. One is the expert who promises the can't-fail franchise, and prominent among these are the MLM — multilevel marketing — programs offered.

This is not to condemn all such offerings. Obviously, many people are engaged successfully in such programs. But many lose money and time and may even become completely discouraged and lose whatever entrepreneurial spirit they had, as a result of bad experiences buying into such programs.

There are thousands of "experts" ready to take your money. Some give good value; others give next to nothing, are fraudulent in making promises they do not (cannot) make good. When a headline makes a promise that is too good to be true — e.g., HOW TO MAKE A MILLION DOLLARS A YEAR — GUARANTEED! — that is exactly what is wrong with it: it is too good to be true. Such advertisements are, in fact, fraudulent, in violation of several laws, but the authorities are simply incapable of keeping up with and policing all of the offending advertisers. In fact, many are probably on the edge — fraudulent but difficult to prosecute because of technicalities.

You must use your own judgment in assessing these claims. At the least, do some checking, if the purchase represents a substantial investment. And there are several ways to do this:

- Sometimes these advertisers publish short sentences that purport to be endorsements from satisfied customers, with the notation that the full letters are on file. Ask for copies of those letters.
- Whether the advertiser does or does not claim such endorsements, ask for the names of satisfied and successful customers in your locality and talk to those people. If the advertiser resists your efforts to get at least a half-dozen names and addresses, with stalls and excuses, be alarmed by that. There is no reason an advertiser with a legitimate product or service to sell would evade such a request.
- Inquire of Better Business Bureaus and Chambers of Commerce if there have been complaints about the advertiser. Inquire not only in your own city, but also in the city where the advertiser is located.

This kind of checking is not only to verify the honesty of the advertiser, however, but also to verify his or her competence. Many self-proclaimed expert copywriters, marketing consultants, direct-mail counselors, and others prove to be considerably less expert than they claim (and, presumably, truly believe themselves to be) at their chosen skills. Such people are not conscious frauds; they truly believe in what they claim they can do for you. But that does not mitigate the damage they can do you and your venture. Bear in mind at all times that the relationships among the quality or virtues of a product or service offered, the effectiveness of its marketing, and the success of the venture in the marketplace are far from linear or direct—are not even a cause-and-effect relationship. Poor products and services that are marketed effectively may be—and probably will be— more successful than good products and services that are marketed poorly. So don't allow the apparent or even real success of what you are offered throw sand in your eyes. Judge the product or service on its merits, not on how persuasive the seller is. Gather in a reasonable amount of information before you attempt to make a judgment, and never make a judgment without having gathered some objective information—hard facts.

Chapter Six

Can You Do It Yourself?

*Certain things you ought
to do for yourself not only to
save money; there are even
more important benefits in
many cases.*

SPECIALISTS AND SUPERSPECIALISTS

As we saw in the last chapter, today might fairly be called the
age of superspecialization, an age in which even specialists
specialize. Whether you practice law, medicine, engineering,
technical writing, plumbing, or almost any other profession,
craft, or trade, the practical advantages of specializing within
your specialty soon become apparent. And some fields have
multiple levels of specialization as a result of increasing knowledge and economic advantage. In many situations it is simply
more profitable to be a superspecialist: You may be able to operate with greater efficiency and may be able to command a larger
fee for your services.

Yet with all this increasing vertical specialization, our society has kept its strong do-it-yourself ethic. This holds for more
than assembling a TV stand, repairing a leaky faucet, or panel-
ing your basement, however. We have already discussed the
ease with which you can handle your own incorporation or
registration of a fictitious (dba) name for your venture and buy
a ready-made corporate kit of bylaws, forms, stock certificates,
and seal, for one thing. And even a casual survey of bookstore

shelves reveals books offering to guide you as a lay person in handling your own divorce suit or bankruptcy, writing contracts, dealing with bank officials, and managing your investment portfolio, among other tasks. You can now buy do-it-yourself kits for pregnancy tests in the drugstore, use a simple desktop computer to publish your own newsletter, and do a great many other things that were once the exclusive province of the specialist.

These opportunities lead to the inevitable problem of trying to decide what you can and should do for yourself versus what you should entrust only to the hands of an experienced professional. This is no small problem.

Most of us have an almost childlike faith in the expert specialist. A physician, especially one who looks the part and has a charismatic manner, we esteem no less than a god. We are awed by the self-confident lawyer who comforts and reassures us when we are worried about some problem with the authorities. We are even impressed by the TV serviceman who understands the magic of picking pictures out of thin air and can get that ailing set performing this magic again.

Perhaps we have a need for such awe and faith, finding comfort in it. And perhaps it is justified in certain individual cases. But I am reminded of the preface to a textbook on calculus in which the author urged his readers to lose any fear of the subject that they might have. "What one fool has learned, another fool can learn," he argued. And that is true for all fields. Obviously, you cannot take out your own gall bladder, nor should you argue your own case in court, but always bear in mind that the specialist is a fallible human being, too, despite his or her specialized knowledge, training, and experience. Many of the things a specialist can advise you on or do for you, you can do for yourself, as in the case of establishing a simple close corporation or registering a fictitious ("dba") business name, discussed earlier. Not all the things the specialists do require years of training and experience; many require only normal intelligence and readily available guidance.

The issue, however, is not entirely one of whether you *can* do some of the specialized functions yourself; the question remains of whether you *should* do some of these things yourself, whether considerations other than the economy of doing it for yourself are involved. Let's take the case of the accounting function.

YOUR FRIEND, THE ACCOUNTANT

The firm of H&R Block has become a large and highly successful corporation, almost an institution, by providing a relatively simple service, preparing tax returns for individuals. This service continues to be the main subject of their advertising, although H&R Block is today a conglomerate corporation, encompassing a number of companies.

By far the majority of all tax preparers' customers could make out their own tax returns, although many claim an inability to do so. They are mystified by the bureaucratic language and structure of the forms and awed by the mental gymnastics required to translate the cryptic IRS instructions into practice. Because it is far more convenient to have a specialist prepare the return, millions go to professional tax preparers.

Convenience alone is a powerful motivator, but professional tax preparers are not reluctant to add motivation by encouraging fear of the complicated forms and possible audit. Nor do they shrink from using fear motivation to point out that those who prepare their own returns often fail to take advantage of all exemptions and deductions to which they are entitled, and thus may overpay their taxes and fail to get refunds.

A great many people who undertake a business venture also have a fear of attempting their own accounting in general. Many of us cringe at the idea of tackling anything even remotely connected with mathematics, and we are further intimidated by the jargon of the accounting professionals. Even when accountants use terms we think we understand, such as "cash basis," to refer to the accounting system, we often find, ultimately, that the word does not mean what we think it means.

Public accountants provide their services in a number of ways. Probably most accountants, especially the larger firms with a number of employees, do everything on their own premises with their own computers. Individual accountants, who may themselves maintain their offices in their homes, sometimes will call on their clients at regular periods to do the postings and other such work in the client's office, using the client's computer and software. This practice of working on the client's premises is not as common today as it once was, however. Generally, you deliver or send your records to your accountant at some regular interval, and he or she does with them whatever mysterious things accountants do.

There are several possible variants of this procedure, and my own experiences are enlightening. My first accountant handled all my records, in his own office. He kept the books there and posted the various invoices, records of receipts, and other relevant information. Every month he sent me an accounting, a financial report. The problem was that the report described events and conditions that happened about three months earlier. That is, on June 1 I had the opportunity to discover whether I had turned a profit or lost money in February. Now that may be acceptable to a corporation that is doing well enough generally to settle for this, but it was not acceptable for me: As a small business—as one of what the U.S. House Small Business Committee once wanted to identify as a "mini-small business"— I could not tolerate a wait of three months to find out whether I was being successful or not. I needed to know continually how things were going, so I could take immediate remedial action when necessary.

When I began to understand the direct shortcoming of this method of operation, I tried another accounting firm, one recommended to me by others. This accountant, who was a partner in a firm with four principals, immediately wanted to design a system for me, handle my checking account reconciliations, and generally take over all the accounting and bookkeeping functions of my tiny firm.

I balked. I had decided to use a simple proprietary system that was designed for small business, do-it-yourself bookkeeping. (I chose the Dome System, but there are others, of equal merit, sold in office supply emporia.) I was capable, I believed, of handling my own bank reconciliations, journals, and postings, if not of coping with the IRS. (Illuminating details of these functions will be offered in the following chapter.) It was only the latter service, filing tax returns for my midget corporation and coping with the requirements of the IRS, that I really wanted an accountant to do for me from this point on. And so I stubbornly opposed his ideas and resisted his efforts to convince me that he was right.

It was only after a valiant (and unsuccessful) effort to win me to his view that my new accountant surrendered and accepted my conditions. And it has been that way ever since: My spouse does all the postings, with the simple system we use, and our accountant makes out our corporate and personal tax returns. We know at all times how we are doing, in terms of costs and profits, because we are posting and balancing accounts every week.

Probably you can find several ready-made accounting systems that will serve your needs; most provide ample flexibility to satisfy individual needs. You may believe, however, that your venture is so specialized or so different that no proprietary, off-the-shelf accounting system will do for you. You can still handle your own postings: Any good accountant will set up a custom-designed system for you and instruct you in posting it, if you wish to do this yourself. (In fact, some accountants prefer this and will suggest it to you.)

Of course, in today's world you do not need to do any of this manually. Dome and others have computer versions of their systems, versions that will run easily on most desktop computers. You enter items via a keyboard rather than a pen, and the program does the calculations and postings for you. There are also accounting programs that will calculate your taxes.

In short, it is no longer necessary to be an accountant or even a bookkeeper to keep your own accounts; you don't even have to know how to calculate percentages or subtract line 4c from line 4b. You have many easily available practical options and alternatives to the traditional methods. You *can* do it yourself, if you wish to. But aside from whether you can or cannot do it yourself or whether you should or should not do it yourself, there is that important and often overlooked question of the whole reason for using accounting in your venture. *Why* must you keep records? The answer to that question bears most strongly on the issue of doing it yourself.

THE TRUE PURPOSE OF ACCOUNTING

A surprisingly large number of people believe that the prime purpose of accounting systems is to keep records for tax purposes, as required by law. It may be that the IRS is a beneficiary of your accounting system, but the objective of accounting is to benefit you by providing information to help you manage your venture: accounting is an essential management tool. That is what is really at stake here. Business is inevitably about dollars; they are the only accepted measure of success and failure in the business world. And so they are a basic tool of top management.

Many years ago, a friend and associate who was himself the owner of a small but successful business remarked to me, "In principle, business is quite simple: Keep doing whatever shows a profit, and stop doing everything else." That is sound advice, as sound as the advice of the successful Wall Street financier of some years ago, Bernard Baruch. Asked for advice on how to make money in Wall Street, trading in securities, Baruch responded, "It's easy; buy low and sell high."

Of course, both gentlemen were being a bit satirical, because the advice was obviously easy to give but a good bit more difficult to implement. And yet the advice had a serious side, for there was a message in the irony: A proper accounting system is supposed to give you the kinds of information to do what my former associate suggested. The whole point of an accounting system, any accounting system, is to provide feedback to you as the manager of your business. Inadequate accounting information is a fatal weakness because it conceals the true state of the business and thus misleads the management. In many cases businesses lose money for a long period of time before management becomes aware of the situation. By the time the losses become clearly apparent, even without proper feedback, it is often too late to save the venture.

It works the other way, too: If the accounting system fails to provide the right information when the information is timely, management may miss important opportunities. This is analogous to the story, probably apocryphal, of the executive who says, "I know that one-half of my advertising dollar is wasted; the problem is that I don't know which half." Perhaps there is no accounting system that would help that executive discover which half of his advertising dollar is wasted, but it is important for every business owner to do everything possible to learn where his or her money is going, and that is especially true for the fledgling small business.

THE INEXACT SCIENCES

In accounting, as in most things, nothing is as easy as it seems. The jargon is not pointless; it is a special language, used by accountants to describe various conditions and situations that we will discuss in the next chapter. Nor is accounting an exact science, despite the fact that it is based on the exact science of mathematics. There are many imponderable factors in accounting, such as placing a value on inventory that has been on the shelf a long time or on capital equipment that has long since been totally depreciated. Sometimes you need to estimate overhead when you either have not been in business long enough to calculate actual overhead costs or you have made changes that have that same effect.

In the next chapter we will discuss the basic subject matter of accounting: costs, prices, profit, and loss. There you will begin to appreciate the truth that accounting is not an exact science any more than the practice of law or medicine is. Even engineering is not quite as exact a science as we would like to believe it is; that is why bridges and buildings sometimes collapse, even before they are completed, and why electronics engineers have been known to joke that there are three steps in engineering: design it, build it, and find out why it doesn't work.

This is also why I exhorted you, in an earlier chapter, to regard lawyers, consultants, and anyone else you turn to for help as advisors only, rendering opinions for *your* decision; the decision is always yours. The advisor cannot possibly be as conscious of the pros and cons of each decision and action as you are. Even when the advisor has nothing to gain either way, he or she also has nothing to lose either way; the risk is yours. And all decision making involves a weighing of the pros and cons and a judgment of how much risk is justified.

DECISION MAKING

That brings up a most important element of all business: decision making. Unfortunately, decision making often paralyzes progress because many people are overly fearful and ponder too long, hesitant to make the commitment that a decision imposes. Often that is simply because the person overestimates the importance of a decision. In fact, however, there are ways to judge and assign a degree of importance to all your decisions.

For example, let us suppose that you are faced with a decision that involves the expenditure of what to you is a large sum of money. (Remember that "large" is a relative term, and what is large to you may be miniscule to the head of some large corporation.) We will assume that $100,000 is involved. That is usually a quite substantial sum to the small business, especially one small enough to still be home based.

The real issue here is not the total amount of money involved, but the risk involved. If there is a serious risk of losing the entire $100,000, yes, this is probably an important decision for the small business and merits some careful thought. But if the risk only involves losing $1,000 or $2,000, that is another matter. And if the risk involves earning only 6 percent against the possibility of earning 7 percent—that is, a decision about what investment is likely to pay a better return—that is yet another matter.

Time is valuable, and your own time as a business entrepreneur has a definite value. To spend many hours pondering a decision that involves only a few hundred dollars at most may be a bad trade. You should place a value on your time, too. One way to do this is to ask yourself what you would charge a client for your time if you were a consultant. And let me hasten to assure you here that any well-qualified consultant is "giving the store away" if he or she charges less than $100 per hour today. (And even that is a relatively low figure; a great many consultants would not find that an acceptable fee.)

Faced with a decision, then, and unsure about how long you should ponder it, ask yourself this question: What are the best and worst possible consequences of a good or bad decision here? That is the true measure of importance. You have two decisions to make, and you can't make the second one until you make this first one, an assessment of possible consequences.

Remember, too, that procrastination, avoiding or delaying a decision indefinitely, is a decision in itself, a decision to do nothing and hope for the best. Still, delaying a decision is not always wrong, either, if the delay is a justified one. And the chief justification for delay is the conviction that you do not have all the facts you need.

Lack of information is another matter that often calls for soul searching. How can you be sure that you are not deceiving yourself into believing that you need more information, hence more time? We often find it easy to deceive ourselves when we want to do something or, as in this case, avoid doing something. If you find yourself succumbing to that temptation to evade making the tough decisions, start asking yourself why: Is there some special bit of information you lack? Have you a reasonable hope of getting that information soon? Will you, in fact, be better informed a few days or a few weeks from now and thus be better qualified to make the decision?

BUSINESS IS RISK

Accept it as a premise that any business venture represents risk. It is probable, perhaps almost certain, that all successful entrepreneurs are risk takers and that the most successful are usually the most venturesome risk takers, the people with the courage to think big. Russ Perot, no small thinker he, left IBM to found a multibillion-dollar enterprise. Henry Ford dared what was then the revolutionary idea of paying workers a dollar a day. Charles Kettering believed in the "impossible" (according to others) automobile self-starter motor, just as Thomas Edison believed in the "impossible" incandescent lamp, Fulton in his steamboat, and Marconi in his radio. No success of note is achieved without risk. But there is no stopping the truly dedicated person who is determined to succeed and secure in his or her faith in ultimate success. Chocolate king Milton Hershey and aluminum king Milton Reynolds, like a great many successful individuals, suffered numerous business failures, even bankruptcies, before ultimately achieving success.

Success, then, often means coming back from bad decisions, setbacks of many kinds, and even bankruptcies. It means conviction that you are right, that your plan is right, that you will ultimately prevail. It means that you can "roll with the punches," adapt to the realities you encounter, and come back from every reverse of your fortunes. Only those who can carry this off are successful in the end.

But let us go on to the hard-headed realities of accounting now, a few harsh, cold-water-in-the-face facts to be presented in the next chapter.

Chapter Seven

Accounting, Costs, and Pricing

Simple though accounting is in its principles, costs, pricing, and other basic accounting matters can be confusing if you do not have a firm grasp of those principles.

THE MYSTERY OF ACCOUNTING

Accounting is not a black art, although it may appear sometimes to be so, and perhaps not entirely by chance: The accountants may find it beneficial to tell you less than you ought to know. But it is a discipline that a great many very ordinary individuals master in conventional and quite ordinary courses of study in conventional and quite ordinary colleges and universities. This is not to derogate the status of accounting as a important and necessary activity of our modern society. But it is important to put things into a proper perspective: Anyone who can cope successfully in modern society is capable of mastering the basic concepts of accounting and need not be at the mercy of the professionals of the ledger and the balance sheet.

Before we venture into the accountant's sanctum, let us establish some fundamental truths, for I do not wish to mislead you: I am not an accountant and have never had any formal training in the art of keeping books. Further, let me make it clear that this is not a course in accounting. I would not attempt that even if I were qualified to teach the subject, as I certainly am not. I am trying here merely to remove some of the mystery that surrounds accounting for most lay people. I am compelled by my own limitations to explain what little I know of the subject in simple, everyday language, sans jargon. Frankly, however, I believe that the completely amateur status I enjoy is an advantage for both of us: I am not compelled to use that special jargon of the accountants—I wouldn't know how, in any case— so I am obliged to try to explain accounting in the simple lay person's terms in which I think and that, I hope, we both can grasp easily.

Accounting Is about Money

In accounting, all the numbers refer to money, although money is represented in many different ways and by many different terms. These terms are supposed to indicate different things about the money—for example, *depreciation, assets,* and *liabilities.* In accounting, it is the jargon and some of the manipulations that are confusing and difficult to understand, not the concepts and principles; the latter are quite simple and sensible. (If your accountant cannot help you to understand these after the little orientation session here, you ought to begin to wonder whether the failure is a result of his or her inability to explain or to a self-serving desire to keep you in the dark.)

How Many Kinds of Money Are There?

Most of us, in our private lives, know only two kinds of money: income and outgo. The businessperson and accountant, however, know many kinds of money, each identified and labeled to help in understanding what is happening in the business and what decisions should be made. This is especially true of costs, because there are many kinds. To get a good understanding of this principle, consider first two broad kinds of costs, direct and indirect. Even before that, however, understand one most basic principle, a most commonsense one that still seems to be overlooked by some people in small businesses: Income must equal outgo to break even. That is, every nickel you spend to conduct your business you must recover in your sales. Never lose sight of that fact, no matter how the nickel tends to become disguised or lost sight of in the welter of jargon used to describe it.

DIRECT AND INDIRECT COSTS

If you buy an item for $10 and sell it for $15 or at whatever markup you place on it, you have experienced a direct cost of $10 for that sale. That is, you know that you incurred $10 of cost for that sale, a $10 *direct material cost* that you can attribute directly and exclusively to that sale. If you pay someone $150 to do work for which you collect $300, you have a $150 *direct labor cost*. If you pay a messenger $5 to deliver that item you paid $10 for, you have a $15 *direct cost*. This principle applies to any kind of a venture. If you manufacture the item you sell and you know the cost of the materials and labor that went into the manufacture of the item, those are direct costs.

In short, any cost you can attribute directly and solely to some given sale, a cost you would not have incurred had you not made that sale, is a direct cost. That is another requirement of our definition of direct cost: You must be able to identify the cost as being incurred solely for or in direct connection with that sale.

We identify direct costs as a category simply because there is also such a thing as indirect costs: costs for rent, heat, light, telephone service, advertising, insurance, taxes, repairs, postage, printing, bookkeeping, depreciation, and a great many other items. They are real costs, too, of course, and part of those costs must be charged against items or services sold. The item that costs $10 and is sold for $20 does not produce $10 profit because these other costs must also be recovered. That is, the item cost you more than $10 because all the accompanying costs must be charged to it as well.

A problem arises here. We do not know how much of the rent, heat, light, insurance, taxes, and other costs should be charged to that item. Those costs are necessary to conduct the business, but we can't assign any of them directly to the item. So we refer to them as *indirect costs*, and they, too, must be recovered, of course. But how much of those costs must we recover in that $20 sale?

This is where the idea of overhead comes in. *Overhead*, a term you have undoubtedly heard many times, is the general cost of doing business. Some organizations include in the category they call overhead all those indirect costs, whereas others have more than one pool of indirect costs. For example, some organizations have a pool of indirect costs they call overhead, but they exclude the indirect costs associated with payroll, including sick leave and vacation time, Social Security payments, other payroll taxes, holidays, and insurance. They call that latter set of indirect costs *fringe benefits* to distinguish them from other overhead or indirect costs. For convenience in discussion, however, we will assume that all indirect costs are segregated in an expense pool called overhead.

To recover those indirect costs, most businesses establish an overhead rate, which is a percentage of direct costs added to make up the total nominal cost of whatever is sold. And the rate is established, usually, as a historical rate, a rate based on experience. For example, let us suppose that your records reveal that last year your total direct costs were $100,000. To keep the mathematics simple, let us assume that your indirect costs for that same period were $60,000. That is an overhead rate of 60 percent, easily calculated by simple arithmetic:

$$60,000/100,000 = 0.6$$

$$0.6 \times 100 = 60\%$$

That means that for every dollar of direct cost you experienced 60 cents of indirect cost, so you must add that 60 cents to arrive at the true cost. The $10 item thus actually costs you $16, and selling it at $20 means you have a $4 gross profit—a pretax profit, that is.

That is a simplified example to illustrate both principle and practice of establishing and using an overhead rate. Practices vary, however, from one organization to another and from one type of business to another. The simple example offered here is based on the premise that you are in some kind of retail business in which you resell merchandise you have bought at wholesale prices. Your labor (what you pay yourself and/or others) in such a venture is normally an overhead cost, and the rate is applied to the merchandise you sell. However, in ventures in which you sell a service, such as consulting, the principle still applies, but the practice is a bit different. That is because the principal item you sell is labor, and you usually sell it in units of time, generally hours or days. Here the labor is a direct cost item, and you apply the overhead rate to that labor.

Suppose you find that last year you billed $100,000 in direct labor, and your indirect costs amounted to $78,000. Your overhead rate is 78 percent, of course $(78,000/100,000 \times 100 = 78\%)$. If the materials you use in connection with your venture are an insignificant part of your cost, you may choose to include all costs of materials in your overhead. If materials are an important part of what you sell and you can identify most of them as direct costs, you may apply an overhead rate to them, too. It would not, however, normally be the rate established for labor overhead but would be calculated separately and would be based on what your records tell you are the indirect costs associated with materials. It is not unusual for business organizations to have more than one indirect rate, as noted earlier, or to have more than one overhead rate. A major objective is always to identify all costs and price what you sell so as to recover all costs and turn a profit as well.

The accounting system, of course, has other objectives. At least two of them are worth noting here. One objective is to minimize your costs; the other is to minimize your taxes.

Is the Difference Significant?

By now, you may be wondering whether it helps in any way to identify costs as direct or indirect. There is no single answer to that question, though—in government contracting, for example, you may be required to analyze and identify both direct and indirect costs. For general purposes, however, there is a more basic reason for distinguishing the two from each other: Making the identifications helps you make sound management decisions. In many business situations you cannot control direct costs; they are dictated by the nature of the business. But in most business situations you do have a measure of control, perhaps even a large measure of control, over the indirect costs. That, in fact, is largely what the next few paragraphs are about.

MINIMIZING COSTS

Business success usually depends more on success in marketing than it does on any other single factor: Being competitive in your prices is important. Yet trying to be the cheapest guy in town (offering the lowest prices) can be deadly; it has been responsible for the demise of more than one business. But that is usually when the prices are set below actual cost—when the business managers do not know their true costs or have some unrealistic notion that they "can make it up in the volume," the increased sales they expect will result from lowered prices.

This injunction, by the way, does not apply to the loss-leader marketing promotion. That is a type of sale in which you offer to sell something at cost or even below because you wish to attract buyers in the hope of selling them something else, something profitable. This is a marketing ploy widely practiced by large retailers, especially department stores, to create traffic in their stores. It does not represent a loss, however, because whatever it costs you is or should be charged off as a marketing expense.

But running sales at greatly reduced prices (still well above direct cost, however) is an interesting idea because overhead does not have a linear relationship to sales volume or direct costs. Some overhead costs are variable, but others are fixed or at least vary only a little. There is some relationship of indirect costs to sales volume: A busy store, for example, needs more employees than one that is less busy and it incurs other additional expenses, such as increased telephone and delivery costs.

But increasing sales and increasing direct costs by 50 percent, let us say, does not increase your overhead dollars by 50 percent. For example, let us suppose that your overhead costs are $50,000, your overhead rate is 60 percent, and your overhead costs break down along these lines:

Rent, heat, light:	$ 8,000
Office supplies:	5,000
Depreciation:	2,000
Overhead labor:	35,000
Total:	$50,000

Now let us suppose your business begins to catch on or you are running special promotions, and sales increase considerably. That raises your direct costs by 50 percent. But overhead increases too, as follows:

Rent, heat, light:	$ 8,000
Office supplies:	6,000
Depreciation:	2,000
Overhead labor:	50,000
Total:	$66,000

Something has happened to your overhead rate: It is now calculated as $66,000/150,000 = 4.4 = 44\%$. Despite the increase in overhead dollars, your overhead rate has actually decreased. That is because the large increase in sales volume brought a large increase in direct cost dollars, but only a small increase in indirect costs: Your rent, heat, and light, for example, did not increase. Actually, for a 50 percent increase in direct costs, you experienced only about a 24 percent increase in the overhead dollars, so the indirect costs in *dollars* increased, but the overhead *rate* dropped by nearly 16 percent. That means that the $10 item is not burdened with $6 in additional, indirect costs but is rather "loaded" with $4.40 in indirect costs. That is why increased sales volume enables you to lower your prices without sacrificing profit. And, of course, it explains the benefits of keeping your overhead as low as possible.

If this reasoning seems to be anomalous, look at it this way: The cost of being in business (overhead) is shared by all the sales and the direct dollars. The more sales or direct dollars there are to share the cost of being in business, the lower the amount each sale or direct dollar must be "taxed" to pay for rent, heat, light, and so on.

But do understand this about the benefits of reducing your overhead: Increased sales and increased profits are attractive prospects, but even they are not the most important factors. A more important benefit is greater business security: the greatly increased probability of business survival in a competitive world.

Aside from this, the close control of overhead generally is an important issue: Many businesses succumb to the disaster of excessive overhead. Some begin with great enthusiasm and great faith in instant success, and so spend freely to have impressive and expensive stationery, rich furnishings, elaborate equipment, and other symbols intended to convey an aura of success to prospective customers and clients. How much such trappings contribute to business success is impossible to estimate accurately, but it is certain that they do contribute substantially to the overhead costs of doing business and so are inevitably a burden.

To gain and keep control of your overhead and, for that matter, of your business overall, you must have a true picture of all your costs. You must know precisely what you are doing at all times, not guess or whistle hopefully in the dark when you lower your prices to induce an increase in sales or make other business decisions.

This points up another issue, that of minimizing overhead in general by eliminating unnecessary costs, as well as by increasing the direct cost base on which the overhead rate is calculated. Proper accounting systems with proper reports are an essential tool in this process. You may accept it as an article of faith that in almost every business venture the overhead rate is directly proportional to the distinct effort made to control it. That is, when no specific and directed effort is made to control overhead, it rises steadily and unrelentingly. You may depend on that. As Murphy's Law makes abundantly clear, left to themselves, things get worse. Always.

An appropriate paraphrase, then, is: The price of minimal overhead is eternal vigilance. Watch those telephone bills, especially the toll calls you didn't make, the printing expenses for stationery and literature that wound up being thrown in the trash or used as scratch paper, the advertising that produced zero results, the charitable contributions made for no known reason, the subscriptions to magazines you have no time to read, and all those other expenses that add not an atom of support to your business. Be sure that you get and read a report of income and expenses each month. You may find it to be rather shocking literature.

THE BUSINESS AS AN ENTITY

The law recognizes a corporation as a legal entity with an existence of its own, separate and apart from its stockholders (owners). When the latter pass on from this world, the corporation continues to exist. And good business judgment suggests that even the sole proprietorship ought to be regarded and treated as an entity of at least some independence. Still, the founders/owners of any business, incorporated or not, tend to regard themselves and the business organization as the same entity. This kind of identification, especially prevalent in the one-person business, can lead to certain problems best avoided.

One problem that sometimes stems from overidentification is the inability of the principal to perceive his or her compensation as part of business cost, rather than profit. Small business owners often tend to count everything but their own salaries or personal draw from the business as costs, which inevitably leads to the notion that their own salary is part of profit.

Many business difficulties result from this false idea that the proprietor draws compensation from profits. As the proprietor or principal stockholder in your corporation, working full time to make it succeed, you are an employee of the organization, and your salary is a cost. Profit is what, if anything, is left after you have paid yourself and all other costs.

It is quite possible, especially in the early days of a new venture, that the business cannot pay you at all or can pay you only a portion of what you have decided your salary is to be. That does not change anything: The business entity should owe you that unpaid salary, to be paid at some future date. In the meanwhile, it is a debit, a liability that the business must one day pay. You may consider (and record) this as either a loan to the business or as a further investment. (Either way, the business incurs a cost and an obligation to repay you.) That is the businesslike way to do it. But however you handle the practical problems, do regard and treat yourself as an employee. And if you have a spouse or other family members involved in the business, the principle applies to them also: all salaries, commissions, and related items (e.g., FICA, withholding tax, and fringe benefits) are cost items, direct or indirect. Don't even think *profit* until all those cost items are satisfied.

PROFIT AND RETURN ON INVESTMENT

The questions of prices to charge customers, investment in your venture, salary to pay yourself, and reasonable profit level are interrelated ones. Even calculating investment is not always a simple matter. It's easy enough to determine how much cash you furnished to start the business, but in most cases that cash up front is not the total investment.

Other Investment

You may furnish to your new business property you already own—desk, typewriter, computer, tools, automobile, and/or other items the business requires. The value of those items represents a part of your investment. Set a fair value on those items and enter them into your records as assets of the business and part of your investment.

Logically and morally, the business should not succeed at your personal expense, such as by means of your working free or for coolie wages. Still, personal sacrifice is often a necessity in the early months of a business and even for as much as a year or two. A new business venture can be almost stillborn if the principal imposes excessive salary demands on it. Many start new businesses by drawing no salary at all for a long time.

That does not mean that the business really gets free or nearly free labor. That labor is *sweat equity*. Labor, yours or anyone else's, has value. If your new business cannot afford to pay you the salary you ought to be getting, the difference ought to be placed on the books as a growing investment.

Setting Your Salary

How much should you pay yourself? That is, what should your salary be, regardless of whether you collect it or not? Of course, you may set it anywhere you want to, especially if you are not actually paying it to yourself. But that is not good business; your salary ought to be set at whatever is a reasonable level, at "the market" for whatever you do and the size of your venture. Do what you can to determine what chief executives of similar small ventures are worth to their organizations, or at least make your own estimate. Add the difference between that estimate and what you actually draw to your original investment.

Setting Prices

In some businesses, prices are set by the market (what the item or similar items are selling for generally) and/or by list prices. Some businesses, such as upscale department stores, charge list prices for most items, although they run sales at which they discount some prices. Today, however, many businesses sell everything at discounted prices. If you are selling items that are standard, sold by many others, it is possible for customers to determine what the market is by shopping around. Competition may therefore force you to sell at a substantial discount and may even determine what the price is that you can get: what customers will pay.

That's not an unvarying truth, however. A certain well-known FAX machine that lists for $900 is offered widely for prices ranging from about $625 to $750, and these prices appear in many advertisements in the same publications, where it is easy enough to do the comparison shopping from your easy chair. Yet many people will pay $750 for this machine despite the fact that some dealers offer it for far less. (I bought one of these machines for $600.) Why is that? There are many imponderable factors: Some people simply like and trust a certain dealer and will pay what that dealer asks, regardless of competitors' prices. Some just won't bother to shop around. And some are unaware of the models and brands and operate on the premise that the higher-priced machines must be better products. In any case, do not assume that you must always meet the competition; in many cases you do not have to, especially if you have other inducements than price to persuade prospects to become your customers. You must evaluate your own situation and not necessarily be driven by what competitors are doing.

On the other hand, you may be selling something that offers no convenient means for comparison shopping. If you buy a specific brand and model computer, you can seek the lowest price and know, at least, that you are getting the same machine, if not the same service. But if you buy a machine from someone who builds it, it is a unique item; comparison shopping becomes more difficult and perhaps not possible. If you know enough about computers, you can seek out other models that have similar features and make a judgment, but you cannot make a direct comparison.

If what you sell is of that nature, you can set your own prices, but you are not free to charge whatever you like. There is still a market on that class and category of product. Even if you are selling your services as a consultant, a truly unique item, prospective clients are certain to have some idea of what similar consulting services are worth.

Other factors are involved, too, such as the economic climate of the area in which you sell, the way in which you merchandise and market, and your basic business philosophy. For example, the individual I buy my computers from runs a small company, employing only a few people, and has no desire to grow large. He prefers to select and use only high-quality components, assemble and test each system thoroughly, and charge what he needs to charge for building a high-quality system. He sells to the appropriate market for such systems — to those who prefer to pay for what they agree is a high-quality product.

In short, there is always a general market of some sort for whatever you sell. But there are usually several markets for all kind of goods and services. You may therefore choose the market in which you wish to sell.

Return on Investment

People have many standards by which they judge business activities and whether a given business, or even a given marketing campaign, is viable. People in direct mail, for example, tend to talk about "response," which means the percentage of the total prospects reached (number of names and addresses mailed to) who responded with an order or with whatever the solicitation asked for. That may have some merit as a yardstick to measure success, but it is not entirely reliable because it is possible to turn a good profit on less than 1 percent response in one mailing while losing money on a 5 percent response in another.

Return on investment or *ROI* is considered by many to be a more reliable measure. Put as simply as possible, this is simply a determination of how much your investment is earning. If, for example, you invested $50,000 in your venture and it shows you only $500 net profit at the end of the year, the ROI is only 1 percent, less than your money would have earned you in a simple saving account. (Large corporations often show 2 to 5 percent as net profit, but that is also often after paying stockholders a substantial dividend.) And regardless of the response percentage, the ROI on a direct-mail campaign is more reliable than a response rate an indicator of success.

Of course, you may derive other benefits, such as a good income and tax breaks, and you must consider these gains. But the ROI is a specific, easily determined factor, and it is widely regarded as a valid measure. It can thus serve you as a guide to determine whether your venture or campaign is running as efficiently as it ought to and producing acceptable results.

Markups and Discounts

Markup is gross profit, the difference between direct cost and selling price. It is the factor by which you increase the price you pay for something to arrive at the price you charge your customers. It can be expressed as a percentage or in dollars. For example, you might mark up an item 25 percent: If it costs you $10, you add $2.50, selling it at $12.50.

Most industries have a more or less standard markup, often following the suggestion implied by the prime supplier's list price and discount. But do not confuse discount with markup; they are not the same thing. The term *discount* applies to the list price and how much under that list the item is priced. The term *markup* applies strictly to what the item costs you in direct cost and how much you add to that to cover your indirect costs and earn profit.

For example, if your supplier sells you what you buy at a 40 percent discount, that $10 item costs you $6. The supplier's list price suggests that you should mark it up 40 percent, selling it at $10. But you may decide that it is wise to sell it at $8, which means marking up your net price of $6 by $2 or by 33 percent, one-third of $6. And that applies to labor, too: If you pay yourself $25 an hour and you sell your services by the hour, you must mark up that $25, setting the price to the client to perhaps $75 an hour or more, as necessary.

Let us go on now to talk a little about taxes and insurance.

Chapter Eight

Taxes and Insurance

*In today's litigious and
statute-saturated world, the
need for insurance—and that
is insurance of several kinds—
is almost as inevitable as
death and taxes. Operating
without taxes is impossible,
and operating without
insurance is reckless.*

TAXES AND THE HOME OFFICE

One characteristic of our democratic form of government is that
you are required to pay taxes at many levels, federal, state, and
local. Moreover, you get to (are *required* to) collect some of the
taxes for these governments and you even get a pittance for
doing so. (That is usually the case with sales taxes.) The major
tax advantage of doing business in and from your own residence, however, is the tax benefits you can claim as business
deductions. If you understand the IRS rules and handle things
properly, you can achieve a weighty chunk of relief in your
tax burden.

As in the discussion of the accounting systems and functions earlier, I claim no expertise and certainly no special
qualifying experience as a professional expert in the relevant
field of taxes. For details and qualified legal opinions, you must
consult an experienced public accountant and/or a lawyer. My

experience is entirely as a taxpayer, and I do claim a fair amount of experience in that capacity; I have paid a variety of taxes to a variety of governments over a very long time! Despite my amateur standing as a commentator and mentor in tax matters, therefore, I can pass on some useful experience-based information to illustrate typical cases and my own personal fortunes and misfortunes in fencing with tax collectors.

Again, as in the case of accounting, the public at large subscribes to a certain widespread mythology, naiveté, and plain wrongheadedness about taxes, tax obligations, and tax exemptions or deductions.

The consequences of believing some of these myths too readily and thus being wrong about these matters are sometimes quite unpleasant. Hence I offer these observations about what I have learned and what you ought to do to verify any uncertainties you may have about what you may or may not do about your tax burdens. This is especially the case with the main tax base, the one the IRS insists on collecting as a tax on our earnings.

Unfortunately, it is possible to encounter misunderstanding and plain ignorance of the tax laws among the employees of tax bureaus themselves, even those who are charged with giving out counsel and guidance to honest taxpayers, and the tax officials believe themselves to be not at all obligated by the false counsel of their own experts. For example, when I had a question about the admissibility of expenses I incurred that exceeded the allowance made by my employer at that time, I was assured by an IRS counselor that I could deduct the excess. My subsequent plea of misleading guidance availed me absolutely nothing, as it fell on the stone-deaf ears of a tax official who disallowed my claim. (I, of course, urge caution in following the counsel of even the tax offices.)

On the other hand, I have not found it to be true that all agents of the IRS are cruel, unscrupulous, and unforgiving— as some gossip reports. Quite the contrary. Though I have no more love for tax collectors than most people do, I have found it not especially difficult to reason with IRS representatives, and I have managed always to resolve my tax problems without extreme actions or bitterness beyond that which many of us feel for what we sincerely believe to be an unfair system generally.

DEDICATED SPACE FOR BUSINESS

The most important tax question for anyone working in an independent venture at home is that of tax deductions for business expenses. The IRS policy is fairly clear on how much of your home expense you may deduct as a business expense. The basic principle is simple enough: The space must be *dedicated*, which means devoted exclusively to your business use. Opening the morning mail at your dining room table does not qualify you for a deduction of the dining room as a work space if you are still using it as a personal dining room. But even that principle is not quite as clear-cut as it seems and you will find some exceptions to it, although its application to special circumstances still makes good sense.

If you take some room of your residence and fit it out as a full-time business office or other business work space, you are on safe ground in claiming the cost of that space as a business deduction. You deduct the cost of that space on a pro-rated basis. For example, if you are maintaining a residence of 1,000 square feet and the room or rooms you convert for business use represent 250 square feet, you are entitled to deduct 25 percent of the cost (rent, taxes, interest, etc.) of that 1,000 square feet as a business expense.

When the space you dedicate for business use is not clearly separate, as in the case of using only part of a room, the distinction is less clear. But the principle still applies: The space must be used exclusively for business, as if it were at another location than your home, such as in an office building or industrial plant. But it is more difficult to demonstrate to an IRS auditor, should it become necessary, that the space that is only part of a room is truly dedicated to and used solely for business. If, for example, you use a *portion* of a room, such as a corner of your bedroom or basement, for business, you must somehow demonstrate clearly that the use is entirely for business. Do this by equipping the space with a desk, filing cabinet, workbench, or whatever furniture and equipment you need for and is obviously suited to your business venture. Keep your personal items out of that area. If you can, separate it physically with a portable partition or room divider of some kind. The physical evidence of dedication will always be more convincing than your verbal arguments.

There are, of course, many kinds of possible ventures and thus a wide variety of situations. Some kinds of ventures require keeping an inventory, merchandise for resale, a supply of raw materials, shipping supplies, or other items that you must have on hand in bulk. You may thus find it necessary to devote a significant amount of your residence (a garage or basement, probably) to storage of inventory. The same rules apply here: Take steps to make it abundantly clear that the space used for storage is used entirely and exclusively for business storage (don't store your bicycles and garden tools in the same place), is used regularly for that purpose, and is necessary to (a regular element in or part of) the conduct of that business. (Always assume that any IRS agent who visits you is a profound skeptic, probably made so by experience, and so requires that you produce hard evidence to support your claims.)

Allowable Exceptions

There are exceptions, as always. If your business is day care of children in your own home, for example, you may very well be using several residential rooms or spaces in your home for business on a part-time basis—say, from 9:00 A.M. to 5:00 A.M. five or six days a week. That is reasonable enough for that kind of enterprise, so stick to your guns if you are unfortunate enough to meet an unreasonable IRS agent and force that agent to go to his or her superiors for final judgment, although even that is not your last resort of appeal. (We have been fortunate enough to deal with reasonable ones, but that may very well be because we have always made it clear that we are confident in our position and have nothing to hide or even to defend.) Again, pro-rate the cost on that basis and be prepared to demonstrate that such is the case, that the pro-rating makes good sense by ordinary logic. Keep careful and detailed records, for one thing. Always bear in mind that the IRS agent expresses his or her own opinion, not necessarily official policy, and may very well be wrong. (In fact, there is an excellent chance that you will never actually be called on by an IRS agent, so this is a "just in case" discussion.)

Principal Facility

Deduction of cost for work space in your home is allowable only when that space represents your principal place of business, although even that has exceptions. If you have an office somewhere in an office building where you spend most of your time, you are not entitled to charge off desk space you use at home occasionally for business purposes. There are some exceptions to this rule also, however, as in the case of professional people who meet with clients in their (the professional's) home. (This use requires face-to-face meetings with clients on a more or less regular basis to qualify.) But there are also cases where individuals divide their time between an office at home and another elsewhere, and this is a normal and necessary business procedure. If you do this on a regular, scheduled basis, you can probably justify the home office expense. Or if you maintain an office somewhere and your spouse works with you as a partner but in an office in your home, you may have an arguable case for deducting the cost of that office at home. (Believe it or not, the IRS does not always win disputed cases such as these, and a firm stand on your part may very well pay off in a conciliatory IRS response.)

Other Deductible Expenses

The basic cost of the space is usually the major tax deduction for an office at home, but it is not the only one. You can deduct a reasonable portion of other expenses that are shared between your business and your personal life. If you keep a separate telephone line for business, its total cost is deductible; if your business shares your personal telephone line, pro-rate its cost. Apply this principle to all shared costs, such as that for water, trash collection, real estate taxes, interest on your mortgage, utilities, insurance on your property, maintenance of your property, and others. (Of course, insurance on business property only and maintenance of business property or business space only is fully deductible.)

This applies in principle to all items. If you buy new furniture and depreciate it over five years, that simply means that you take 20 percent of its cost as a business deduction each year. At the end of five years, you have recovered the cost of the furniture and take no more deductions for it, although it will probably be useful for years to come. But suppose you take to your office and use some old personal furniture that you have had for years and have charged your business for it by paying yourself some sum of money for it. It doesn't matter how old or even decrepit the furniture is, you can and should start a depreciation period on it as though it were new. Depreciation is an accounting convenience, a method for ensuring that the business is properly credited with an expense item represented by the furniture. It has nothing to do with real useful life of a capital item, but only with how you will charge its cost to the business—that is, primarily over how long a time you deduct and recover its cost as an investment.

That brings up the matter of "expensing" versus depreciating capital items. *Expensing* an item means writing it off in the year it was bought. *Depreciating* it means writing it off over several years, usually five or ten, more in the case of real estate. But depreciation is applied to capital items, which are generally items costing above some specified amount and having a useful life of one year or more.

First of all, you must define what a capital item is in your own system. It is largely arbitrary. You set a value as the minimum, perhaps $200 or $500, and all items costing more than that amount and having an extended useful life, usually of a year or more, are "capitalized." If the item falls within the IRS guidelines for maximum value of an item that may be expensed. When I bought a modest computer system for $2,500, I chose to write it off immediately; the IRS permitted me to do so with any capital item not in excess of $5,000 cost. (This is an accounting policy decision, but it is not out of place in this chapter because it illustrates that tax obligations have a great influence on accounting policies and procedures.)

Limitations

If your business is a part-time venture and you have regular income from a job, you cannot use business tax deductions to offset taxes you owe on your regular income from your job. That is, the deductions you take for use of space and other facilities at home cannot exceed the gross income from that business venture based at home. If your venture brought in $25,000 in gross profit and you can itemize $26,000 in deductible expenses, you may still deduct only $25,000. You have no business profit to tax, and you have a loss, at least on paper.

That brings up another interesting point: When is an at-home venture, especially a part-time one, a business and when is it merely a hobby? The IRS position has been that your home-based business may show losses or, at least, zero profit for three years at most. After that, if it continues to show no profit, the IRS believes that your activity is a hobby and not a business venture at all. That is on the margin, for even venture capitalists who invest and risk large sums of money on others' ventures tend to the conventional wisdom that it is not unreasonable for a new venture to require three or four years to reach breakeven and begin to show a small profit. In any case, be prepared for the IRS to be somewhat jaundiced in their view of your deductions for a venture that is not earning or about to earn profits by the end of a third year.

State and Local Taxes

By now, a great many state and local government impose a sales tax on their citizens, and they normally demand that the retailer collect the tax for them, allowing the retailer-cum-tax-collector 1 or 2 percent of what he or she collects. Of course, the retailer would far prefer to not be bothered with it at all, but the government would almost surely collect virtually nothing if each citizen was expected to calculate and pay 2, 3, or 5 percent of everything he or she spends to acquire title to worldly goods. So it is necessary to burden the seller to the ultimate consumer with the problem and unpleasant duty. That means that you do not pay the tax when you buy your materials or products, if you buy them for resale, but you require your customers to do so.

Generally, when you register with your government and get a "tax number"—a certificate and identification as a seller who will collect taxes and turn them over to the government—you are exempt from paying the tax yourself. When you buy your products or supplies, you furnish your tax number as an exemption and your supplier does not charge you. For example, if you buy cosmetics in bulk and repackage them in smaller packages to sell to consumers, you are exempted from paying the tax on what you buy because you are going to charge your own customers tax and turn that money over to your government.

Whether you buy and resell finished goods or buy materials that somehow go into the finished goods you sell, you are exempt from paying the sales tax. The sales tax is collected from the ultimate consumer, so only the retailer, the ultimate seller, collects the tax when making sales, and then must turn that tax money over to the government. On the other hand, if you are not the seller to the consumer but sell to those who sell to consumers, you use your tax-exempt status and never pay the sales tax because your customers are people who sell to ultimate consumers and thus must collect the taxes from them.

A Few Miscellaneous Taxes

Of course, the income tax is the big tax bite, but for the self-employed today, the Social Security taxes are no small consideration, either. In fact, for many individuals the FICA (Social Security tax) is even greater than the income tax because there are no exemptions or deductions on FICA. It is levied on gross income to the maximum provided by law. (Currently, that is on the base of $42,000 income.)

When you are employed by someone, you pay half, well over 7 percent of your earnings, and your employer pays the other half. When you are incorporated, you pay both halves: You are an employee of your own corporation and are handled on paper as such, getting a W-2 form, for example, as when you work for anyone. Your corporation pays the matching FICA. If you are in a self-employed status (unincorporated), you pay the total amount (currently 15.02 percent) as a "self-employment tax."

There are some miscellaneous taxes, such as that for unemployment insurance, but they are more an annoyance of extra recordkeeping and reporting than a financial burden.

Of course, your state may impose an income tax on you also, as many states do today. Even cities—Philadelphia, for example—sometimes do so.

As an employee of your own corporation, you receive a paycheck, with FICA and income taxes deducted. Your corporation makes the quarterly returns to the IRS and other governments, as required. When you are a partner or sole proprietor, you are required to make quarterly estimates of your taxes due and pay the estimated amount.

The tangle of taxes grows steadily more complex, so that it is more than the question of difficulty that impels most home-based businesspeople to seek professional help with taxes; the sheer amount of work required is itself a burden when you are struggling to get your main work done every day.

SPECIAL SITUATIONS

There has been a trend toward the steady elimination or relaxing of laws that have prevented employers from having employees working at home on piece work and other arrangements. In fact, except for the garment industry, as a result of the historical case of child labor laws, most of the relevant laws are gone or greatly moderated. In an increasing number of situations, therefore, you may be able to deduct home office and other expenses even when you are not self-employed. For example, if you are a telephone solicitor on a commission basis, working from your own office at home, and that place of work is a required condition of the job, you can probably qualify for a tax deduction. The office must meet the conditions described earlier, and you must not have been compensated by the employer for any expenses of maintaining an office, telephone, and other costs necessary to your work.

Whatever is absolutely necessary to the work you do at home and is not directly compensated by an employer – tools, special clothing, training, manuals, utilities, shipping, postage, repairs, equipment, or other items – is probably deductible.

INSURANCE

Once again, I am compelled to furnish the now familiar *caveat* that I speak from personal experience and not as a technical expert on insurance. In fact, I have often been mystified by the language of the policies and the explanations of the agents. Like most people, I tended to throw up my hands in the face of this incomprehensible phraseology and accept what I was being told. That may or may not have been a sensible thing to do, but it appeared to be the only course open to me. And so I must stand before you as not even a dilettante in the field and relate my notions gained from my own experience.

In this case, that may be an advantage to you because I have no axes to grind here: I am not a champion of, an apologist for, or a critic of the insurance industry. Quite the contrary: I will try sincerely to be entirely objective in discussing insurance generally, within the limits of my understanding of this arcane field. Fortunately, I have had both good and bad experiences with insurance companies, and that helps me to present a reasonably balanced view.

First of all, we must accept that insurance has become an absolute necessity in today's world. Two factors make it absolutely necessary to maintain insurance policies of several kinds: Ours has become an excessively litigious society, and the costs of almost everything have skyrocketed. Nor are these two considerations unrelated to each other, for the cost of defending yourself in a legal battle, even when you are entirely blameless and win the suit, can easily mean financial ruin. ("Winning" can be a sardonic term, with definite Pyrrhic overtones.) It has, in fact, meant just that for many individuals. But everything is excessively costly today, and a burglary, fire, or other casualty loss can impose an intolerable burden on you and on your business venture.

The kinds of insurance you need depend to at least some extent on the nature of your venture. Some businesses, for example, include significant possibilities of being sued for large sums of money. That means that you must have liability insurance, and in large enough amounts to protect you adequately against a judgment. Suppose you package and sell some kind of consumer product, perhaps computer software. What are the possibilities that a customer might sue you for damages? They are probably not great, for computer software is not likely to injure anyone seriously. But there is the possibility that some other packager of software may decide that you have infringed on his or her copyright or trade name, and decide to sue you. (Such occurrences are not at all rare today.) And if you package and/or sell a cosmetic, food, or food supplement of some kind, the risks increase immediately.

So serious is the problem of liability and related litigation today that rates for coverage in some fields have reached critical levels. Many lawyers and physicians, the latter especially, have found that they simply cannot afford the malpractice insurance necessary today and have quit their practices. So it is a matter for careful consideration: Many people, perhaps almost all, need some kind of liability insurance.

Probably you maintain some kind of general coverage for liability in the event someone is injured on your property, as well as general fire and burglary coverage. These measures may or may not protect you. You must check them carefully to see what restrictions they include. They may, for example, exclude coverage if your property is used for business purposes, or they may include limits that are not adequate. In my own case, for example, I carry extra policies to cover the computer, FAX, and other special equipment I use to conduct my freelance writing activities. I also insist that they pay me full replacement value rather than some depreciated value that would compensate me only a fraction of what I paid out for the property and what it would cost me to replace it. For example, we were burglarized some years ago, and we recovered only about one-third of the original value of what had been stolen, so we were put to considerable expense to replace our property.

Group Insurance

Health insurance is as much of a must today as all other categories of coverage, for a health or sickness problem can do you in financially as quickly as can a lawsuit or major casualty loss, if uncovered and uncompensated. My own unexpected, lengthy illness some years ago resulted in medical expenses of over $40,000 in a few weeks. We would have been in straits for some time paying that had we not been covered adequately.

The answer to this need for medical coverage, hospital and major medical emergencies, is group insurance of some kind. It is a necessity for most of us, who could otherwise never afford the cost of a hospital stay of even a short duration.

The problem is that a one- or two-person business is hardly a group, for insurance purposes. But there are numerous approaches to a solution.

The usual, and quite a practical, one is to join a group via some other group connection. One is a trade or professional association of some sort. Many of these have today set up plans to provide group insurance to members. But this does not have to be an association connected with your business. It can be an automobile club, a veterans' group, or even an ad hoc group organized entirely for group insurance coverage. Today, most sponsors of such coverage will accept groups of as few as six members, although it is always a good idea to form or join as large a group as possible.

There is always the possibility that you may continue coverage under an older policy that covered you in prior employment or under the policy of a spouse already employed and covered elsewhere. In my own case, my wife had been a government employee and belonged to a large HMO (health maintenance organization). We have belonged to this group together, under direct billing, ever since.

Disability Insurance

The self-employed individual has no sick leave; you must get sick on your own time. That means without compensation, of course: when you are ill, your earnings stop. For brief illnesses of a few days, that is tolerable; for lengthy illnesses, it is not.

There is insurance to guard against the worst financial effects of falling ill. *Disability insurance* is insurance that will provide you with an income in some prescribed amount for some prescribed period of time when illness or accident renders you incapable of working. If you are entirely dependent on your earnings from your business venture, it would probably be wise to investigate disability insurance and sign up for a policy.

Policies vary widely in cost and benefits, and these two factors are related to each other, of course. You must find some acceptable balance between the minimum set of benefits acceptable to you and the maximum you cost you can afford.

Miscellaneous Insurance

The foregoing is by no means a complete description or discussion of all kinds of pertinent insurance, although it does cover the major categories. If you are in a partnership, you may wish to insure both partners so that the surviving partner is protected against heirs taking over a deceased partner's interest and harming the enterprise or otherwise making continuance participation difficult. This insurance may provide the means for paying off heirs and assuming complete ownership, for example, or for getting out yourself. Product liability insurance and special insurance coverage of other kinds are also available.

Choosing Insurance and Insurers

The insurance industry is regulated in every state by an insurance commission of some sort. These agencies are supposed to protect the common welfare with regard to insurance because hardly any lay person is capable of fully understanding either the language or the laws that concern insurance. And yet you cannot rely on these commissions to protect you against predatory underwriters: Some are quite honorable, quick to honor their contracts, but some are not, and the latter try to find ways to evade their contractual obligations. I had excellent experiences with two insurance companies who paid claims cheerfully and quickly and even urged me to send in every scrap of paper because I might have additional coverage I was not aware of. (I did, and I was sent an additional check.) But I had quite distressing experiences with others, who struggled to avoid paying their claims and sometimes succeeded in doing so.

Predators in the insurance industry appear to be especially active in the areas of health and disability insurance. You would be wise to move cautiously in buying this kind of insurance. And one way to do so is to buy insurance through established brokers, either those you know or those who have been highly recommended by friends who do know them well. Brokers have a vested interest in protecting your interest, for you are *their* customers. Our own insurance broker has been writing all our insurance for more than a few years, and he will continue to do so because he is more than an insurance broker and agent: he is our friend and protector in matters of insurance. He guides us away from mistakes in insurance and works hard to explain to us why he recommends what he does. He listens carefully to what we want and then counsels us accordingly. If we have a claim, he handles it, fighting our insurance battles for us, if necessary. We feel comfortable with Jerry. He handles all our insurance problems quietly and efficiently so that we can concentrate on doing what we do for a living.

There is one more highly important subject to discuss before we go on to Part 3. We need to talk about financing your venture and handling the typical cash flow problems that plague even some large organizations as well as a great many small ones.

Chapter Nine

Financing and Cash Flow Management

Funding the new business and managing the cash flow can be the most serious and most difficult problems of any business ventures. They are, however, problems related to each other, and thus some of the solutions help to solve both problems.

DEFINING THE PROBLEMS

There are many problems in business, as you no doubt already know, but the most serious ones are the money problems. In a sense, a business needs two kinds of front-end financing. First, it needs the capital for start-up, for purchasing equipment, supplies, furniture, and whatever else is necessary to get ready to do business, to "get the doors open." But it also needs operating capital for the months until the business begins to produce enough income to stand on its own feet.

It is essential that you have at least a little money of your own (banks are notoriously unwilling to provide 100 percent financing), but you may well have to raise considerably more capital than you can provide on your own. In that case, you will need a business plan.

A great many individuals get brilliant ideas for business ventures and then are stymied by lack of capital. Many businesses are stillborn because of this problem. Many others are launched despite the problem of insufficient capital but ultimately perish because of that lack of financial depth.

THE BUSINESS PLAN

Many new ventures require capitalization by banks, venture capitalists, private investors, and/or other investors. Even established businesses often need to pursue lenders or investors for fresh capital to finance expansion and other necessities of a growing business. And to raise that capital for even the tiniest of new enterprises a *business plan* is a necessity. Briefly, a business plan provides information to prospective investors and/or lenders to persuade the lender/investor of the soundness of the venture and the high probability of success. In short, the business plan is really a sales presentation (sometimes referred to as a *proposal*). Bear the objective firmly in mind when and if the time comes to prepare a business plan. (A guide and outline appear in Part 5 of this book, as do names and addresses of government agencies who can help with financing and free services.)

SELF-FINANCING AND CASH FLOW MANAGEMENT

Perhaps you can manage to provide enough of your own capital to get started on a modest scale, improvising fixtures and furniture, carrying a small inventory, and practicing extreme frugality in other ways. Still, you may soon find that you do not have enough operating capital to pay daily expenses and draw even a modest salary while the business is growing slowly.

That's a problem of cash flow, and yet it is a separate problem in that many beginners in business know that they must have at least a little investment capital to start doing business on even a modest scale, but they often do not recognize the need for operating capital. They assume, naively, that income will begin to flow as soon as they open their doors.

Alas, they soon discover two factors they had not counted on:

1. Business does not always start with a great rush. Quite the contrary, although that does happen occasionally, it is more often the case that business (and income) grow slowly and take a relatively long time before showing enough profit to take care of daily expenses. And that is usually especially true for a home-based venture, which is often home based of necessity — because of a shortage of capital.

2. Even when business is good and grows fairly rapidly, "collections," as they used to refer to what is now called "cash flow," are often slow. That is, in many businesses much of the sales volume is with customers who maintain open accounts (charges) and who will probably not pay their bills for thirty days or more. (Even large organizations who, presumably, can easily afford to pay their bills on time often deliberately "age" their payables to benefit their own cash flow and may thus take as much as sixty to ninety days to pay you.) Before long, you can have a great deal of money "on the street" — owed to you — so that even though you are doing a satisfactory volume of business, you are being choked by the lack of cash flowing in while the bills continue to mount.

This is especially difficult for the young business with steadily growing sales. Suppose that you do $5,000 in sales the first month. By the end of the second month, we will assume, you have collected that $5,000 and have the gross profit in the bank. But you do $6,500 of business the second month, so that original $5,000 has long since gone into the inventory and other expenses incurred in doing more business. And that can continue to grow for some time, the cost of doing more business growing more rapidly than the cash flow grows. Even for the moderately well-financed new business, the pinch of the cash flow problem can reach crisis proportions in the first year.

It is because of this, among other typical problems, that you must expect your new business to take at least a year or two to begin to earn a net profit. In fact, venture capitalists looking at potential investments in new businesses tend to study them on the basis of whether they are likely to become profitable in three to four years.

A FIRST ATTACK ON THE PROBLEM

Cost reduction is a worthy activity in any business, new or well established. Cost avoidance is even better. That means not buying anything you really do not need, and it is especially better for the fledgling new business.

As critics say to hopeful young singers and comics auditioning for their first shot at show biz, don't quit your day job. Not if you can help it. If at all possible, run your new home-based venture on a part-time basis and don't draw a salary. Put every dollar of income back into the business to help it grow.

The typical mistakes many make are understandable. You start out flushed with enthusiasm for your "can't miss" idea and cheered on by friends and relatives. With this base of self-assurance and confidence, you start out in great style: handsome new furniture, shiny new equipment, expensive stationery and other office supplies, and a generous advertising budget.

Of course, almost all of that expense is not absolutely necessary, except, perhaps, the advertising. You can do as much business at a second-hand desk or even a kitchen table as you can at a new $1,200 solid oak desk and "president's chair." (I once worked for the owner of a company that started at his mother's kitchen table and now is headquartered on New York's Park Avenue with sales of well over $300 million annually.) Expensive stationery does not produce a penny's worth of business more than modest stationery. (I wish I could produce figures on how many tons of expensive stationery wind up being used as scratch paper.) And the same may be said for those expensive copiers and other shiny new office machines, which often wind up gathering dust in closets.

You can't really anticipate with complete accuracy what

you will need. I once had a regular and substantial copying expense, taking my typewriter-prepared manuscripts to a local copy shop almost daily. I was tempted to invest as much as $3,000 in my own copier. I resisted the temptation, fortunately, for not too much later I bought my first computer and word processing system. From that time on, I have had only occasional need for copying, and that rarely for more than a single sheet or two. (My little FAX machine provides that as an incidental convenience.) On the other hand, I was entirely mistaken about how useful a computer would be to me; to my surprise, it became absolutely indispensable. I would be benefiting today if I had bought a system earlier, for I would then have more of my manuscripts on computer disks. When I did buy my first computer, however, I investigated the field quite carefully before deciding what was most suitable for my needs.

LABOR INTENSIVE VERSUS CAPITAL INTENSIVE

Most business ventures require an investment of some sort. And yet many businesses can be launched with very little cash up front. Most business ventures fall into one of two categories, in terms of costs: *labor intensive* or *capital intensive*. These terms refer to the major costs in capitalization costs and operating expenses. What that means, in simple terms, is that the business is based either on selling services of some sort, usually a business that requires relatively little front-end investment, or on selling something requiring substantial capital investment and, usually, substantial operating expense.

Capital-intensive businesses include manufacturing and wholesaling, which usually require major investments in physical facilities—plant and equipment—and/or in inventory. The heavy cost of all the equipment and/or inventory, not the labor, is the major factor in the cost.

Labor-intensive businesses include supplying engineering specialists and office temporaries, house painting, and freelance writing. They require only modest investments in physical facilities and equipment, and most of the cost of what is sold is for labor, often high-priced labor.

There are exceptions, of course, where a venture falls into a gray middle ground—for example, if it is essentially labor intensive but has substantial capital investment, or if it is capital intensive but has a significant labor cost. Most ventures, however, fall distinctly into one or the other of these categories, and this furnishes a clue to one thing you can do if you have not yet decided what your home-based business is to be and you do not have much capital to invest. If you can offer a service as the basis of your business—writing, drafting, illustrating, training, programming, decorating, consulting, and so on—and especially if the service is one you can personally perform, you can probably start your business on an extremely modest basis as far as initial investment is concerned. You will probably need very little in the way of physical facilities, and you may very well be providing the services in facilities provided by clients—on the client's premises, that is. (Even in performing on federal government contracts I was sometimes provided a government office, secretarial services, and free access to copying machines, computers, and other facilities. That is even a more common practice in providing services to corporations in the private sector.)

FINANCING BY CUSTOMERS

Many businesses are financed by the customers, although the customers may not realize this. These are the many businesses that operate on a cash-only basis, requiring payment when the order is placed. But it also is true of a situation you may not have been fully aware of: In many cases, the customer finances the entrepreneur by making payment *months* in advance of the delivery of the service!

The U.S. Postal Service, for example, is always paid in advance—often many months in advance—of providing its service. In fact, the Postal Service has many millions of dollars paid in advance and financing operations: Every stamp in your desk drawer, every dollar of credit in your postage meter, every dollar of deposit for bulk mail and permit mail is an advance to the Postal Service against services to be delivered when demanded.

Not only the Postal Service enjoys this privilege, however; many ventures in the private sector are also paid in advance, sometimes well in advance, of providing the services. Here are a few examples:

Airlines and other transportation services get paid immediately in advance of providing their services at full list prices, but they also offer many special arrangements where they get paid well in advance of providing those services. They offer special rates during their off-peak hours but require reservations and payment—deposits, at least—well in advance.

Travel bureaus and tour packagers get paid—with deposits at least—well in advance.

Most periodicals get paid in advance, as much as a year and sometimes several years in advance of their service.

Periodicals and other advertising media—radio and TV—are usually paid in advance for advertising services. Periodicals are often paid three or more months in advance.

Most mail-order dealers are paid in advance, when the merchandise is ordered, and even if it is not shipped for several weeks. (Under current law, a mail-order dealer may take up to thirty days to fill the order.)

All these policies give the entrepreneur use of the customer's money for some time, ranging from days to months. That is a significant business advantage, and one you may wish to consider in choosing a business. But that is not yet all. Even when long-term advance payment is not the customary way to do business in some fields, you can sometimes contrive to do so.

Some kinds of ventures are cash in advance by their nature. Mail order and direct mail are among these. Although there are some exceptions, normally all orders are paid for in advance by currency, check, money order, or credit card.

A FEW EXAMPLES

A great many imaginative entrepreneurs have devised all sorts of ingenious ways to minimize costs, avoid costs, and get paid in advance. Here are a few examples that ought to suggest some ideas to you.

Joe Cossman is one of the legends of the mail-order business. Enormously successful, as he deserves to be, here are a couple of principles he follows:

He set $500 as his *top limit* (he probably has raised that figure in these inflated times) to try out, test, and evaluate a new idea—and he usually spends less than that before deciding to go on with or drop the idea. He says that the one time he made an exception to that and set his limit higher, he dropped $60,000.

He says, also, that you should get slightly sick to your stomach each time you have to spend money, especially when you are spending money unnecessarily. You can get so much simply by *asking* for it.

Let's take advertising, for instance. It's one of the most expensive, probably *the* most expensive item in your budget. But you can get a great deal of *free* advertising. Free advertising is called *publicity*, and not only is it free, it is many times more effective than paid advertising. You can't buy the kind of advertising that publicity gives you.

Take that fellow Gary Dahl, for example, with his pet rocks. He became a millionaire in only ninety days, he says, and he didn't spend 10 cents in advertising. *He got millions of dollars' worth of free publicity.*

Cossman does the same. He always manages to get reams of publicity for his products and promotions by being clever, resourceful, and *asking for it.*

In other words, when you can get editors, publishers, TV talk-show hosts, and others to give you free publicity, you are using *their money* for your advertising, money you do not ever have to pay back.

The trick is to give your product or promotion an angle. If it's truly new and different, use that angle. Write a story about it, and tell what it does for users. Send that story out, with photos, if it's a product that needs illustrating, to editors, news people, and others who communicate with the public. But don't expect to get your story into *Time* magazine, unless it's truly unusual and you happen to get lucky (as Dahl did). Settle for the "trade press," those many magazines and newspapers or news-letters that circulate among the practitioners of a given trade. (Go to the library and look them up. You will find them listed in reference books, such as *Writer's Market* and *Ayer's Guide to Periodicals*.) If you mail your story to enough of these journals, you will almost certainly get enough publicity to be worth many times your cost in doing this.

In just one of my own promotions, for example, I sold books and newsletters dealing with selling to the federal government. I made many deals with associations and other newsletter and trade magazine publishers to get free advertising (publicity) in their publications while I gave their members and readers special discounts.

That is not the only kind of financing help available to you or the only way to use some creative imagination. In many businesses you can use *the customer's money*, paid in advance, to fill the order.

One way to do this is by *drop shipping*. You don't invest in stock at all. You get the orders, make up a shipping label, and send it to the *prime source* with the wholesale price (usually about one-third to one-half the retail price). The prime source ships the order under *your label*, as though it came straight from you!

In some ventures you can be the prime source and use variants of the idea, investing little or no money of your own. Take the information or self-publishing business as an example of this tactic. You publish how-to-do-it reports, which are not formally typeset or bound in fancy covers. You can walk down the street to a nearby print shop and have copies printed overnight to fill the orders, if you do not wish to carry a stock. In fact, with today's high-quality computers, printers, and copying machines, you can run a copy every time you get an order; you don't ever have to carry a stock if you don't want to! You can use customers' money *every time* to print copies, if you wish to work that way.

You can also sell your information reports through dealers in a variety of arrangements. You can supply your reports to dealers willing to stock them. (The usual arrangement for this, if the dealer stocks an appreciable inventory, is to sell reports for approximately twice the printing cost.) You can also be the drop shipper, having others get the orders for your reports and send them to you, with their labels and the wholesale price, for you to ship out. Or, as a further variant, you can use the per-order or PO system with publishers. You prepare a camera-ready advertisement or, if the periodical does not carry advertising (most newsletters do not), prepare an editorial ("news" type) announcement for the publisher to run, with the orders to come to him or her. Then it is a standard drop-ship arrangement.

The singles club is another small business in which you can use the principle. You work with your members' dues, which are advance payments. You don't need your own money even to get started.

The résumé-writing business is still another example of a cash-up-front venture, whether you do it by mail order or by face-to-face transactions with your customers.

Lots of businesses — practically all mail-order ventures, for example, but many others as well — are cash-in-advance or cash-with-order businesses. The trick, however, is to manage things so that you use those advance payments to fill orders.

It's a matter of cash flow, and it is not difficult to choose a business that enables you to work with customers' money. But even that is not all there is to it; there are other ways to spare your own cash.

Postage costs are quite high and still rising. They are a major cost element in many ventures today. Here are a few tips in that area:

Far too many novices mail out a single sheet or two in an envelope, paying 25 cents (the current first-class rate), which is far less than the full ounce you are allowed. Actually, you can mail up to five sheets of ordinary typewriter paper for 25 cents, and you are wasting postage if you mail less than that. (I am referring to advertising literature here, of course.) The same consideration applies to second- and third-class mail, too, where the rates are based on 2 ounces. If you cannot take advantage of the extra sheets you can utilize for your postage stamp, you can get others to pay your postage by offering "piggybacking"–charging others for the privilege of sending their circulars along with yours! Or, as the other side of the coin, if you don't want to be a mailer, you pay to have your own circulars piggybacked in someone else's mailing, at a substantial reduction in your own mailing costs.

There are many other deals offered to save you money. One mail-order printer offers to print four pages for the price of two, if he gets every third page for his own advertising. You save on printing, he saves on mailing.

If you run inquiry advertising–invite people to send for free information so you collect names to mail your sales literature to–you can ask for an SASE (self-addressed, stamped envelope), eliminating the postage cost. It also saves your time and labor, of course. (*Tip*: When someone sends you one of those little 6-inch envelopes, and some people will, simply cut the front panel off and paste it to the front of one of your regular business envelopes.)

Many publications that carry a "new products" section will describe your product without cost, if you send a news release (some call it a "product release").

If you sell your product or services locally, stop and see the editors of your local newspapers. Stories in the local press can bring in a great deal of new business; the right kind of publicity is much more powerful than advertising. One man in the Washington, D.C. metropolitan area works for the federal government but runs a little moonlight business selling smoke detectors. He managed to get a nice writeup, with his picture, in a local newspaper, and was all but swamped with orders immediately.

You can also send news releases and/or news stories to any of the many newsletters published regularly in the United States. The editors of these periodicals are usually hungry for news, and it is relatively easy to get a plug for yourself in these little journals. Most of them have limited circulation, but if you are in enough of them you can reach a great many prospects. (A plug I got in only one of these, a rather popular and successful newsletter, brought in over $2,500 worth of orders.)

One of the best promotions I ever ran was an announcement of a book I was in the process of writing. I invited readers of a popular newsletter to send in orders, with advance payment, but cautioned that they would have to wait about ninety days. In return for waiting, however, they were guaranteed immediate shipment of the first copies off the press, plus a bonus, which I did not define. (I did not know then what it was to be, but I later decided to publish a newsletter, and I gave those first buyers free subscriptions.) I received enough orders, with advance payment, to finance the printing and shipping of the books and the new newsletter! That demonstrates what can be done with a bit of imagination.

The processors of pork like to say that they make use of every part of the pig but the squeal. A shrewd mail-order entrepreneur can do as well. You can even make money out of the curiosity seeker and other inquirers who do not buy but do make inquiries. You should save those names, putting them in a list of inquirers or "opportunity seekers." Those who buy, on the other hand, become names on your customer list. You can make money from these names.

You can rent both sets of names. You do *rent* them; you do not *sell* them. The customers' names, should you choose to rent them, are those of *buyers*, and thus are more valuable than are those of inquirers. Rent them at whatever rates you can command. The market is usually on the order of $20 to $35 per 1,000 names *for each use*. Rent buyers' names for about one-third more. But remember, you are *renting* them, and can rent them over and over. Good mailing lists are money makers.

Practically speaking, you need a computer to handle your mailing lists effectively, but nowadays you can handle it with a small desktop computer and a suitable software program. A simple database management program is fine for the purpose, but you can get a special mailing list program if you prefer. (Suggestions will be offered in Part 5.) There are also companies that will market your list for you, if it is large enough to be worthwhile for them. But you will make more money if you handle them yourself, and that is not hard to do with a modern desktop computer.

Deposits, Retainers,
and Progress Payments

Any custom work, such as writing rèsumés, consulting, or public speaking for fees, has the built-in hazard that what you are doing has no value to anyone but the specific client for whom you are doing it. Even if the work results in a product of some sort, as in the case of rèsumé writing or design work, the product has no application elsewhere, hence no alternative value. If the client fails to pay you, you have a 100 percent loss. Be aware of that possible hazard in undertaking custom work of any kind. The best insurance against loss is getting paid up front.

It is not always possible to get paid your entire fee up front for at least two reasons: Not every client is willing to pay the entire fee in advance, and in some arrangements you must charge by the hour or day without being certain how many hours or days will be required to complete the work. In such cases, you should arrange for progress payments. If the work is to be long term, you should get an agreement to bill and be paid periodically, perhaps once a month or once every two weeks, with at least a first payment or retainer in advance. If the work is relatively short term, a good plan is to get about one-third the estimated amount in advance as a deposit or retainer, another third at some predetermined midpoint (such as on completion of a draft), and the final third on completion or delivery.

There are always exceptions because there are always exceptional circumstances. If you are undertaking a task for a major organization whose ability and willingness to pay are beyond question, you may wish to forego advance payment. For a short-term assignment, it is sometimes impracticable because the job will be completed before the large organization can complete the paperwork and get a check drawn for a retainer. Even so, ask first for the retainer, if only to help your cash flow. Sometimes even the largest corporations have facilities to make on-the-spot payments of what are to them small amounts of money. Be sure, however, that the client has made a firm commitment both to the work and to retaining you. A retainer or advance deposit is certain evidence of firm commitment, but it is always a good policy to have some form of written agreement or purchase order as well. There are enough horror stories to illustrate the soundness of that admonition, such as one related to me by consultant Steve Wilson:

Steve works in the energy field and was invited to handle an assignment for a large coal company in West Virginia. Accordingly, Steve drove for many hours from his home in Michigan to the offices of the client company. He had to wait a while for Mr. X, who had retained him verbally by telephone. When Mr. X arrived, Steve sat down in his office and stated that he was ready to go to work. To his dismay, he was rebuffed by Mr. X, who now claimed he had not actually retained Steve but only discussed with him his availability for possible retention and assignment.

Steve realized at this point that he had been victimized by an employee who had acted without authority and was now denying his action, and so he had to return home empty-handed. (The story had a happy ending because Steve took some wise action promptly, but that is beside the point here.)

I confess to having myself been a victim of similar circumstances more than once. I later learned to ask for a purchase order or, at least, a confirming letter, as well as a retainer, before doing anything. I found, over the years, that when I was able to get a retainer I never had problems collecting my bill later. It was only in those cases where I crossed my fingers and gambled with an unknown small organization that I sometimes suffered a loss. (Unfortunately, I learned, even a written contract with the client is no guarantee that you will not be victimized and suffer a loss.)

I found, also, that in most cases I could preserve my own resources by requesting the client to furnish an airline ticket when the assignment required travel. If there is not time enough to have a ticket mailed to you, the client can always arrange to have a ticket waiting at the airline counter of your own airport or issued by a travel agency near your home. Too, clients can and often will arrange your hotel reservations and bill your accommodations to their account.

These measures make good sense because otherwise you

must tie up considerable cash of your own, without profit to you, for perhaps as long as thirty to ninety days. So far, I have never had difficulty in making these arrangements with an out-of-town client. In fact, on some occasions the client provided these services without being asked to, anticipating the need to do so as a routine.

OTHER CASH FLOW RESOURCES

There are some simple and easy ways to handle some of your problems of financing and cash flow, if the sums you need are not great ones. They may cost you a bit more in interest charges than conventional business financing, but sometimes it is worth that cost to solve the immediate problem. Moreover, some of the expedients are much faster than applying for bank loans and represent, in fact, a small but standing and ever-ready line of credit.

I refer to the gold Visa and MasterCard bank cards, which usually carry a $5,000 limit each and which enable you to do more than merely charge purchases to them: They also enable you to withdraw cash at the ATMs (automatic teller machines), and many provide checks which you can use as you would any check. (The Discover card also offers this convenience.) You can have more than one of these cards and use each independently of the others. Obviously, it is necessary to use these cards responsibly and avoid that hazard of becoming a credit-card junkie. The money is perhaps *too* easily available, and the interest rate is high; caution in use is essential.

If your business is such that you run open accounts with customers and get into that problem of too much money on the street, there is another alternative, one used by companies large and small. It is the practice of discounting your "paper" or selling it, as some put it, to a lending institution. You may have noticed that when you bought a major appliance from some local dealer you got a payment book later from some bank. The dealer had discounted its note at the bank; that is, the bank gave the dealer the money represented by the note you signed, less some percentage that represented the lender's interest or profit on the transaction.

You can do the same, although you will not have the bargaining power of Sears or the Ford Motor Company to get the most favorable terms. You may also have to agree to *recourse*, meaning you are responsible for any accounts that prove to be uncollectible.

It is also possible that you will run into difficulties getting a commercial bank to handle your small account. As in the case of business loans, most banks are not especially fond of handling the accounts of small businesses, whose total volume is not very large. But where the U.S. Small Business Administration and, in many cases, local and state agencies help small businesses get loans, there is no equivalent program for discounting your receivables for cash. Therefore, you may wish to turn to individuals known as *factors*, who will buy your receivables but only at a greater discount than that imposed by a bank.

It is also helpful in several ways to be able to offer your own customers the convenience of using credit cards in making purchases from you, and this is not difficult to arrange. You can become authorized to handle Visa and MasterCard charges at some local bank. When you deposit the slips, they are like cash deposits. Because the money is immediately available, from the viewpoint of cash flow alone, charges are more convenient than checks. Of course, they are also essentially without risk.

You will have to pay some fee for the privilege, probably 5 percent or more, depending on volume and prime rates in effect at the time, but the beneficial effect is that the convenience to your customers helps encourage sales. Some people report as much as 25 percent of their sales made on such charges.

With care and the use of as many of these approaches as are applicable to your own venture, you should be able to solve most of your financing and cash flow problems.

PART THREE

THE ESSENCE OF BUSINESS SUCCESS: EFFECTIVE MARKETING

Perhaps the highly successful book *In Search of Excellence* misled you into believing that the "revelations" made therein were new discoveries. That is not so. If anything, they were *re*discoveries and reinforcement of the truth that every good businessperson has always known: Business exists to serve customers, and it survives, prospers, or perishes as a result of how well or how poorly it does so. Unfortunately, many of us forget the lesson at times and we need to be reminded of it. Perhaps that was the real secret of the success of that book: It reminded us once again of the difference between the businesses that do well and those that do not. Unfortunately, many tend to forget that truth, or perhaps fail to learn it to begin with, when we have a period of such economic buoyancy that even those who neglect customers can survive and prosper for a time. But it is always a limited time, as we discover when the mighty fall or approach collapse, as did Chrysler Corporation, rescued only by federal government intervention.

BUYERS VERSUS CUSTOMERS

Peter Drucker, well-known authority on management, has said that the objective of business is to create customers. But what is a customer? Is everyone to whom you sell something a customer? Or is there something more to that term and its meaning?

I buy many of my supplies and equipment by mail from firms I know nothing about before I make my first purchase from them. So far, I have found all courteous, cooperative, and reliable except one. I bought a computer keyboard from that one, and had a great deal of trouble with it. I returned it and got a replacement, which also proved defective. I tried to return that for a refund, unwilling to accept another replacement. That dealer was surly and defiant, rejecting my claim entirely. Investigating, I found a number of others who also found this supplier disagreeable and noncooperative. This explains his extraordinarily heavy advertising: He is making sales, but not customers. He must find new buyers constantly to replace those he has driven away after a first sale. Making sales and making customers are not the same thing.

It seems obvious that every business is created to sell something to someone and that creating customers means also *keeping* those customers so that they will come back and buy again. Every business has competitors, and mistreating or neglecting your customers can only result in sending them into the arms of competitors who are more caring of their customers. Moreover, the loss of the customer is not the only penalty: Dissatisfied customers grumble to their friends and neighbors, dissuading others from buying from you.

A first sale is made to a buyer. The buyer who is satisfied and returns to buy again, and even to recommend you to others, has become a customer. It costs money to create customers. It may cost even more to make a first sale to a buyer than the profit on that first sale. The investment you make to win that sale is therefore justified only if and when the buyer is made into a customer. Profits will come eventually, when the customer has made enough purchases from you so that you can recover the investment you made in winning the customer. That is why it is almost always *cheaper* to keep a customer than to create another one, even when the customer is wrong or it costs you money to keep the customer happy. (That's why it is an immutable truth that "the customer is always right.")

Chapter Ten

Business Success Requires Hard-Headed Practicality

*In the business world
no one cares to hear about
the storms you met at sea. They
only want to know whether you
brought the ship home.*

THE BUSINESS WORLD IS UNFORGIVING

In every sphere of human activity, but in none more than in the world of business and industry, management faces this acid test: With unlimited resources, anyone can get the job done. The real test of a manager is the ability to get the job done despite totally inadequate resources.

That is a harsh reality because business is itself a harsh reality, and it is no kindness to deceive anyone, yourself least of all, about it. Business is competitive, and in more ways than one: There are direct competitors, selling essentially the same thing you are selling, and there are indirect competitors selling other things but still competing for customers' dollars, which are always limited.

That means, in essence, that you almost never enjoy a truly

exclusive position. Even if you offer a service or product that is totally proprietary and unique, the prospective customer is almost inevitably pondering the spending of his or her supply of dollars on your service/product versus another service/product. Most people cannot afford everything they want, so their purchases are almost always compromises between desires and practical possibilities.

BUSINESS SUCCESS IS A SIMPLE CONCEPT

There is a simple explanation for why the business world is, overall, a harsh reality. Unlike all other human activities, success in any business hinges ultimately on a single, decisive factor: profit or the lack of it. Public schools, associations, government bureaus, military departments, and other organizations can be and often are highly inefficient, and yet they go on and survive despite all shortcomings; efficiency is not a prime goal for them, and profit is an unknown and strange concept. But traditional businesses must all meet that acid test of profitability, sooner or later; it is the irreducible must for business survival, and lack of it is a certain prescription for death.

Nor is it enough even for a business venture eventually to achieve profitability after a lengthy struggle between costs and marketing. Most businesses are expected to need one to three or four years to establish their viability; the most hard-headed venture capitalists accept that. But even then the business must continue to show profits over the long term, or it perishes. Many landmark and well-established businesses whose names are known to all have suffered this fate. In recent history, these have included Robert Hall, the clothier; W. T. Grant, the novelty and general merchandise store chain; and E. J. Korvette, the discount department store chain. These are only three examples of highly successful firms that failed to maintain their vigor and permitted rigor mortis to set in prematurely. And except for the relentless energies of Lee Iacocca and the intervention of President Jimmy Carter to win an infusion of federal taxpayers' money as a loan, the venerable and mighty Chrysler Corporation would have gone the same route to extinction.

The business world is unforgiving of major mistakes, especially of weakness in marketing. It is no respecter of past glories. The consequences are harsh ones even for the former giants of the business world.

WHAT IS MARKETING?

One of the problems, perhaps a major problem in business, is that *marketing* tends to be a rather vague and general term. Most people who do not know better, and even those who ought to know better, tend to use the word interchangeably with *sales*. They are not quite the same thing. Simplified as much as possible, it is fair to say that *selling* is the act of asking for and getting the order; marketing is the process of deciding what order to ask for and how to go about getting it. And even that does not really explain the difference, for marketing addresses an entire universe of related questions that must be answered even before you begin to quest after sales:

Just what is it that you are really selling?

To whom are you, or should you be, addressing your offers and appeals?

Why ought they to buy this item from you? (What will it do for them?)

How will you reach these prospects and present your offer/appeal?

How will you make them understand their need for this item?

How will you induce them to order now?

Even these questions are somewhat premature, in a sense, for there are questions that should precede them, should precede even actually initiating the venture. In fact, marketing analysis should be the second step in planning and making the initial decision to launch the venture. The first step is formulating the basic idea upon which to found the venture.

Step 1: The Seminal Idea

Every business venture starts with an idea. Unfortunately, many entrepreneurs launch a venture, investing time and money, without a truly clear idea of what they are doing. Perhaps they make a vague assumption that once their doors are opened, everything will fall into place, that they can feel their way as they go along. That is often the basis on which someone opens a retail store of some kind, assuming that sales will follow of their own accord. It works sometimes, usually when the individual is able to survive during what is likely to be a lengthy trial-and-error period before success begins to set in or when pure chance favors the venture.

James is a superb Chinese cook. He learned his trade in Hong Kong, and he claims to know how to prepare a thousand Chinese dishes, a claim I won't dispute, having dined on his culinary creations many times. I cannot recall ever tasting better Chinese cookery, although we have dined in many fine Chinese restaurants. All the friends and relatives I told about James and his tiny new restaurant sampled James's cooking, and they agreed: James has few peers in the art of the wok.

Unfortunately, James was forced by lack of funds to choose a tiny location in a remote corner of a small and obscure shopping center, and his restaurant languished there. James thought that the excellence of his cooking would be enough to ensure success, as it has for other restaurants in remote locations. It was not. He did no advertising or promotion, depending entirely on word of mouth, but he also did not have financial backing sufficient to carry his establishment until word of mouth did enough promotion. He was gaining slowly, but he could not hold out long enough; he was forced to close before he reached the breakeven point and had to go back to working in someone else's kitchen.

Millions of individuals make similar mistakes, launching mail-order, store front, and other ventures without very much thought to marketing or anything else. They make the commitment, that is, without a clear idea of what will make their venture successful — that is, who will buy from them or, for that matter, just what it is that they will sell and why anyone ought to buy whatever it is. Success in such circumstances is more often the result of chance than of design.

Suppose, for example, that James had decided to specialize in some way, even if only with a distinctive, attention-arresting descriptor of some sort, such as *Secret Emperor Minoan Recipes*, and then had taken out a few inexpensive advertisements in a local neighborhood newspaper. (In fact, James prepared a delectable and distinctive shrimp dish we have never been able to find anywhere else!) Suppose, in fact, that James had made some special offer in those advertisements, perhaps a contest to name one of his dishes, with the prize a free dinner for four. And suppose, further, that James had sent out special invitations in the form of press releases to the food editors and restaurant critics of all the local newspapers. It is almost inevitable that he would have drawn more customers than he did, even if they came out of sheer curiosity, and he would have gotten at least a little publicity. Then the excellence of his cookery would have had a fighting chance to lure customers and make his little restaurant a success. (The location now houses a successful small Japanese restaurant.)

James never asked himself the questions "Why should anyone patronize me, rather than others? Who are these prospective customers? How can I reach them and let them know about my restaurant? What am I offering that would induce them to seek out my remote little establishment?"

The answers to these questions are not unrelated. Quite the contrary, they bear directly on each other, because they are connected to the main question: What is the basic idea on which the venture is to be based?

Young Montgomery Ward had a new and different idea: He launched a retail business in which he guaranteed satisfaction unconditionally. Ward pledged a complete refund, no questions asked, to any customer who was not satisfied for any reason at all. It was a revolutionary idea at the time, dismaying his competitors, who promptly forecast his immediate failure in the world of commerce. They were wrong, of course; this was an idea whose time had come, and the angry competitors were soon forced to emulate Ward's example, as they do to this day.

Gail Borden thought it terrible that the public was forced to buy dreadfully adulterated milk, a common condition a century ago. He set about to find a way to preserve milk, and he succeeded eventually, but he did not succeed in persuading the public to buy his canned condensed milk immediately; that required a long and difficult fight. He prevailed eventually, however, as the survival of his company and name now attest.

Milton Hershey had more than one failure of his candy-selling enterprises until he returned to Lancaster, Pennsylvania and specialized in selling chocolate. The identification of Hershey with chocolate needs no comment or explanation today.

Joe Sugarman had many good ideas when he launched his mail-order business selling new electronic devices, but one as far-reaching as Ward's unconditional guarantee was to accept credit-card orders by telephone and mail, a practice then thought to be excessively risky that has now been almost universally adopted by merchants.

In most cases, probably, the desire to launch an independent venture of some kind comes first. Then comes the quest for an idea for a venture. This is the time to ask yourself certain basic questions, such as whether you ought to stick to some field in which you have experience or to strike out in a new and different area. Along with these considerations comes the question of specialization versus generalization.

Where Do Business Ideas Come From?

Shortly after World War II, two young veterans met in a Los Angeles restaurant for lunch. They were astonished at the tender, flavorful steak they were served at an unbelievably modest price. They soon discovered that the secret was that of the restaurant's chef, who had somehow learned that marinating meat in papaya extract had the effect of tenderizing it. The two men made a deal with the chef, paying him a royalty for the use of his extract and name, launching the successful product Adolph's Meat Tenderizer.

Note from this and other stories that getting an idea is not enough. You must *believe* in that idea enough to pursue it, even when others try earnestly to discourage you (as in the case of Montgomery Ward, Gail Borden, and many others with bold, new ideas). It takes a great deal of fortitude and faith, especially the latter, for faith is what enables you to persist when it is so easy to become discouraged.

Specialization Versus Generalization

The immediate tendency in planning a venture is to generalize, to offer everything in the hope that casting a wide net — running a general store — will maximize sales opportunities and, consequently, sales and cash flow. Alas, the result is often the opposite. When you are generalized, prospects see no distinction in what you offer.

On the other hand, specialization carries a risk also: Will there be enough prospects interested in that specialty you offer? You must be clear on that point.

The answer lies, usually, in moderation. Avoid the extremes of being so general as to be almost formless and colorless, yet avoid the opposite extreme of being so specialized that you have too limited an appeal to generate enough of a customer base for viability. Find that point where you are specialized enough to be distinctive, yet generalized enough to enable a substantial base of customers to identify with what you offer.

When Is an Idea Not an Idea?

An employee came to see me one day with what he said was a great idea. He told me that he had been studying our operating problems in the department where he worked, and he could see that the operations there were not efficient. He was letting me know that much time and effort were being wasted there, and a more efficient system was needed. His idea was to reorganize that department to improve efficiency.

I had listened to my share of such "ideas" before, and I had learned to cope effectively with them without discouraging employees' efforts to be helpful. I responded to this employee as I always responded to such suggestions. My response was approximately as follows:

"Jerry, I am sure that you are right and that we need to make a few changes. I thank you for bringing this to my attention. However, before I can move on this, I need more information. Here is what you can do for me: Draft a full reorganization plan in detail. Tell me just what changes you would make and how you would organize the department. Then I will let you know what I think of the plan."

In the years I managed that organization, I responded that way many times to employees bringing me a variety of ideas for reorganizing departments, getting new business, starting new services, and other well-intentioned suggestions. But I waited in vain for any of those people to follow up my response and bring me a plan of any kind.

What these people were bringing me were notions, not ideas. A notion is not worthy of the title *idea* if it contains not even the beginnings or suggestion of a plan of action. Of what value is a notion that merely states a general goal or general complaint without even the suggestion of some approach to implementation? You should certainly not gamble your money, your time, or your reputation on something that nebulous.

When television came along in the early 1950s, furniture dealers, department stores, and others quickly added TV receivers to the lines they sold. But more than a few people who had not been in business rushed to open TV stores, retail establishments that sold nothing but TV receivers. Most failed in a short time because the sale of TV sets alone was not enough to support a full-time business. The people who leaped into that kind of venture simply had not thought things out. They had acted on a notion. Had they "done their homework" by doing some research into how much profit they could expect to make on TV sales, what their costs would be, and how much business they could expect to do (make a conservative estimate of sales and then cut that figure in half), they would have been less eager to leap into this new business with nothing else to support their venture.

Such information is not easy, but equally not impossible to come by. There are many places to get help. One is the U.S. Small Business Administration. That agency of the federal government operates over eighty district offices, so one is almost surely listed in the telephone directory of some city near you. But other federal, state, and local government agencies can also help you gather information and develop market estimates. Many of them will furnish brochures, pamphlets, and even complete manuals. More information on finding such agencies is supplied in Part 5 of this book.

That is not the only source of information and help. Check your local library, for one. Most libraries have reference works that will supply useful market information. Check also with local services such as your local Chamber of Commerce, business association (Rotary or Lions Clubs), trade association, and others. (Check your telephone book under the heading *associations*.)

Some other suggestions are offered in Part 5.

Chapter Eleven

Marketing: The True Test of Viability

In the end, after all your planning and preparation, it is the buying public who determines how viable your business proposition really is.

MARKETING VERSUS SALES

After recognizing that *sales* and *marketing* are not the same activity in a technical sense, we must also recognize that selling—creating customers—is the ultimate and true objective of marketing. Everything you do in marketing must be designed to help make a success of the sales efforts to come later when you offer your goods or services. Deciding what those goods and services are to be, to whom they will be offered, how they will be offered, and under what kinds of terms and conditions are all part of setting the stage for the sale. Marketing is largely preparation for selling, so sales success depends to a large degree on the effectiveness of the marketing.

If you review the previous discussions of marketing activity, you will see that all address that objective of helping make the ultimate sales that are the objective of all business. At some point in the process, then, *marketing* becomes *sales*. There is no clear demarcation between these two activities, nor is it necessary that one exist. What is necessary is that you recognize that your effectiveness in selling will definitely depend on other factors than your personal effectiveness as a salesperson. The old cliché about a salesman being so good that he could sell an icebox to an Eskimo is a gross exaggeration. In fact, you cannot sell anything to someone who does not really want to buy it. Even the high-pressure salespeople accomplish their sales by first persuading prospects to want what they sell (although sometimes the want fades as "buyer remorse" sets in).

SALES: AN ACT OF PERSUASION

Selling is without doubt an act of persuasion, but one point must be emphasized: Selling does not consist of persuading someone to buy what you sell, but of persuading someone to *want* what you sell. Buying is simply the prospect's way of satisfying that want; once the want is firmly established, the sale is not difficult to consummate. As the late Elmer Wheeler, often acclaimed as "America's greatest salesman," said in his own piquant way: If you want to sell lemonade, first you have to make people thirsty. In the end, it comes down to a question of wants and needs. Strictly speaking, *want* means lack of, but modern usage has made *want* synonymous with *desire* and I will therefore use the word here to mean desire.

Need is another word used freely in discussing sales and marketing. Again, as in the case of *want*, the word is not without its ambiguities. As most of us use the word, it does not refer to something that is an absolute must in a practical sense; in a practical sense, *need* is almost synonymous with *want*. That's because when we humans desire something ardently, we are able to easily persuade ourselves of the urgency with which we must have that item. So although one may have two dozen pairs of shoes, he or she may easily discover a need for yet another pair. We tend to think and say, "I need it," when the literal truth is, "I want it." Needs are therefore a direct factor in the thinking and planning of marketing and sales activity.

NEEDS, FELT AND CREATED

Marketing experts sometimes speak of *felt needs*. Felt needs refer to the mental state of a prospect who is conscious of a desire to own some item or buy some service, as contrasted with someone who must be "educated" in his or her "need" for some item. The prospect with the felt need might be the customer who has decided that life cannot go on without a new color TV or red sports car and so begins shopping for the item. Does that mean that he or she will walk into a place of business and point to the item, whipping out a checkbook or credit card? No, it is rarely that easy. That customer has probably not decided yet between Brand X and Brand Y, and even if he or she has decided on the brand, he or she has probably not yet decided which dealer offers the most attractive deal. You will get some sales without a fight, but those are more often the exception than the rule; you have to work to win most of your sales successes, even from the customers with the felt needs.

Of course, the other side of that coin is creating needs. That task is not quite as clear-cut. Can you really create a need? Can you make someone want something he or she did not want before you showed up on the scene?

In one sense, yes, you can create needs, especially if *need* and *want* are interchangeable terms. If you somehow induce a prospect to want something you sell, you have created a need. Suppose, for example, that you invent an easier way to cook. (Let's call it a microwave oven.) Suddenly a great many people who had never expressed dissatisfaction with their gas ranges decided that they must have one of the new microwave ovens. Obviously, the availability of a better (or, at least, easier) way to cook has created a new need. Of course, the need for a microwave oven could not have existed before the microwave oven itself existed, so it is the introduction of this new item that created the need for it. Or so goes the conventional thinking.

But let's look further at the business of creating needs. When microwave ovens first appeared on the market, they were quite expensive, beyond the means of many buyers, and so the "need" for them grew slowly, felt only by those who could afford them. When the prices began to fall and microwave ovens came within the reach of many more than before, the "need" increased sharply.

That, of course, is the pattern that has characterized the introduction of all kinds of new goods and services—automobiles, radios, TVs, VCRs, spas, air travel, and many other features of modern living. The need for these items rose in direct proportion to the ability of individuals to pay for them.

More than a few years ago, department stores introduced "charge plates," forerunners of today's credit cards. Charge plates created needs for items that many buyers could not afford before but now decided they could, because they could charge the items and pay in installments. So the charge plates and the credit cards that followed have created many needs.

You create needs, then, by introducing new products and services that people like and find attractive, but you do so only to the extent that you make it possible for people to own the items and use the services.

Is There Such a Thing as a New Need?

All this suggests that you can create a need where none existed before. Obviously, there could not have been a need for radio before radio existed, nor for airline transportation before passenger airplanes existed. But stop and consider: In the long-range view, do these things truly satisfy newly created needs or are they really better ways of satisfying old, classic needs?

Humans have always had a need for entertainment. The ancient Greeks had their sporting events, the Romans their games, and these diversions have evolved into the many sports played and witnessed today. The theater was also an ancient entertainment, from at least the time of the ancient Greeks, and it survives in some form today. But within the memory of many living today, radio was a novelty enjoyed by only a few. After a while, radio receivers came within the grasp of most consumers, and soon radio was the chief means of entertainment at home. The pattern was repeated with movies, TV, and videocassette recorders.

These modern miracles do not represent the creation of

new needs as much as they represent newer and better ways of satisfying old, classic needs. But interpret that word *better* carefully, for it does not necessarily mean more effective, more efficient, or at lower cost; it means more desirable to the users. Looking at stereo pairs of photos in the parlor was more comfortable and more convenient than sitting on a cold stone bench in a windy stadium watching gladiators butcher each other. But radio was far superior to that, as TV was superior to radio. And videocassette recorders and players were better than TV and far better than going to the movies—much cheaper, too.

Look at how we heat our homes, for example: From open fireplaces, to central heat via coal, then oil, and more recently gas, each system cleaner, more efficient, and more convenient than its predecessor. That is what accounts for the swift success of each new method of heating private homes. The progression has paused there, however. Electric heating has been introduced, but it has not caught on because it offers no real advantages—it is not significantly superior to gas heat in any way, and is considerably more costly to operate.

The success of modern express services is another example. It is due not only to the service they render, but at least partly as well to the dissatisfaction many of us have with the U.S. Postal Service. Private express services offer a better way to rush things or to make sure that they will arrive in time. Lately, FAX—facsimile transmission—has become the newest success story because it is even better than express deliveries for some things. It is faster and cheaper, and the public is embracing it most enthusiastically.

What is the significance to us of all this? Just this: The "secret" of successful marketing, especially of outstandingly successful marketing, is to create needs by offering prospects a better way to satisfy their classic, traditional needs.

WHAT DOES "BETTER" REALLY MEAN?

One thing you must always remember in business is that there is only one truth, the *customer's* truth. The ancient expression that "the customer is always right" simply means that you must cater to the customer's perception of fact, for, as another old expression has it, "you can't win an argument with a customer." In the business world, "better" is whatever the customer finds better. There are, for example, many instances where the less expensive product appears to be of higher quality than the more expensive one. It would be foolish for a printer to contest a customer's choice of paper, for example, because the printer knows that it is not the better grade. He might explain that fact, but he stops there if the customer does not wish to be persuaded: Winning an argument might easily mean losing the customer.

Convenience is a great motivator. What is more convenient is usually better, as far as the customer is concerned. And convenience includes speed of service, in this high-paced age. Customers are often motivated more by speed than by price, paying a bit more than necessary to avoid waiting. Convenience is what impels many customers to patronize the 7-11 stores (which are, in fact, referred to as "convenience stores"), although they might find a wider selection and lower prices in the supermarket. But they would have to park their cars well away from the store and march up and down many long aisles to find what they want. Many items are available at considerable savings by mail order, but ordering by mail, or even by telephone, means waiting for delivery. The preference of many customers is to pay a bit more and enjoy the benefits of at-the-door parking, speedier consummation of the purchase, and the generally more intimate atmosphere of the small establishment.

A fairly sure way to win customers is to offer them goods and services that they recognize as being better. Montgomery Ward offered something better when he offered the no-questions-asked, money-back guarantee. The first mail-order dealer offered a better service when he made it possible to buy something without leaving home. Automobile maker Ransome Olds knew that "better" in automobiles at the time meant an automobile that did not have to be cranked by hand to start, and so he commissioned inventor Charles "Boss" Kettering to create the first self-starter for his Oldsmobile. (Note how many advertisers stress only that special better feature of whatever they sell, ignoring all else about the product or service.)

"Find a Problem and Solve It"

One popular piece of advice offered as an unfailing formula for success is, "Find a problem and solve it." This adage makes good sense when properly interpreted, but it does require interpretation. At first glance it seems to suggest that one ought to try to discover what troubles a great many people and then seek a remedy or create a great new invention. That may work, but there is an easier way to apply this principle. It is not necessary to do anything revolutionary. (In fact, it is a platitude in engineering that progress, meaning sound engineering practice, consists of evolution, not revolution.) It is sufficient that you make an important improvement in anything many of us use or do, in even the simplest product or practice.

What this means is simply this: We often do not recognize that a problem exists until we learn of a better way to do something. We accepted the condition as normal and necessary prior to the change. For example, in my own youth a small, hand-held device known as a *can opener* resided in everyone's kitchen drawer. It was used laboriously to cut through and pry open the lids of cans. Probably few of these exist today or find use except where there is no electricity. No one complained that opening cans was a problem, arduous and crude as the method was, as long as they did not know of a better way to do the job.

But you don't have to do anything as dramatic or as difficult as inventing a self-starter motor or an electric can opener to "find a problem and solve it." Nor does "better" necessarily mean better only for the customer; it can also mean better from your viewpoint as a marketer: a better way to advertise or a better way to promote sales in general, for example, especially when that better way also offers the customer some benefit. The first merchant to accept credit card orders by mail and telephone had a better marketing idea, and it also afforded his customers a convenience they had not enjoyed before. In my own case, I sold how-to reports, newsletters, and other materials by mail order. I wrote and published these myself, an advantage in direct cost of the product. It took, at the time, as much as thirty days for an out-of-town check to clear, and most mail-order dealers would not ship merchandise ordered until the customer's check cleared. However, the nature of what I sold and what it cost me to produce it was such that my actual out-of-pocket loss was not great when a check failed to clear. So I shipped publications ordered immediately and cheerfully accepted the occasional bad check. There really were not that many of them, and the good will generated by prompt fulfillment was worth the occasional small loss I suffered.

There are many practical approaches to finding better ways to do and make things. Consider each service or product you might consider as a business basis from several possible angles, including at least these:

- How can you make it more effective or more efficient in doing whatever it is supposed to do?
- How can you make it more convenient (or faster, where that is relevant, as in delivery) for the customer to use it? To order it? To get delivery of it? To pay for it?
- How can you give the customer greater assurance of satisfaction or protection, such as a better guarantee or a free trial period?
- How can you provide the customer something extra, going the extra mile to serve buyers?

Think about the complaints that are common knowledge. One, for example, is that instructions that accompany many items are usually badly written and hard to understand. So they are of little help to the user trying to assemble, operate, or service some item. But it doesn't have to be that way. When I bought my first computer, the dealer invited me to a free half-day seminar as a training session, supplementing the manufacturer's written instructions, with an opportunity to ask an instructor as many questions as I wished. He also had a service department, and his technicians answered questions and provided additional guidance via telephone. And when I bought a modem in that establishment, I was given free communications software to accompany it. It is probably no coincidence that this dealer has been one of the most successful ones in the area, growing steadily by adding branch stores in other metropolitan locations.

Making Lemonade Out of Lemons

What the computer dealer did illustrates an important principle, often expressed by the philosophy that problems are not problems but opportunities. That is, within every problem is the seed of an opportunity for the alert and resourceful individual. So what I am exhorting you to do here is not to seek out problems but to seek out opportunities.

Bear in mind at all times that problems are a routine, everyday part of life: You may rest assured that every prospect you approach has problems and will always turn a sympathetic ear to offers or even to vague suggestions of help in solving the problems. You may have heard or will eventually hear the bit of wisdom that every successful salesperson is a consultant. What that means is simply that (1) the truly successful and fully qualified salesperson is completely knowledgeable about his or her own field—what the service or product he/she sells is and can do for customers. And (2) that salesperson has, as a first interest, a desire to determine what the prospect's needs and problems are and then a goal of determining how he/she (the salesperson) can help the prospect solve those problems (through buying whatever the salesperson sells, of course).

This approach is sound in all applications. If you are selling a commodity, you seek to determine what common problems are and offer all prospects a solution. If you are selling a custom service, you do the same thing for prospects on an individual basis. Here are some examples of that approach in practice — in *successful* practice:

Suppliers of parts in high-tech industries usually employ engineers as salespeople because their salespeople must talk to customers' engineers. When a small company in Philadelphia contracted to design and manufacture the first Citizen's Band radio for RCA, the Shirley Coil Company's own engineers/ salespeople worked with the design engineers to help them design the coils they needed and supplied sample coils for the prototype equipment. That kind of direct and substantial support is quite common in technical industries. Today, design engineers know that they can get considerable technical aid from the sales personnel of the various vendors.

The Warner Electric Clutch and Brake Company of Beloit, Wisconsin enjoys an estimated 95 percent of the market for their major line of products. They sell these products through the salespeople of well over 500 dealers throughout the United States. But they recognized as a major problem that in the booming post–Second World War years that their dealers were forced to hire many salespeople who were not knowledgeable enough in the directly relevant technology of industrial plant automation. They (Warner) therefore undertook to create a training program for these salespeople. The objective of the training was to make them capable of serving prospective customers as consultants. That is, they were to be trained in how Warner's products could be used to modernize and improve aging industrial plants and how to analyze prospects' problems and show them how Warner products could solve their problems. They were, simply, to serve prospective customers as technical consultants, in the best tradition of modern sales techniques.

This approach to marketing is highly effective, as the following personal example demonstrates: Some years ago, I decided that OSHA, the Occupational Safety and Health Administration of the U.S. Department of Labor, needed nothing more urgently than my services as a writer. I did claim expert knowledge in some areas of industrial safety (e.g., electrical), if not in health. I therefore visited the Washington, D.C. offices of OSHA and worked my way through a series of departments searching for an opportunity to make a connection.

Eventually I reached the office of an executive in charge of developing training services for the organization. My approach, after the conventional exchanges of self-introductions, pleasantries, and platitudes, was to inquire into this department's (really, this executive's) problems. I wanted to learn as much as I could of their day-to-day operations and needs, but I especially wanted to learn what problems they had and which were of greatest concern.

I did not ask specifically for identification or descriptions of problems, of course; that is not the way to do it. Effective salespeople are primarily good listeners, asking an occasional question designed to draw the other out and produce useful information. I therefore made a series of general inquiries, with the dual purpose of learning both how the organization functioned generally and what their typical needs and/or special problems were. I was a shoulder to cry on and an attentive ear, a convenient and often highly effective role for marketing purposes.

As I heard the tale of woe unwind, I was thinking rapidly, developing in my mind an informal and spontaneous presentation of how the problems might be solved through the services I could provide. I held my counsel until the flow of information slowed to a trickle. My prospect had evidently completed his dissertation of distress. In this case, the unhappiness centered on a training program in the form of two manuals written for them by a contractor that had not been accompanied by any kind of implementation or administrative guidance. The agency was at a loss as to how to put the manuals to work effectively. At the least, they wanted a curriculum plan that would utilize the manuals.

Fortunately, I was able to respond directly and spontaneously with suggestions of what I could do to solve the problem. I was immediately invited to submit an informal proposal describing in summary what I had just stated at some length, describing what I would do for the organization and what it would cost the government.

The result was a purchase order, the first of a number of lucrative purchase orders and contracts. They came about because I focused carefully on what I would *do* for the organization (for the individual in charge of the organization, that is), rather than on what I wanted. Here the pertinent wisdom is this: The way to get what you want from anyone is to help him or her get what he or she wants. A key objective of all selling, therefore, is to learn what the prospective customer does want and work on ways to help him or her get whatever that is.

Marketing Ideas Abound

The idea of the salesperson as a consultant is a rather well-established principle of modern marketing. But it is also a subset of a more general principle that effective marketing consists or is based always on service to the customer. (Remember that the customer is always motivated, whether consciously or subconsciously, by the idea, "What's in it for me? Why should I buy it?")

In practice, that means—always—that you market effectively only when you think from the customer's viewpoint. The key is to consider, always, what services you can provide. And it isn't difficult to get ideas to enhance your marketing. There are lots to be found if you simply keep an eye and ear open for them. Here are just a few:

A prominent mail-order supplier of office and related supplies offers an interesting case of a business that started at home, in the basement of founder Jack Miller, in fact. The firm is Quill®, a large and prominent firm today, operating out of a large facility in Lincolnshire, Illinois, a Chicago suburb. I have watched this firm grow over the years and have noted that the management not only started with services that made it attractive to deal with, but has continued to add such services steadily over the years.

First, from the beginning Quill did not ask for payment with one's initial order nor offer a lengthy credit-application form, but asked only for a bank account name and number. Credit for the first order was then extended automatically, a most gracious and appealing gesture. The order was filled promptly, something of a novelty in itself in this era, and an invoice followed as a separate communication. (This is itself an unusual practice; many firms shipping on charge accounts enclose an invoice with the shipment.) The entire approach—granting credit instantly, without a formal application asking for a financial statement and multiple credit references, and guaranteeing the customer's right to return merchandise for any reason at all—was an interesting innovation in itself. Who could resist trying the firm out? What, in fact, could anyone lose in trying the firm out with an initial order?

This policy was complemented by freely inviting and almost begging the customer to return anything he or she did not like or want for whatever reason. (I think Quill outdid even Montgomery Ward in this!) A form was supplied so that it was not even necessary to make arrangements or get advance authorization for a return, as it is with a great many mail-order firms.

Eventually, Quill offered a free newsletter to customers, and later still they added a new feature, a column in their monthly catalogs (which supplement the thick semiannual catalogs) called "Quill Business Tips," which are just that, helpful tips. The current catalog, for example, discusses how to maximize the success of business meetings. Of course, these features, the newsletter and the business tips column, suggest and promote items Quill sells. The purpose is not only to promote good will generally, but more pointedly to sell specific items the firm handles.

But there are many other ways to serve your customers well. When I had problems with a modem I bought by mail order, the firm replaced it with a better product that sold for less money and sent me a refund check for the difference while also paying the freight charges for the exchange. It is hardly necessary to say that I was impressed and have done further business with that firm. I trust a firm that exhibits such honesty and concern for its customers.

Marketing is not just selling: It is creating customers, and that means creating relationships. Marketing is a "people business." You must *serve* your customers, and serve them well.

The principle of service to the customer is applied in more than one way: It is not necessarily only what you *do* for the customer that impresses and persuades him or her, but possibly *how* you present your ideas as well. That is, you can present your ideas in such a way that you persuade the customer to perceive that you are addressing his or her most direct interests. Note cosmetic advertising, for example: One advertiser may address the exotic nature of the product, but a better marketer addresses the power of the product to create an atmosphere of romance or otherwise to attract the opposite sex.

The point here is that you ought not to expect your customers to make the logical transition from the beneficial characteristic you claim for the item to the direct benefit they will experience. Most customers will not make that logical transition. You must make it for them. You must show them, in the most direct terms, what the specific benefit will be. With that philosophy in mind, I do not stress that I help clients write winning proposals; that is an afterthought or supporting argument. My emphasis is always on my ability to help clients win contracts. That is the end result they want, and that is the promise they want to hear me make and validate.

Think always in terms of the end result the customer wants and focus on how you can help get that result. You can never go wrong with that approach.

Chapter Twelve

Marketing Methods

*No more popular subject is
taught in our business schools,
presented as lectures and
seminars, and written about
in books and articles than
marketing, especially the many
methods of marketing.*

THE PRINCIPLES ARE IMMUTABLE

The principles of marketing do not change, although the methods do. There are many marketing methods, and new methods or innovative variations of established methods are constantly being introduced. Too, with modern methods of communication and travel—radio, TV, automobiles, and airplanes—the public in general is steadily becoming more knowledgeable and sophisticated about advertising. Thus appeals must likewise become more sophisticated, and they have done so.

It is important to know this fact and to know and understand all the various modern marketing methods. But despite changes in methods, you must never lose sight of the immutable truths of principles in marketing, which are based on the unchanging characteristics of human emotions and reactions. All marketing methods, regardless of their differences, are simply alternative ways of reaching prospects with your messages and appeals. Some methods reach more people than others. Some reach certain kinds of prospects more effectively than others do. Some are more efficient than others. Some have greater impact than others. And some are especially suited to certain products or prospects. But all effective marketing methods appeal to the same basic human desires and drives: In the end, people are still motivated by the same kinds of appeals, regardless of the media or sensory approaches used to deliver that appeal.

There are, in fact, several basic avenues of marketing, although we may disagree on what that term "basic avenue" means. You can assign the avenues from the viewpoint of the advertiser, who may classify the various methods in this way:

Print media — newspapers and magazines

Broadcast — radio and TV

Direct mail — salesletters and brochures

Direct marketing — personal calls via door-to-door, telephone, direct mail, and other direct methods

The prospect may perceive the basic methods this way:

Eyes only — print media and "junk mail"

Ears only — radio

Ears and eyes — TV

Personal intrusion — salespeople at the door and on the telephone

You may have noticed that the prospective customer's subjective view of these media and marketing methods is considerably different than the marketer's probably more objective view. For this reason, it is really not possible to make parallel classifications. Nevertheless, let us consider first the basic media or methods from both your viewpoint as a marketer and from the prospect's viewpoint. Later, we will discuss and explore these media and methods in greater depth.

Print Media

Soliciting the patronage of prospective customers through advertisements in various periodicals is one of the oldest marketing methods. Magazine advertising has the advantage of being relatively easy to do, and it does reach a great many people. It has two disadvantages: It is essentially a passive method, and it is a method in which the advertising is largely wasted because you are charged for using it in a mass medium that reaches a large population, relatively few of whom are truly good prospects for whatever you are selling.

You overcome this problem by advertising only in media that reach the population group you wish to target. If you are selling tools, you would find a far greater percentage of the readers of *Popular Mechanics* good prospects than the readers of *Playboy* magazine, although in both cases the readers are principally men. There are periodicals for almost any group of people you can name, and you can generally get more for your advertising dollar by selecting the right ones for your copy.

Broadcast: Radio and TV

Broadcast media are superior to print media in many ways, and yet the same advantage and disadvantage exist: It is relatively simple to market on the air and you reach many pairs of eyes and ears, but the medium is also essentially passive and a large proportion of your advertising dollar is wasted here, for the same reason. It is possible, however, to choose the most suitable time slots and channels for your purposes. On most stations, Saturday mornings are given over largely to programs for small children, so you would avoid these times if you want to sell items that appeal mostly to adults. But you can also select certain types of programs, such as sports events, for your commercials.

Direct Marketing

Direct marketing is a general term. It means that the marketer pursues the prospective customer individually, through personal visits, telephone calls, and mail. Each of these approaches is a universe unto itself, and we will have to discuss them at some length. But first a brief and general appreciation.

The individual salesperson, traveling about and knocking on doors, is practicing one of the oldest and yet still active methods of marketing. With the great population shift to the suburbs, door-to-door selling is more difficult. Many other changes have taken place also in recent decades, and there are many fewer "Fuller Brush Man" and "Avon calling" types of salespeople than previously. But direct selling has not declined; it is simply practiced a bit differently today. It employs such devices as "dinnerware parties" and "multilevel selling" for marketing consumer goods, but the traditional traveling salesman (and saleswoman) still calls on customer prospects.

Telemarketing, selling by telephone, is a fairly recent innovation, not yet especially well established nor especially successful, because many people dislike the intrusion into their privacy that telephone solicitation represents to them.

On the other hand, direct mail, referred to by many as "junk mail," is a widely used method of marketing many kinds of goods and services, and it has grown steadily in its popularity as a marketing approach. (We will discuss direct mail in much greater detail in a later chapter.)

Each of these basic approaches to marketing has many subsets, which we will examine in turn. For any given situation or set of circumstances, you usually have a set of choices. At the same time, the choices are rarely unlimited but are constrained by the circumstances. Working in or from your own home immediately presents one such constraint. It is impracticable for a business based in your home to conduct certain kinds of marketing.

Several kinds of factors will inevitably influence your marketing. Aside from the physical problems that influence marketing methods, there are the marketing problems themselves. Mail order is an example and, again as pointed out earlier, although many direct-mail marketing experts are fond of claiming that anything can be sold by mail, there are limits to the practicality of selling some things that way. (But that does not rule out using direct mail to support marketing and help create conditions for selling, such as generating good leads for big-tag items.)

Face-to-Face Selling

Face-to-face selling — selling by direct, personal presentation — is the one method that is practicable for virtually all items, and yet even it has limitations for you as an entrepreneur working from your home, depending on what you sell. You can, of course, sell insurance and real estate from an office at home because that usually means calling on prospects at their home or meeting them at a sample house or the house offered for sale, with relatively few meetings in your own office. You could also sell cosmetics and many other items in your home using the party method. You would have a considerable problem, however, trying to sell across-the-counter items, such as vitamins or hardware, in your home except by face-to-face selling or any other method that would require a steady stream of shoppers. There are exceptions to even this rule, however: You can have those dinnerware or cosmetic parties in your home, and you can have lawn sales or garage sales also. (Some people make a business of buying up things they later resell at their own garage sales, as though they were simply cleaning out their own attics!)

TRADITIONAL METHODS

In many lines of business, conventional wisdom about marketing dominates thinking. That is because some given approach to marketing has become traditional and is widely accepted as *the* way to market in that business. Usually, although not always, the tradition is based on experience: The pioneers in that business have found, or claim to have found, that a given marketing method is the only effective one or that it is far more effective than others.

One example is selling newsletter subscriptions. It is rarely easy to sell subscriptions to begin with, and it is generally accepted that direct mail is the most effective method. Other methods, reportedly, do not work well.

You have probably received your share of mail solicitations to subscribe to newsletters and magazines. Although magazine publishers do advertise in their own and others' magazines, most do the bulk of their solicitation by direct mail. And distributors of magazines, those whose entire business is selling magazine subscriptions as agents or brokers for the publishers, use telemarketing frequently, with the major distributors using contests offering multimillion-dollar prizes, conducted by direct mail and TV. The latter type of advertising, however, does not sell subscriptions, you may have noted; it is used to sell participation in the contest—to persuade viewers to enter the contest and send the forms in when they arrive in the mail; ultimately, these distributors rely on the direct-mail solicitation, too.

Insurance agents have long sold life insurance by going door to door and calling on total strangers. They even collect premium payments in this manner, which is a boost to selling more insurance as well as keeping existing policies going. For some reason this practice has been restricted almost entirely to life insurance. Hospitalization, major medical, automobile, and other liability insurance policies are usually sold by direct mail, although print advertising and TV commercials are often used to generate leads for direct follow-up.

Some of these practices are changing. These litigious and increasingly violent times are making many householders reluctant to open their doors to strangers, for one thing, a fact that alone makes house-to-house selling more and more difficult and declining in popularity today. But it is also increasingly difficult to find people willing to knock on doors and endure the many unpleasant experiences encountered inevitably in door-to-door selling.

In some cases, some traditional method of marketing is regarded as the sole dependable method; in others—probably in most others—it is only one of several possible methods, all of which are practicable. Vitamins, for example, are sold widely by mail-order methods as well as by classic retail methods in drug stores, supermarkets, and other such retail outlets.

(Strictly speaking, *mail order* is not the same as *direct mail*, and it is not a direct-marketing method at all. In mail order, you solicit business through print or other advertising, getting your orders through the mail, whereas in direct mail you use the mails to solicit orders from individual addressees.)

All these established patterns of marketing are not necessarily immutable nor ultimate truth. Perhaps there are other effective ways to sell newsletter subscriptions. Perhaps some imaginative marketer will find or invent another approach that proves even more effective than the usual direct-mail solicitation that is supposedly the only effective way to sell subscriptions. Perhaps better ways than those now in use will be invented to sell many other items. Certainly, every new device is considered for its possibilities as a medium for advertising and promotion. (Airplanes were once used to skywrite advertising messages, and at seashore resorts you may still see small airplanes towing advertising banners.) With computers now inexpensive enough for even the small business to own one or more, we have seen other changes come about. There is, for example, an increase in automated telemarketing, where the computer operates a system that dials successions of numbers automatically, delivers a recorded message soliciting a response, and records the response as a sales lead to be followed up. "Junk mail" has been succeeded lately by "junk FAX," with advertisers using automated telemarketing to send FAX messages to a series of FAX numbers.

All these solicitations have their downsides. Many people are offended by what they consider to be invasions of their privacy, and they may become hostile to your product or service. In fact, these kinds of solicitations inspire enough adverse publicity to compel legislatures to create regulatory statutes. Telemarketing has long been regulated by laws limiting the lateness of the hour permissible for telemarketers to make their calls. You may demand to be taken off the mailing list of anyone who sends you direct-mail solicitations. And there is already movement to restrict the use of FAX numbers and machines for solicitation.

Regulation and widespread objection to these solicitations

do not have a great effect on most marketers' decisions to use such methods. In general, their relative success is measured by probability statistics—the benefit of advertising to such large numbers of prospects that a response rate of only 1 to 4 percent will produce enough orders and return on investment to make the marketing campaign worthwhile.

SALES PRESENTATIONS

Almost all contacts between humans include a presentation in some form or other, and most certainly in sales situations of all kinds, even though we do not always recognize that we are making presentations whenever we are talking to a prospective customer and trying to make a sale. The term *presentation* may conjure up a vision of a highly organized and formal process with elaborate aids, and indeed that description fits many presentations. Except for the sale to a customer who knows exactly what he or she wants and selects or orders it voluntarily without the slightest preliminary, however, every sale requires and is made possible or consummated by a presentation of some kind. (Even in the self-service store, displays and signs represent sales presentations.)

But there are many kinds of sales situations and needs, and thus there are many kinds of presentations. They run the gamut from spontaneous and informal to carefully planned, meticulously executed, and formal. Here are brief summaries of typical basic situations and types of presentation required to meet each situation, from least to most formal and elaborate:

- Probably most salespeople, especially those engaged in over-the-counter sales, do not think of their contacts with prospective customers as presentations. They greet the prospective customer; may inquire about the prospect's interests, if the prospect has not voluntarily stated them immediately; display and present merchandise or describe the services offered; explain policies, guarantees, prices; and otherwise respond to the prospect's needs for information while trying to make a sale. That is a spontaneous and informal presentation that a salesperson probably makes many times during the day.

- Some salespeople sell much more big-tag items, such as automobiles and houses, in which a much more extended and elaborate presentation is necessary. In fact, such sales often require more than one presentation on more than one occasion to consummate a sale. These presentations often involve elaborate brochures and charts and usually include displaying and demonstrating models by taking the prospect on a tour of a model house or a demonstration ride.

- Some salespeople sell items that are relatively difficult to sell by calls on prospects in their homes. Encyclopedias are a typical item. The salespeople are generally given a carefully designed presentation and are trained to make the presentation exactly as written (often memorized, in fact), displaying the product during the process.

- Finally, some sales involve truly large projects, usually one of a kind and involving great sums of money. By their very nature, these high stakes and inevitable heavy competition make it essential that the presentation(s) be meticulously designed, painstakingly prepared, and flawlessly executed, usually with more than one speaker and with elaborate presentation devices and aids. These kinds of presentations are jocularly known as "dog-and-pony shows," in recognition of the obvious planning and rehearsal involved.

Written presentations are an entirely different sales situation. The most prominent example of this kind of presentation is the proposal, which may be solicited by the customer or inspired entirely by the proposer's initiative. It, too, may be formal or informal; some proposals can become quite elaborate and be accompanied by such aids as slides, posters, and audiotapes. Often, too, the proposal is a first presentation, and the proposer is invited to make a follow-up presentation, which is often that traditional dog-and-pony show. And often only those whose proposals were outstanding are invited to make follow-up presentations, which are designed entirely to help the customer make a final choice among the top few proposals.

THREE ELEMENTS OF A SUCCESSFUL PRESENTATION

You must keep in mind at least three major considerations in designing and staging a sales presentation, all of which may be studied as strategic areas. These are: the strategy of the sales message, the strategy of the media choices, and the design or organization strategy of the material. Let us look at these three strategies in detail.

Sales Strategy

Previous discussions of sales strategy—the concepts of needs and wants and of motivators in general—apply here as they do universally. Make no mistake about it; the basic principles of selling an ice cream bar are the same as those for selling a corporation or a new shopping center: Prospects are always motivated by their self-interests, regardless of price and other considerations.

The heart of any presentation is the sales argument: The strategy must be a sound appeal to the prospect's self-interest. You must have analyzed the possible benefits of what you sell to the prospect, decided which is likely to be the most important one to the prospect, and built your presentation around that appraisal. The entire presentation is thus organized to stress and even dramatize the promise of that most important benefit and to provide convincing evidence that you can and will deliver it—that if the customer buys what you offer, the benefit will be realized.

Media Strategy

Media of all types are abundantly available to you today. You can make and support your verbal presentation with slides, transparencies, filmstrips, posters, flip charts, handouts, closed circuit TV, audiotapes, models, demonstrations, blackboards, dramatizations, remote computer terminals, and even other media and methods, in addition to personal verbal delivery, which is a most (perhaps *the* most) important element.

In a way, the very diversity of available media is a problem — it offers too many choices. Take the alternatives of transparencies versus slides, for example: Each has its own pros and cons, not surprisingly, although subjectively they appear to be not much different in their impact. But slides can be set to run automatically, they tend to be brighter and sharper than transparencies, and they are much better suited for presenting photographs or other continuous-tone materials. Transparencies, on the other hand, do not require a darkened room, can be written on and used as a blackboard, and are easy to make on ordinary office equipment. Posters, flip charts, handouts, and other supporting aids each likewise have their pros and cons, and your choices will be dictated by necessity and by the strategic considerations of the design you decide to employ. It is also highly desirable, however, that the materials you choose reflect true professionalism so that they contribute properly to the believability of your overall presentation.

The most important medium is, as already suggested, the human voice, delivered in person by someone with obvious authority to speak on the subject. And by *authority* I mean technical or professional credentials that qualify the individual as an expert, if the subject is a technical one. A presentation must be convincing; a completely canned presentation is rarely as believable as one that is delivered by someone who is well qualified to speak. You will probably find it beneficial to base your presentation on, and build it around, a verbal address.

Design Strategy

The design of a presentation should be a logical consequence of the sales strategy and whatever the individual circumstances dictate. Design objectives will usually include achieving maximum impact and professional polish. Striving for maximum impact means designing to stress the two major messages: the main benefit promised and the main proof or reason to believe in the promise. At the same time, anything suggesting that the presentation is amateurish or carelessly improvised will damage its believability seriously, so all visuals must be top-notch and the entire process must flow smoothly.

The Mechanics of the Process

Large organizations no longer have all the advantages over small businesses they had only a few years ago. Today, for example, the smallest offices have in-house facilities to satisfy many of their own presentation needs. With modern desktop computers and suitable software, you can now turn out your own high-quality typography and graphics, suitable for use as posters or transparencies, which can be made on any office copier. Handouts can be prepared via word processors and desktop publishing software, and copies for distribution can be made on office copiers.

If you prefer not to tackle these jobs in your own office, many small letter shops and other vendors equipped with those computers and that software can turn out such work rapidly and at modest prices. And if you need large, poster-sized copies of any of your materials, copies with dimensions measured in feet rather than in inches, try a well-equipped blueprint shop; they can usually accommodate such needs at modest cost.

Delivery of the Presentation

Delivery of the presentation is as important as content and design; the delivery must be equally professional and smooth-flowing. Unfortunately, a great many people still shrink from the public platform, even when the audience is small, perhaps a dozen or fewer. That is a good reason to come prepared with as complete a set of presentation aids as possible: The use of posters, slides, and other presentation devices moves the focus of the audience away from you — and with it much of the stress that makes public speaking so distasteful to many people. If you are uncomfortable on the platform, therefore, use various presentation devices freely. It's a good practice, in any case, to have frequent changes, using a variety of presentation devices. This helps sustain interest in the presentation and relieves the speaker of much of the burden.

It is not hard to speak effectively. You do not have to be a great orator, nor do you have to have a marvelous, resonant speaking voice. What you do need for success on the platform is simple enough: You need to know your material and your subject well, you need to be confident that you know what you are talking about, and you need to be enthusiastic about your subject. If you take steps to ensure that you meet that first criterion of knowing your material, and you really *care* about it, the other things will usually fall into place. Forget about yourself and how you look or think you look standing there in front of everybody. Think only of your audience, of what they want to hear, what they have come to hear from you. Don't worry about what to do with your hands. Don't worry about meeting people's eyes. Forget all those tips for speakers you have read about; most of them are bad advice, anyway. Lose yourself in that subject that is so important to you, and soon you will be grinning at the right places, raising your voice when necessary, waving your arms about to make a point, and getting a big hand from your audience. Nothing pleases an audience more than a truly animated speaker. Enthusiasm is infectious, and you will find that enthusiasm is a sauce that adds zest to any presentation.

WHERE AND WHEN TO MAKE PRESENTATIONS

Up to this point we have not really talked about where and when to make sales presentations, but only about how to make them. The fact is that many occasions, places, and situations govern the making of sales presentations, most of which must be managed, engineered, or otherwise contrived by you. You cannot simply stroll into the offices of prospective customers without an appointment and proceed to make a sales presentation. Yes, there are some such occasions. Sometimes, even in such cold calling, a prospect surprises you with a cordial and smiling, "Come on in. Let's talk." You may have lucked out and stumbled over an easy sale. (It does happen occasionally.) Or you may have met an idle and bored individual who welcomes any break in a dull day but is not a qualified prospect. (That also happens, perhaps more often than occasionally, and "qualified" means someone actually able to place an order, should he or she wish to.) Those occasions aside, however, you must usually work at finding or creating situations that are true opportunities for you to make effective presentations; they do not happen with reliable regularity unless you take the proper steps.

You can create a marketing campaign that will result in a number of specific invitations to appear and present your proposition. That would be a normal consequence of what is often called *inquiry advertising*, the direct purpose of which is to inspire requests for more information. But there are other ways to achieve the same goal.

One of these other ways is to get yourself invited to speak at various meetings, conventions, seminars, and symposia that are relevant to what you sell. If, for example, you offer editorial, typesetting, graphic arts, or other such services, you could reach prospective customers by speaking at seminars and meetings devoted to proposal writing, brochure writing, marketing, and related subjects. Send letters to those presenting such meetings (the "program director" of relevant trade or professional associations, for example), listing your credentials and offering your services as a guest speaker. You will usually be greeted most cordially. Such organizations are almost constantly seeking speakers for such occasions.

You might wish to consider organizing and offering your own seminar. Even if you organize a full program and charge attendees a fee, you are likely to generate sales leads as a result. However, you may prefer to increase attendance by making it free of charge, an open marketing ploy. Many organizations, such as the Evelyn Wood speed-reading organization, have done so with great success. It is possible to reserve a hotel meeting room and run a small-space advertisement in a local news-paper for a small charge, but you can probably persuade your local government to let you use a meeting room at the local library or other public facility, and you can use public facilities to advertise the free seminar. Many associations offer half-day (3-hour) seminars at their annual conventions and welcome ideas and presenters for such seminars. Some convention sponsors, such as *Training* magazine, pay expenses only, and others pay fees and expenses.

You might also send out a letter or even a full direct-mail package to local companies, offering to present a free seminar of some limited duration — probably an hour or two — on the company's own premises and at the company's own convenience. If you are wise, you will provide some useful information in that hour or two while you are also letting attendees know what you offer.

MARKETING OBJECTIVES

You must be aware, in conceiving and planning your marketing, of the marketing problem known as a "not a one-call sale." That is a reference to the fact that although many products can be and are sold spontaneously in a first meeting and presentation, others are rarely sold this way. Those are the big-tag items, usually, such as refrigerators, automobiles, houses, and similar-size items. Prospective buyers of such items usually need time to listen to presentations by various sellers, look at several models, and ponder a bit before committing themselves.

Such purchases are not casual ones, and you, as the salesperson, must usually make a substantial commitment of time to make even the initial sales presentation, let alone the succeeding ones that are usually necessary to finally close the sale. That is, you are making a substantial *investment* in each such sales call and presentation. You cannot really afford to do this with a prospect who does not represent a serious possibility of an ultimate sale.

Recognizing this as a practical reality, you must arrange somehow to develop *leads*, names of people who have inquired seeking more information, thus suggesting that they are seriously interested and worth the investment of your time and effort to make a presentation to.

Your immediate marketing goals, then, are either to win sales directly, as a result of your marketing, or to generate sales leads for follow-up and closing. You must, of course, have decided which is your goal and have structured your marketing to address the proper goal.

PUBLICITY

There is one other, special activity and medium that we have not discussed, although it is usually (but not always) the responsibility of the marketing department. That is PR, the popular short name for public relations. It can easily be the most influential of all the marketing activities, and in the next chapter we will look at some examples as we examine and discuss some of the methods you can use to employ PR in your own marketing program.

Many people regard PR as free advertising, and in a sense it is just that. In fact, when you get a great deal of favorable (or, at least, not unfavorable) publicity for your product or service, you are getting advertising that is not only free but is often far more effective in many ways than paid advertising.

Publicity is free because you do not pay for the space or time devoted to your product, but it does cost something to conduct PR activities, of course, as you will see. The costs are relatively modest, however, if you handle your own PR. (There are many PR firms and PR consultants, if you wish to hire help for this work.)

One important point: There are cases where publicity is a totally unpredictable and chance occurrence, but if you wish to put PR to work seriously to aid your marketing, you cannot depend on random luck. You must plan a comprehensive PR campaign or, at least, establish and carry on some routine PR activities on a regular basis. Among the commonly used PR tools are press releases, product releases, letters to the editor, and other means for getting the name of your product and information about it reported in print and mentioned on the air. In the next chapter, we will have a closer look at these activities.

Chapter Thirteen

Writing Sales and Other Promotional Copy

*The world will not beat a path
to your door merely because
you have a better mousetrap.
You need to beat the drums
for your better mousetrap to
persuade the world to come.*

PROMOTION IS AT THE HEART OF MARKETING

One of the ironies in business is that effective marketing often creates commercial success for products that are not especially noteworthy, whereas superior products languish because they are not marketed successfully. In fact, you may be sure that every successful product has directly competitive products, some of which are of at least as good quality, and even of superior quality in many cases. It is often the quality of the marketing, and that alone rather than any other factor, that is responsible for success or failure of a venture.

In anything that depends on popular approval, results are not always predictable; we cannot ever know surely how the public will react. The Honda automobile, product of a Japanese company, is popular here and highly regarded as a fine car. But a Japanese friend assured me that it does not sell nearly as well in Japan. That is because, he believes, the Japanese have such a firm image of the Honda as a motorcycle that they have trouble accepting it as an automobile! This is a problem the manufacturer probably did not anticipate and has evidently had little success in solving.

That image the public has of a product is its *position*, in advertising jargon, and advertising specialists speak of *positioning* to refer to their efforts to create an image for the product or the advertiser that is in tune with the advertiser's objectives. You'll see other examples of this as we proceed.

The phenomenon works both ways: Advertising or a bit of publicity can sometimes do wonders for a product that might never have made it out of the starting gate otherwise. *Winning Through Intimidation*, then a self-published book by Robert Ringer, benefited from a review in *Time* magazine, which turned it into a success it probably would not have achieved without benefit of this publicity. Much the same can be said for mood rings and many other novelties that flared briefly as they caught the public's imagination, became news, and then died. But there are other tales, tales of more "serious" products that were made successful by effective marketing and assumed a more or less permanent position in the economy.

The name IBM so dominated the electric typewriter market that many people used IBM as a generic term for typewriter. And during the reign of the mainframe computer as the dominant business machine before the arrival of the desktop computer, that name was also almost synonymous with the word computer. Probably a great many people were not more than dimly aware, if at all, that there were other manufacturers of computers besides IBM.

The latest commercial *Wunderkind* at this moment is the FAX, a popular abbreviation for the facsimile machine. This is not a case of a single brand name's catching the public fancy, but that of a *kind* of product. There are many FAX manufacturers, and the general public probably does not know one name better than it does another. FAX machines are not a new invention, although they have been greatly improved and are much less costly than they once were, so why did they suddenly become so popular? It's not possible to know, although many reasons have been proposed. So far, their use here is primarily by and for business, but we are told by the press that FAX machines are so popular in Japan that people are buying them there for personal use. (I find that the FAX has many advantages over a telephone answering machine, from my viewpoint. Perhaps others agree with that!) That may well happen here, too, as prices tumble under the pressures of intense competition and the cost-cutting advantages of mass production.

Such a spontaneous embrace of new products is not unusual. Radio, TV, personal calculators, videocassette recorders, stereo systems, compact disks, and many other products have been ardently received by the public, at least as soon as their prices came within the reach of most people. Advertising is consequently rarely aimed at persuading the public to buy such an item; it is invariably directed at promoting a specific brand or model.

That itself brings up an important point about marketing and promotion generally that merits mention here: In promoting what you sell, you must have a clear view of your *specific* objective. That is, your general objective is always to sell your product or service, but you must know what you are competing against—a similar competitive product versus anticipated buyer resistance (or indifference) to a new and unknown product, for one thing. High-priced competition versus low-priced competition, for another. Strictly functional (no frills) models versus deluxe (with many convenience features) models, for still another. And so on. You cannot focus your advertising or publicity properly without working out the answers to these and other questions bearing on just what you want your promotion to accomplish. But we are getting a bit ahead of the story here. Let's go back to fundamentals.

ADVERTISING FUNDAMENTALS

Those whose income derives from the advertising of others—the advertising agencies and the media whose main income derives from the sale of space and time – are fond of the slogan, "Advertising pays." Unfortunately, *some* advertising pays, but a great deal of it does not. It does not for a variety of reasons, including poor copy, wrong media, wrong season, wrong time slots, wrong placement, and wrong proposition generally, among many other possible flaws.

Advertising is expensive. It is too expensive to waste the money spent on it, at least for the small business. But even large businesses bemoan the waste. I have already quoted the anonymous executive who complained, "I know that half my advertising dollar is wasted, but I don't know which half it is." It is almost impossible to discover which half of the advertising dollar is wasted in a great deal of general advertising, where there is no practical way of relating sales to advertising; one can only judge whether sales have increased generally as a result of spending advertising dollars.

That is a risky and burdensome expense for the small business struggling to succeed. But there are ways to track your advertising dollar rather precisely in circumstances where you have deliberately designed and established a method for doing so. This involves running tests by keying your advertising (using identifying codes that link responses to specific advertising promotions) and monitoring results so as to create a record that relates the results to the advertising as cause and effect. (Although many advertisers do this only with small samples to test copy, periodicals, and other variables, many advertisers key and record results for all their advertising rather than only for test runs.)

Keying Advertisements

Let us suppose I place an advertisement in six periodicals, using the same copy and running all at the same time so as to create as uniform a set of conditions as possible, using these periodicals:

Popular Mechanics
Popular Science
Science & Mechanix

Everyday Electronics

Radio Electronics

Handyman Monthly

I have all responses come to me at my post office box number, but I use an additional designator that is different in each periodical: I direct readers to address me at Departments PM, PS, SM, EE, RE, and HH, respectively. (You have surely seen those advertisements asking the respondent to address some cryptic department, room number, or other key.) That key enables me to determine to which advertisement the respondent has reacted. I can tally the results in a simple record, as shown in Figure 13-1.

The total cost for all advertisements is $650, the total number of responses is 1,015, so the average cost of a response is 64 cents. The most efficient result, however, was from *Handyman Monthly* (35 cents per response). In any case, this indicates directly how each periodical "pulled." I can thus make a sound judgment about which periodicals to use—perhaps all, if all proved profitable, or perhaps only a few. But I then have a good idea of what is happening to my advertising dollar, and I can at least reduce the waste and maximize the results.

That is only one way to key advertisements and only one purpose for which to do so; there are others we will examine

Figure 13-1 *Tabulation of Keyed Advertisements*

Periodical	Cost	Key	Responses	Cost/ Response
Popular Mechanics	$132	PM	231	$0.57
Popular Science	128	PS	195	0.66
Science & Mechanix	79	SM	81	0.98
Everyday Electronics	112	EE	102	1.10
Radio Electronics	134	RE	220	0.61
Handyman Monthly	65	HH	186	0.35
Totals:	$650		1,015	
Averages:	$108		169	$0.64

later. And this example is to test the relative pulling power of the various periodicals, but you might wish to test any of a number of other variables and alternatives, such as the following few examples:

Promises
Versions of advertising copy
Sizes of advertisements
Months or seasons in which to advertise
Types of periodicals
Media
Offers
Inducements to respond
Prices

I can now decide which result directs the best path to follow—which produces the best results. If I want to be really efficient, I will try all these in relatively short runs, conserving capital in that way. The probability is, I have learned, that the results from a short run will be as accurate and beneficial as those from a long run, if the sample is truly representative and random; I need not waste a great deal of money in finding out what works best and what does not work well at all. But we need to take a closer look at just what we are testing and evaluating.

COPY FUNDAMENTALS

Although they are called by different names, there is really no significant difference in kind between *sales copy* and *advertising copy*: Both are created to persuade people to certain actions. That action is buying, in the case of most companies and most situations, and buying is what we are concerned with here. The chief difference between the two, when a difference does exist, is that sometimes advertising copy is directed to persuade people to some intermediate action that is preliminary or ancillary to buying, whereas sales copy is always directed to persuade people directly to buying.

As they do about politics and religion, almost everybody has an opinion about advertising and sales copy, and it is usually a strong and emotionally biased opinion: They are convinced that theirs is a correct appraisal and everybody else's judgment is wrong. It's easy to be so arbitrary and biased because there is no right or wrong to writing copy, except in hindsight: Whatever works is right. The most expert copy writer is often fooled when copy that is beautifully "right" bombs completely and copy that is "all wrong" is brilliantly successful. The fact is that success and failure in sales and advertising copy depend on public reaction (almost like show biz!), and that is never completely predictable. Still, professional sales and advertising experts and their copy writers do know what usually does and does not work. If you learn and stick to sound principles for writing persuasive copy, most of your efforts will be reasonably successful and occasionally something will be outstandingly successful. With that *caveat*, then, let's look at what usually works and the principles on which to base your own sales and advertising copy. To this end we will examine examples of copy for print media, although we will later discuss the application of the principles to visual and aural media.

PROOF AND PROMISE: A REPRISE

You have encountered the concept of proof and promise before in these pages, but it is necessary to reprise the message here. In any case, it cannot be repeated too often: People act out of self-interest, and you get their attention by appealing directly to their self-interest. More precisely, you get the individual's attention by appealing to his or her *perceived* self-interest. And that is usually not the same thing at all.

The simple fact is that most people tend to perceive things through a lens of self-interest that is highly selective, searching for agreeable words and tending to reject or be highly unsympathetic to disagreeable ones. Most products being marketed have their share of "good news" and "bad news"; effective advertising focuses only on the good news. Consider the "before and after" copy in Figure 13-2. Both are honest, but the first example ("before") leads with the bad news, that freelance writing success is not easy, whereas the second leads with the good news that it can be made easier than it used to be. Both paragraphs say the same thing, use much the same words, but what a difference in lead and focus! The first one starts with a headline that is slightly ominous and then goes on to a lead sentence that reinforces that impression with the unpleasant news that it may take many years of struggle for the reader to become a successful freelance writer. Long before the good news is offered the mood has been set, and it is a negative one, reflecting the negative copy.

The second example is much more positive, leading with the good news that early success as a freelance writer is possible. The copy follows up that cheerful mood-setting promise immediately with an expansion that explains and reinforces the headline.

No one really wants to believe that years of struggle are necessary preliminaries to success, and in fact they are not, for some people. The reader would like to believe that he or she is

---

The Truth about a Freelance Writing Career

Most successful writers have first had to spend many years struggling to learn how to succeed in their chosen field. But now there is a way to shorten that struggle. It is a brand-new book, *Shortcuts to Writing Success*, written by a well-known and highly successful writer, Paul Scribble, yours for only $14.95.

Early Success as a Freelance Writer

You can march straight to early success as a freelance writer, avoiding that traditional long struggle others have endured. The methods, techniques, and tips that make it possible are all revealed in a brand-new book, *Shortcuts to Writing Success*, written by a well-known and highly successful writer, Paul Scribble, yours for only $14.95.

Figure 13-2   Examples of Bad News and Good News Copy

one of those who can reach success early, with a little guidance. The promise is not a lie; early success *is* possible. Whether it is possible for the reader is another matter; no one knows. But it is not immoral to promise to reveal all that an experienced and successful professional has learned about the ingredients of success. That is what both advertisements promise, but it is unlikely that the first example will produce as good results as the second one.

The copy in Figure 13-2 is brief, probably too brief to be fully effective, but it does illustrate the principles. In an actual case, the advertisement would have the reinforcement of some follow-up explanation of author Scribble's credentials as an expert and at least a little detail on the content of the book. It might also use such tantalizing teasers as "Insider Secrets and Tips Revealed!" and "Learn How the Experts Do It!" Or, if the copy was intended for direct mail as a salesletter or brochure rather than as a print advertisement, it would present a great deal of detail about both the author and the book, including, possibly, a complete table of contents.

Headline Writing

Advertising and sales copy needs headlines. Many copy writers believe that the sole function of a headline is to command attention so that the reader will be induced to read the body copy, where he or she can be persuaded to buy whatever is being advertised. That belief leads often to headlines that are only vaguely related or even unrelated to the copy, headlines chosen solely for their attention-getting capabilities. It leads also to the even worse bane of advertising—cute and clever headlines that are only vaguely related or unrelated to the copy. An advertisement for Clorox®, for example, is headlined "PACKED FRESH DAILY, Introducing New Lemon Fresh Clorox Bleach"; a photograph that dominates the page shows nine bottles of the product packed in a straw-filled box as though the box contained lemons. In fact, a label on the end of the box does show lemons. Obviously, the copy is attempting to benefit from the current popularity of lemon flavors in many products today, especially cleaning products, but the connection between "packed fresh daily" and the product is rather vague—a reference to lemons rather than to the bleach. (Moreover, in this case, the advertisement depends more on the dominating illustration than on the headline.)

An advertisement for Plymouth automobiles is headlined simply "INTRODUCING THE NEW PLYMOUTH ACCLAIM LX, *A WORLDBEATER.*" The copy that follows is brief and lists five features and the repeated claim that the car is a "worldbeater." And, of course, there is a photograph of the new car. The logical inference is that the words "introducing" and "new" in the headline are expected to attract the reader's eyes. They may or may not, of course; the reader has no reason to stop and read the copy unless he or she happens to be interested in a new car generally or a Plymouth especially.

Another "clever" headline of the worst kind—an obvious pun—is "KEEP POP COOL." It's an ad for Father's Day that shows a man relaxing in a hammock. Beneath the hammock are an insulated beverage cooler and the explanatory copy that makes the play on words of the headline clear, at least to those readers who happen to know that in some places (New York, especially), "pop" is popular slang for carbonated and flavored beverages. Presumably, the reader is also expected to admire the headline writer's pun-writing cleverness as much as the writer does.

On the other hand, an advertisement that is probably highly effective (it attracted my wife's eyes and her order!) offers the headline "COUNT AND WRAP LOOSE CHANGE INSTANTLY!" with the subtitle "'Calibrated' Coin Counters" and an illustration of the item and how to use it. It carries also an inducement in announcing its price as a reduction from an earlier much higher price.

Another headline that probably works is "MARSHMALLOW SOFT!" announcing the sale of women's sandals, with illustrations and claims of ease and comfort of fit and wear.

It's easy enough to find such examples in any newspaper or magazine and to make generalized judgments, as I am doing here. But the truth is revealed only in testing and may come as a total surprise. It often does.

Note an important difference in one characteristic of the headlines cited:

PACKED FRESH DAILY, Introducing New Lemon Fresh Clorox Bleach

INTRODUCING THE NEW PLYMOUTH ACCLAIM LX, *A WORLDBEATER*

KEEP POP COOL

COUNT AND WRAP LOOSE CHANGE INSTANTLY!

MARSHMALLOW SOFT!

Three of these five headlines are about the product, one is about the reader, and one falls between these extremes. Can you judge which is which here? Try mentally installing "you" or "you can" before each headline, and you will see which one talks directly about the reader's interest (offers a direct reason for being interested and buying), and which simply brag about their product and expect the reader to study the copy and infer some benefit. (*You* would fit before KEEP POP COOL, but it is highly doubtful that a reader would identify this as some greatly to be desired benefit.) Even that last headline is talking about the product, although it does imply a benefit rather clearly. Even so, something like "MARSHMALLOW SOFT ON YOUR FEET" would have been more appealing. A headline should always be addressed as directly as possible to the reader's immediate interest and offer a benefit, the benefit you believe to be the most important one.

Chrysler Corporation asks the reader simply to accept their bald claim that their new car is a "worldbeater." Not only do they offer nothing to support that claim, but they use a word (worldbeater) that is meaningless because it is completely imprecise. Their technique could hardly be more wrong. Even DRIVE THE NEW PLYMOUTH ACCLAIM LX, *A WORLD-BEATER* would have been an improvement over the self-serving and rather smug "announcing."

Adding something to the bleach copy would have been a bit more difficult, because it gives no hint of what the lemon is supposed to do for the user. Even a vague claim of benefit—

such as NOW GET LEMON FRESH WITH CLOROX CLEANING POWER—would have been better than the present copy, however, which does not even offer the briefest suggestion for serving the customer's interest.

The other four headlines have the virtue of being emotional appeals, despite the shortcomings of most of them, but all could have been vastly improved by adding the "you" implication to them and giving the reader a *reason to be interested*. Expecting the reader to spend energy analyzing the headline to see if there is some reason to become interested even in reading further is expecting too much, far too much; it won't happen very often.

It is essentially true that if you do not sell your product in the headline, you won't sell it at all. That is, even powerful body copy will not often rescue an advertisement with a weak headline, but the converse is also true: A powerful headline will compensate to a large degree for weak body copy and often rescue it. That is because the right headline stimulates interest and even desire for the benefit, and the reader is already motivated: He or she now *wants* to find justification for buying and is looking to be convinced.

Book titles often function as headlines, not surprisingly. The sales of one book, titled *Five Acres*, was languishing. Maxwell Sackheim, often called the dean of mail-order copy writers, was asked to help. His advice was to change the title to *Five Acres and Independence*. The publisher did so, and the result was immediately apparent in increased sales. The new title carried a clear message that was missing in the original one by suggesting rather clearly a benefit offered the reader. (In a booklet titled "Seven Deadly Mistakes of Advertising," Sackheim also reports a test in which advertising copy was run with two different headlines. One advertisement pulled twice as many orders as the other.)

THE OFFER

Many people in marketing use that word *offer* to refer to the product and price asked—for example, an offer of a magazine subscription for $19.95. We will use that term to mean something else here. In the jargon I use, an offer is what I offer to *do* for my prospective customer, the benefit I promise to deliver. If I am selling a diet drug and I promise that you can lose up to a pound a day with my product, that promise is what I am offering.

What I need to test is that offer. I need to find out if the promise of losing up to a pound a day is sufficiently motivating to make a marketing campaign based on that promise a viable one. Better yet, I need to see how that offer compares in its appeal with other offers I can make.

I consider several possible offers I can make. I can say, "Lose up to 10 pounds in 10 days," or, "Lose up to 30 pounds in one month." What? You say that those all say the same thing? No, they do not. They may all add up to the same result, but they do not say the same thing. Try putting a sign on a pile of cantaloupes in a supermarket saying "33¢ each, 3 for 99¢," and watch how many customers choose three, rather than one or two. *How* you say something can be more important than *what* you say, in marketing. And there is no reliable way to be sure which offer is the most appealing. Only actual testing reveals which has the greatest appeal. It is quite possible that among those three I suggested here, none will be any more appealing than the others, but it is also possible that one of the three will outpull the others by a wide margin.

But those are not the only possible offers I could make. I could try these, too:

Diet the *Safe* Way

You Won't Even Know that You Are Dieting

Dieting Without Tears

Try to make the offer plain in the headline, and don't be afraid to write long headlines. Ted Nicholas, author/publisher of *How to Form Your Own Corporation Without a Lawyer for Under $50.00* used that title as his advertising headline in many magazines and sold thousands of copies of his book. The length of the headline is not important; the clarity and effectiveness of the offer are. And it is the first thing to test, for nothing else about your marketing matters very much if the prospects are simply not interested in your offer. Once the offer is right, you can begin to shape and polish the other facets to improve response, but not before then.

THE PROPOSITION

What others often call the offer I prefer to call the *proposition*. That is what I ask the prospect to do so that he or she can realize the benefit. It includes the terms of the sale, and that can be a bit more sophisticated than it sounds. My proposition for selling my diet drug might be a three-month supply for $39.95, but I might make it a "special offer for a limited time" of a six-month supply for only $69.95. Or I might offer a rebate coupon, redeemable by mailing it to the manufacturer. My proposition may include some ironclad, no-questions-asked, money-back guarantee of complete satisfaction. I might offer a bonus or a free gift of some sort. Any of these inducements might be included as part of my proposition, and I must test that, too, to see what the public finds most attractive.

TEST METHODS

You can test a single headline, a single offer, a single proposition to see whether it pulls well. Normally, however, it is far more effective to test several alternatives to see *which* pulls best. Otherwise, you run the risk of settling for a mediocre choice or dropping the plan because the one option you tested did not work well.

Of course, you cannot test an unlimited number of options, either; you have to establish practical limits. I suggest that three options is a reasonable test assortment for most cases, although there are likely to be occasional exceptions to this rule.

So far, we have discussed advertising as a primary marketing activity. But it is not the only one, nor is it even the main one for all ventures. PR (public relations), mentioned rather briefly in the previous chapter, is an important marketing activity, too, and it merits a comprehensive look at the tools used in exploiting it.

PR TOOLS

There are various tools used in public relations. The most popular include exhibits at trade shows, contests, and releases.

Releases

The *release*, known variously as a news release, press release, publicity release, product release, and, simply, release, is probably the most widely and most frequently used tool of PR. There are two reasons for this fact: (1) It is a direct and inexpensive route to the news services and publications — newspapers, magazines, newsletters, trade journals, and other periodicals — as well as to radio and TV newsrooms; and (2) it is a simple proposition and can be used frequently, almost daily, in some cases.

The simplicity of creating and using releases is this tool's Achilles heel. Many people create what they call releases that most editors will not touch because the release violates all commonly accepted practices. Such a release not only fairly shouts "amateur effort" but is difficult for the editor to work with, as well. Most such releases do not earn even a cursory reading.

The most basic sin in release writing is single-spacing the copy. Rarely is a release published exactly as received, when it is published at all. Usually the editor wants to go over it with a blue pencil, cutting, adding, and changing the copy to suit the publication's policies and the editor's standards. That is a chief reason for all manuscripts intended for publication to be double-spaced, permitting the editor room to make suitable marks.

A second sin is to type or print the release on both sides of the paper. Manuscript copy is typed on one side only.

There are several other common practices that you should observe. Consider the example shown as Figure 13-3. It does not carry the prominent word NEWS or some variant, as most releases do, but that is not a must, although it is probably a good idea at least to type the word in. Organizations that issue releases frequently have a special form, with such items as

---

**RCB
& Associates**

For Immediate Release....

Contact: Richard Bruno
415 239-6162

ONLINE DIRECTORY OFFERS NATIONAL PUBLICITY TO
HOME-BASED BUSINESSES WITHOUT PC'S

Home-based entrepreneurs who don't yet own a personal computer may now register their business with the "National Home Office Business Directory" (NHOBD), according to Jane Rosenthal, spokesperson for the Home Office Business Network, an electronic information and communication network available to small business owners throughout North America. NHOBD is the first online database to offer listing to an estimated 30 million home businesses. In addition to business name, location, and category, registrants may publicize their willingness to grant cash discounts and to barter for products and services with other home business owners. Home business owners with personal computers and modems seeking to purchase products and services or to network with others may use their PCs to search NHOBD and retrieve listings matching their selection criteria. A registration kit is available from HOBN for $21.75 postpaid. Each kit contains instructions and an input data form which when completed is returned to HOBN. Included with each kit is a copy of a 48-page booklet, "Starting and Managing a Business from Your Home." HOBN, 44 Monterey Blvd., Suite 1400, San Francisco, CA 94131.

###

**44 Monterey Boulevard Suite 1400
San Francisco, CA 94131 415 239-6162**

Figure 13-3 *Typical News Release*

their identity, the word *NEWS* or *RELEASE*, and the word *Contact* preprinted. This release is on an ordinary letterhead, which is a perfectly acceptable practice and not at all unusual.

The name and number of someone to contact is a good idea and a more or less standard practice. Its purpose is to aid the editor, who may have questions or want more information generally.

Not all releases carry headlines, as this one does, and not everyone agrees that releases should have headlines. The argument against is that most editors prefer to write their own headlines. That's probably true, but there is no reason the editor can't do so anyway, and he or she probably will. But providing the headline yourself helps the busy editor grasp the story quickly. My belief is that a headline is a great help to everyone concerned.

The "###" at the bottom is one of several symbols used to signify the end of the copy. ("-30-" or, simply, "End," are also used freely.) If there were additional pages, the word "more" should appear here instead and on each succeeding page until the last page is reached.

This release is produced verbatim, as sent to me. The editor who used it would almost surely make his or her own changes.

The sins of single-spacing the copy or printing on both sides of the sheet are the only common mistakes of format that are likely to provoke an editor into discarding a release without more than a glance. By far the worst sin, however, and the principal cause of the failure of even beautifully prepared releases is inadequate content – that is, content with no value for that editor, possibly no value for any editor.

The word *news*, as used in the context of a release, is not always what a journalist might call "hard news," an item that would interest a great many people, the general public. For example, when a committee of Congress issues a release (and they issue many every day) reporting on an action or a decision concerning important legislation, that is often news indeed, and a newspaper editor might immediately assign a reporter to seek more information. Or a columnist (who is usually on everybody's distribution list for releases) might begin his or her own more intensive investigation, in quest of "the news behind the news." But when you announce a new product or a special sale, that is not news in the same sense at all, and an editor might yawn at it.

In short, it is up to you, in preparing a release, to do two things, if you expect to have your release published:

1. Offer something that is "newsworthy" in the sense that the editor is likely to find it something in which his or her readers would be interested. (Those readers are whom the editor serves, and their probable interest or lack of it is the editor's chief criterion of what to use and what to discard.)
2. Choose the right publications for your item, publications whose readers would be interested in your information.

For example, if you sell cosmetics, don't send a release about your product to *Field and Stream*, a publication for Nimrods and Izaak Waltons, nor to *Popular Computing*, a publication about computers.

You might go the other way, however, and *slant* your release to the publication. If you have a piece about the use of computers to help women choose the right cosmetics for their physical characteristics, that might be suitable for *Popular Computing* and other computer periodicals. Always bear in mind the interests of the readers, for that is what concerns the editor.

Too often, marketers try to use releases to do nothing but promote their own interests—that is, get free advertising and give nothing in return. This tactic will not fly; editors are quite alert and knowledgeable, even intelligent. They easily perceive an effort to simply steal free space in their publications and pay nothing for it. The payment you are expected to make is in useful information, information that contributes to the editor's publication and makes his or her job just a bit easier. And that is as true for the radio or TV news director as it is for the newspaper or magazine editor.

It isn't really difficult to develop "newsworthy" releases. Remember, first, that even daily newspapers use a great deal of

material that is not hard news by even the most liberal definition. They are "features," and they appear in many special sections of the newspaper, but sometimes they are even on the front
page. Some of them are "shaggy dog" stories—stories about
UFOs and Bigfoot; some are simply human-interest pieces; and
some are merely amusing or novel. There is only one criterion:
Will the subscribers find it worth reading?

From another viewpoint, consider your own interest: Are
those readers the people you need to reach? Will the readers of
Radio Electronics be good prospects for vitamin tablets? How
likely are the subscribers to *Senior Citizen's Digest* to buy the
latest in radar detectors?

Play the game honestly: Give the editor/news director
something useful for his/her needs, and you will get the free
advertising in return. It is a swap, something for something.

Where it is appropriate, you may wish to include a photograph with your release. In fact, the inclusion of a photograph
or any other graphic illustration usually increases greatly the
probability of the release's being "picked up" (published). Editors of periodicals are usually fond of illustrations and will often
accept an item they are not exactly crazy about if they like an
accompanying photo or drawing well enough. True, it can get
expensive to make up large mailings of photographs, but it is
possible to restrain the cost somewhat. For one thing, it is no
longer necessary, as it once was, to make the photograph an
8 × 10. Today, 4 × 5 photographs or even slightly smaller ones
will reproduce well, and most editors will accept smaller ones.
But do send glossies, for editors prefer glossies by far to matte
or other finishes. (As an alternative, although a less desirable
one, you can send releases with a note that photographs are
available on request.)

Treat the business of getting publicity releases published as
you would any other marketing or sales effort, for that is what
it is. You are trying to sell editors on using your releases and
giving you the publicity that represents valuable free advertising, so it is very much a *quid pro quo*. Like any other customer,
the editor wants to know, "What's in it for me? Can I use this in
my publication or on my broadcast?"

You may also address releases to columnists, and you probably have no idea how many columnists or how many kinds of columns there are. There are, in fact, dozens of syndicated columnists. Here is a mere sprinkling of the kinds of columns to be found:

Advice

Automotive

Beauty and fashion

Books

Bridge

Business

Careers and jobs

Decorating

Ecology and animals

Education

Entertainment

Food and wine

Gardening and farming

Hobbies

Medical and science

Music

Sports

Travel

Having your release picked up by a widely read columnist can produce surprising results. When I persuaded one columnist to tell her readers that I would send them a useful brochure if they sent me an SASE (self-addressed stamped envelope), I was swamped with over 3,000 such envelopes! And by the way, that is an excellent way to begin compiling a good mailing list. (Certainly, 3,000 names is a good start!)

Television and radio news anchors are another target for releases, but here it is usually the producer or news director, rather than the anchor, who controls the program and therefore should be addressed.

Releases are also used commonly as mailers to individuals, usually as an element in a complete package. That will be discussed more fully in the next chapter.

Product Releases

The product release is a first cousin to the news or publicity release. If you look in the back of many periodicals, you will find a "new products" section. Here you will find descriptions of new products, with sources and prices. And where it is helpful to know what the product looks like, you will usually find a photograph of the item. Prepare a product release as you would a news release, and send it to the appropriate editors. But here you must include a photograph if it is important that the reader see what the item looks like.

Press Kits

The press kit is built around a release or perhaps several releases. It is usually a folder with one or more releases and other items, such as a salesletter, photographs, brochures, reprints of published articles, and other such items. Whenever you have an important enough announcement to justify a press conference, you prepare and hand out these packages to attending journalists. When a journalist or other writer calls or writes and requests information, it is appropriate to send him or her such a package. It is also appropriate to have such packages on hand and give them out at trade shows, conventions, seminars, and other gatherings.

Associations and Memberships

For most entrepreneurs, "getting around" is important. That means being highly visible by being active in many associations and events. It usually helps to belong to a number of relevant associations and to take an active role in all the events so that you become well known yourself while you come to know a great many people. And it also leads you to conventions, conferences, trade shows, and other such events that represent special opportunities for PR and sales promotion generally.

Exhibits and Trade Shows

An exhibit or booth at a trade show or convention is an excellent PR tool. Such a well-attended conclave is an opportunity to meet many people, distribute information, and perhaps get some newspaper or magazine publicity as well, for the press attends all such events.

There are some other things you can do in connection with trade shows and conventions. Many of these events are staged in large hotels or resorts, and many companies set up hospitality suites on the premises, whether they do or do not also have exhibits or booths. Here you can meet and talk with prospective buyers without the distraction of competing exhibitors by receiving them in a suite you have set up with refreshments, literature, demonstrations, or whatever you choose to offer. You must, of course, take steps to let people know about your suite, and you can do so in several ways. One is by taking a small advertisement in the convention program guide. Another is by distributing printed invitations freely. Still another is by posting signs in appropriate places.

Some companies host parties or dinners for conventioneers or exhibit attendees who appear to be important prospects for business. The parties may be on the premises or in a nearby hotel or other facility. This is, of course, an extension of the hospitality suite idea on a grander scale.

Some Miscellaneous Ideas

Seminars are an excellent occasion for you to become known, if you are a presenter. You may stage seminars of your own, or you may be a guest speaker at others' seminars. Aside from seminars, take advantage of every opportunity to speak at meetings of associations, whether you are a member or not. Cultivate your speaking skills. All you need is practice.

One final idea: A newsletter of your own is an excellent PR tool. Handled properly, it is neither expensive nor difficult to produce. We will discuss newsletters more thoroughly in the next chapter.

Chapter Fourteen

Mail Order and Direct Mail

Despite the problems with the postal service, there are many reasons why doing business by mail is still popular. What is surprising is that so many businesspeople have not discovered this method of marketing.

THE "MAIL-ORDER BUSINESS"

We have made frequent references to the "mail-order" and "direct-mail" businesses, and a great many people do think of these activities as businesses. And yet that is not strictly correct, for there is really no such thing as a mail-order business or a direct-mail business. In the hardware business, you sell hardware. In the restaurant business, you sell meals. In the maintenance business, you sell maintenance services. But in the mail-order or direct-mail business, you sell almost anything, but you sell *by* mail. Therein lies the difference: mail order is not a business but a way of doing business, a way of selling and completing transactions as an alternative to the more classic face-to-face selling. Mail order offers great advantages in a number of ways, and it has opened the doors of opportunity to many who might never have found success otherwise. Mail order is a different kind of arena in which to do business, and direct mail is a way literally to pursue business — a way to go out after the customers instead of waiting for them to come to you. Doing business by mail is aggressive marketing rather than passive marketing.

MAIL ORDER VERSUS DIRECT MAIL

Many people refer to both mail order and direct mail as "mail order." Both activities utilize the mails, of course, but there is a distinct, if fine, difference that is worth noting, if only to ensure a clear understanding of the marketing philosophy and method: Mail order consists of advertising in various mass media (some of which even feature a special section titled *Mail Order*), whereas direct mail consists of soliciting orders from individuals by mass mailing sales literature directly to them.

Originally, merchandise ordered from advertising in the media was sent to the customers by mail, and that was the real significance of the term then: People living in rural isolation relied on the mails for much of their shopping. (It was before the modern telephone, automobile, and other conveniences ended the isolation of dwellers in rural areas.) Today other shipping methods are used, and orders are often placed by telephone. In fact, direct solicitation is also carried out by telephone today in what is called *telemarketing*.

To further confuse the issue, major catalog houses, such as Spiegel, Sears, and Fingerhut, are commonly called mail-order firms, although they use direct-mail methods, with their principal sales literature the catalogs they send customers and inquirers. But they do some media advertising, too, so they use both methods, as many businesses in mail order/direct mail do. For example, many use mail-order methods to gather and compile mailing lists for direct-mail solicitations.

So the differences are less distinct (and less important) now. The major difference is between marketing by advertising in mass media (*mail order*) and marketing by individual solicitation (*direct mail*). (Mail order may not use the mails at all today, in many situations!)

WHAT CAN BE SOLD BY MAIL?

You may recall the platitude I mentioned earlier to the effect that anything can be sold by mail. We must define what *sold* really means, however, before we can say flatly that the platitude is true or false. I doubt very much that you can *close* a major sale without direct, face-to-face contact, but I think you can certainly employ mail-order and direct-mail techniques to help make the sale. The salesman who sold me the automobile I now drive has continued to remind me that he is interested in my business by periodically sending me cards, brochures, and catalogs. I certainly am not allowed to forget where I bought that automobile. In my case, at least, such energetic and aggressive care ensures that this dealer and salesman will see me the next time I am ready to shop for an automobile.

Whatever your business, you can make use of mail-order or direct-mail techniques in your marketing. Depending on the kind of business you are in, you can sell by mail, use the mail to help develop prospects for what you sell, or use the mail in still other ways, such as ensuring that customers cannot forget you. Our main focus in this chapter, however, is mail-order and direct mail per se, or using those ideas and facilities as a principal way of marketing, which means selling goods and services by mail.

Because the distinctions between mail order and direct mail are less than absolutely clear, and because most entrepreneurs marketing via the mails and other special methods use both mail-order and direct-mail marketing methods, I will make no effort to separate the terms henceforth: From this point forward, both will be used interchangeably, as so many dealers in mail-order ventures use them.

ADVANTAGES IN MAIL ORDER

Mail order is one of the most popular home-based businesses because it is almost ideal for this setting: You can conduct it entirely by mail and telephone, either full or part time, and entirely in your own home, at least in the business's formative stages. In most cases, you can start with a modest amount of capital, the risks are small (if you are properly conservative), and the base is highly flexible: You can make changes—add to, delete, or modify—the products or services you sell; carrying a large inventory is usually not necessary; and hours are whatever you wish to make them.

MAIL-ORDER ITEMS

Although it is true that you can sell by mail many items that are also sold widely through retail stores and other means, certain items are peculiarly mail-order items—that is, they are sold almost exclusively by mail for one reason or another, either by tradition or, more frequently, because mail order has proved to be the most effective means for marketing them. (In some cases, it is the *only* effective means.) You might thus justifiably refer to these as "mail-order items."

Magazine subscription sale is one such case, as I mentioned earlier. Magazines are sold as individual copies on newsstands everywhere, but subscriptions to them are sold almost exclusively by direct mail, although a few publishers (notably *Time* and *Fortune* magazines) have used TV commercials.

Newsletter subscriptions, also noted earlier, are sold almost exclusively by direct mail. Efforts to sell them by other means, such as media advertising, have rarely produced satisfactory results. Occasionally newsletters appear on newsstands, but they seem to languish there.

Jim Straw is one rather remarkable success story in this field. He publishes the now venerable and widely circulated *Business Opportunities Digest* in Dalton, Georgia. He took the newsletter over some years ago, after his discharge from military service, buying it from its founder, who had been badly injured and incapacitated in an automobile accident. Straw made a number of changes in the newsletter, upgrading it in many ways and ultimately installing in his home modern equipment to turn the publication out as a much more professional product. Today he employs a full-time editor for the newsletter while he devotes his own time to an offshore bank he founded and many business matters related to that and other ventures he has undertaken. (Among these is another newsletter, *Offshore Banking News*.)

The mail-order and home-basing orientation appears to be not confined to newsletters alone but to small specialty publications in general. There are a great many home-based small publishers of such publications, usually how-to-do-it reports or brochures, and they sell exclusively by mail.

Some people visit a local print shop to order business cards, but a quite large proportion of all business cards sold are sold by mail. Many printers specialize in mail-order printing — that is, they do most of their business with mail-order dealers and they sell their printing services by mail. Paul Alexander, of Chantilly, Virginia, built his present mail-order business by first specializing in brokering the printing of business cards as an authorized dealer of several printing firms. Later, with his base of customers and repeat business firmly established, he branched out into other items he sells as a broker, working out of his tiny mobile home in suburban Virginia.

The support of small mail-order dealers is a mail-order industry in itself that includes the many mail-order printers and specialty publishers but also those who specialize in one or more of the following support services to mail-order dealers (and to others):

Manufacturers of rubber stamps, identity badges, plastic laminating, and other such devices and services

Publishing of ad sheets and full-scale advertising tabloids

Mailing services, including cooperative mailings

Rental of mailing lists

Typesetting services

Sale of office supplies generally

Brokering of many products and services, including those listed here

Even this list does not include all the services available in this field. For example, the publishers of the ad sheets and the more ambitious advertising tabloids sell advertising space as their primary venture. (Typical circulation of these periodicals, which are mostly monthly, is 3,000–5,000.) Most of these publishers, however, sell items of their own through advertising in their own periodicals, and most will enclose your advertising literature with their mailings for a suitable fee.

MAIL-ORDER MILIEUS

There are at least three broad classes or categories into which mail-order dealers should be classified, if you are to gain a true insight into this field. These classes refer primarily to size, but partially to market orientation and business philosophies as well.

The bottom dwellers in the world of mail order are those referred to generally as the *inner circle,* so called because they focus their efforts primarily on providing others in the mail-order business with the support services and products listed a few paragraphs ago. A great many of these dealers and merchants are part-time operators—housewives in some cases and people with jobs who moonlight as mail-order dealers in other cases. Some will eventually graduate to larger and full-time enterprises, but many others will not.

The operations of the inner circle are always suggestive of parasitism. Perhaps that is an unfair suggestion, for these are mostly honest and honorable individuals trying to conduct fair business. But the connotation is inescapable, and unless the operator makes an effort to eventually break out of the constraints imposed by being part of the inner circle, his or her business can never grow substantially.

Others break out to market to a much broader world with much broader interests, although they are not rivals of the mail-order giants. One couple who bought an old house and restored it to its original beauty and grandeur were forced to search out many little-known sources of classic plumbing fixtures, door knockers, and other devices that characterized the stately homes of several generations past. That search inspired them to launch a highly successful mail-order enterprise in which they sold such hard-to-find items to others who wished to restore, rather than modernize, old homes.

The third class or category is, of course, the heavy hitters in mail order — L. L. Bean, Walter Drake, and other firms that do many millions of dollars in sales every year.

The Verities and Conventional Wisdom of Mail Order

Mail order has its share and probably more of clichés and platitudes reflecting the conventional wisdom of the industry. Here are just a few of those firm beliefs you are likely to encounter as soon as you begin to communicate with others in the industry or read what they publish on the subject:

- You must get a 3 to 5 percent response from your mailings to succeed.
- You must be able to mark up your costs at least three times — and that is cutting it a little too closely — to make a profit in mail order.
- It will cost you about one-half the selling price for each order you get.
- The quality of your mailing list is the most important factor in mail-order success.
- You must enclose in your mailing a "response device" — e.g., a postage-paid return envelope and/or an order form.
- Two- or three-color printing produces better results than black-and-white printing.
- Better-quality paper will produce better results.
- Making it easy for the respondent to order increases the response rate.
- Getting the respondent "involved" — making him or her *do* something, such as moving a sticker from a form and fastening it to the return envelope — will increase the response.

The most charitable thing I can say about all these cherished beliefs (or claimed beliefs) of the self-appointed mavens of mail order is that they are mistaken. For each of these alleged verities can be argued against quite easily on logical grounds alone, as well as questioned on the grounds of experience. Let us consider them, one by one:

- The response rate: Mailing will cost you well over $250 per 1,000 pieces, if you can even get by that cheaply. (The postage cost alone, by the least expensive means, is well over $100 per 1,000.) That means a cost of $8.33 per order at a 3 percent response rate, and $5 per order at a 5 percent rate. And that is just the cost of getting the order. It does not count the cost of fulfillment—filling the order—and general overhead. If you were selling a $10 item at even a 70 or 80 percent markup, you would lose money. On the other hand, if you were selling a $100 item at a 50 percent markup and getting only a 1 percent response, you would turn a tidy profit. (Per-order cost of $25–30, gross profit of $20–25 per order.) The response rate is meaningless without reference to the other cost factors.
- The markup myth is likewise flawed, as just shown. In our example, we marked up two for one, rather than three for one, and still turned a profit. Fancy? No. This is based on fact, on our own promotions.
- Will it cost you half the selling price for each order? Maybe. So what? It's a meaningless idea, at best. More on that shortly.
- The quality of your mailing list: That is an important factor. But so are the quality of your copy, your offer, your merchandise, and your general reputation. One factor does not signify greatly without the others.
- Response devices, color printing, and paper quality: These factors bear on the results by fractions of percentage points and are therefore significant only when huge mailings are involved. But they are also significant only when everything else is right, and they never have any decisive effect on the success or failure of a campaign.
- Making it easy to place the order: This runs counter to that last item, which says that forcing the respondent to "get involved" in some manner increases the response rate. But we can't have it both ways. The fact is that prob-

ably neither has any decisively large effect: If a respondent is captivated by your offer or what you are selling and truly wants it, no amount of trouble necessary to order it will deter him or her; but if he or she definitely is not interested and does not want it, nothing will induce him or her to place the order.

Most of these notions, in fact, appear to be conclusions culled from random experience and never truly tested on a practical scale. The occasional test results that purport to prove the validity of these notions invariably report gains in tiny fractions of percentage points, which means that they represent insignificant amounts of dollars for most applications. Consequently, they do not appear to be important for any but the truly large mailers who send out millions of pieces, where 0.003 percent may amount to a few thousand dollars.

Sales or Customers?

There is another side to this issue, one that many small mail-order dealers appear to overlook: Are you trying to make sales or customers?

It is not a frivolous question. All the platitudes and alleged wisdom just cited are based on the premise that each sale must produce its own profit. But a great many mail-order dealers, especially the majors in the industry, lose money on virtually every first sale to a new buyer because it is simply not possible to mark up many kinds of merchandise by a factor of several times its cost. It is more likely that at best you will be able to buy merchandise at 40 to 50 percent below the list prices, so the best you can do, under the conventional wisdom, is to mark up the item by a factor of two, thereby ensuring a loss.

But wait a minute. It is a verity of business generally and of mail order especially that acquiring a new customer is always expensive. Losing money on a first sale to a new buyer is not really a loss; it is a marketing cost, part of the cost of acquiring a new customer. Or will be if you succeed in converting that new buyer into a new customer, someone who will return to buy again. For precisely that, making customers, is the secret of success in some kinds of businesses. It is certainly the secret of success in any mail-order venture in which you simply cannot mark up what you sell several times its cost, as when you sell standard commodities or "name brands." Your profits come only later, in bounceback orders and repeat business. (*Bounceback orders* are those you realize as a result of inserting catalogs and/or other sales literature in the package when you fill the original order.)

In short, you must decide in advance whether you are in business to make sales or make customers. But that decision is linked to what you wish to sell, for that may dictate whether you can afford to focus on making sales or are compelled to make customers and win repeat business. If the latter, you must have a line of merchandise and/or other conditions that inspire other sales and repeat orders.

It is possible, happily, to have both. Items such as the specialty publications alluded to earlier usually offer the opportunity to make both profit on first sales and repeat business. Generic items, such as "privately branded" vitamins and other nostrums, also often offer such great discounts that you can realize profits on first sales to new buyers and yet get repeat business also. Too, if you are a good buyer as well as a good marketer, you can often find closeouts where you can get name brand items at large enough discounts to have it both ways.

WHAT WILL YOU SELL? TWO APPROACHES

Quill Corporation, mentioned in an earlier chapter, is a seller of office supplies and other business necessities, selling primarily by mail through catalogs sent out regularly. There are a thick general catalog, issued semiannually, a slender monthly catalog of specials, and unscheduled special flyers and other sales literature, including a monthly newsletter. Quill sells an ever-broadening range of products to an ever-widening circle of customers and has built a large mail-order organization.

Joe Cossman became a wealthy man in mail order, as did the late Joe Karbo. But there is a significant difference in the way Cossman and Quill address mail order and conduct their businesses. Cossman is essentially a one-man business, as Karbo was, selling only one item at a time and expending all his energies and efforts in selling that one item. (Among his better-known items was the ant farm, for example.) When he finds an item he thinks has a good potential, he designs an offer and tests it. If the tests turn out well, he promotes the item as energetically as possible. And when sales slow to a point where it appears no longer worthwhile (an almost inevitable event in this mode of operation), he closes out the promotion and begins a search for the next item. (Actually, he is always alert for new ideas and probably has several candidate items at any one time waiting to be tested.)

Customers and *repeat business* have different meanings for entrepreneurs like Cossman than they do for such mail-order organizations as Quill. The buyers of Cossman's ant farms might or might not have been good prospects for the next item he chose to promote and sell. In any case, he certainly cannot count on it and so must inevitably turn a clear profit on each sale he makes. His business is definitely making sales.

This is, of course, a perfectly valid approach to business, but it is necessary to be aware that in such a mode of operation you cannot take losses on first sales and charge them off as investment in building a mailing list and a customer base. It would be risky to assume that the next single item you sell will be attractive to the same buyers. (In fact, mailing lists age rapidly, and by the time you promote another item much of your list will be obsolete with *nixies*, undeliverable or invalid names on the list because people have moved, died, or other changes have made the name and address useless.)

There is one exception to this rule: If the item you sell is a consumable item, such as a diet preparation, a food, a vitamin, or other such item, there is the prospect of repeat business from buyers.

TESTING

Testing media advertising is somewhat laborious because of the time required to consummate the tests. Even with simultaneous test advertisements it takes several months because most periodicals work at least a couple of months ahead. By the time you make a few tests and run the final copy you decided on, more than a few months have passed. Moreover, other factors are involved, factors over which you have limited control. One of these is the placement of the advertisement, for example. You can request certain positions, but you may or may not be able to get them. That lack of control interferes with creating nearly equal conditions for all test versions, because variations in placement may affect results.

Here direct mail offers a substantial advantage: Testing material in direct mail is relatively swift and easy, and you do have control. You can send out several different versions of your headline, offer, proposition, or whatever you wish to test, keying each, and have results in enough quantity to form judgments within two or three weeks. (Not all responses will arrive that soon, but enough will to give you a fair comparison among the several versions of whatever you wish to test.) Moreover, you do not have to make large mailings. I have found that a mailing of 500 pieces for each version I wish to test will usually tell me as much as would a mailing of 5,000 pieces for each. In fact, in two cases I was able to get definitive results in mailings of only 300 pieces.

There are certain rules you must follow to make the test results significant and reasonably reliable:

1. You must test only one thing at a time. If you want to test different offers, such as different promises or different forms of the promise, for example, don't try to test different prices at the same time. If you do, you will not know which variation was responsible for a difference in results.
2. Each sample mailing must be as close to the others as possible, except for the item you are testing, for the same reason: You are trying to gauge the effect of what-

ever variation you are using. The mailing lists should be as similar as possible. The best way to ensure this is to use portions of a single mailing list for all the test mailings.

3. Each sample should be a random sample, to guard against any unconscious or accidental stacking of the deck. A good way to accomplish this is to select each test list at random throughout the entire mailing list rather than dividing the list in some logical manner. If you have a list of 1,500 names, for example, and want to mail three batches of 500 each, you might choose every third name for one list, then every other name to divide the remaining 1,000 names. The idea is to have each test mailing a representative sample of the entire list.

4. Of course, each mailing must be keyed in some manner. It is a good idea to enclose an order form and key that form to identify the list it came from. If you are testing different prices, you need no special key: The amount of money remitted will indicate which list the individual responded to.

Keep a simple record, such as that shown in Figure 14-1, for each list. (Modify this design to suit your own preference or need, of course.) Record the number of orders and money received each day and the cumulative total of orders. Use the remarks column for whatever purpose you wish, such as to mark the breakeven point when it is reached, the cumulative total of dollars received, or whatever else you think worth noting. Some people like to calculate the percentage of responses, although it is not truly significant for the reasons explained earlier.

The purpose of this notetaking is to keep a record of test results to determine what works best. I think it is a good policy, however, to keep this kind of record of all orders received, even after completing the tests and "rolling out" the main mailing. That enables you to keep track of what is happening and so alerts you immediately to changes, such as a decline or increase in responses, seasonal fluctuations, the quality of a mailing list, or any other significant information. (You may find it helpful

Test List ID:_____

Date	No. Orders	No. $$$	Total Orders	Remarks

Figure 14-1   A Simple Record of Test Results

later to graph or chart the campaign over its life as a guide to
future campaigns.)

MAILING LISTS

Mailing lists come from two sources: lists you rent from list
brokers and lists you build yourself from various sources. By
and large, the lists rented by list brokers belong to others. If you
read the leading periodicals serving the direct mail industry
(*DM News*, a tabloid, and *Target Marketing*, a smooth-paper
magazine) you will find yourself offered the lists of such firms
as L. L. Bean, Dun & Bradstreet, Dartnell, *Ladies Home Journal*, Time-Life Books, and many others. The list brokers, who
prefer to be called "list managers," referring to the service they
perform for the owners of the lists, may own a few lists of their
own ("house lists") but most of their lists are the property of others and the list broker markets the rentals of the lists on a com-

mission basis. As a user, you can therefore rent lists on either the basis of some demographic characteristic you specify— engineers, housewives, book buyers, upper-income group, or other such tag—or you can rent lists on the basis of the firm whose customers the list represents.

Building your own lists is a different proposition. You may or may not be able to rent the kind of list you want. In my own case, I wanted lists of government contractors who were most likely to be interested in proposal writing, but I was never able to find lists specialized in that manner, and the rental lists I tried never worked well for me. As a result, I developed my own lists, compiling them from various sources, including newspaper advertising, public information available from government sources, news items, and membership directories of certain relevant associations, among other sources.

The most valuable lists are always those of your own customers. When you rent lists from a broker, you normally rent the list for one-time use and you must pay for each additional use. Anyone on the list who responds is your customer (or inquirer), however, and that name belongs to you. It is therefore added to your own house list.

There is a mail-order platitude that maintains that compiled lists are of little value. I can't agree with that, at least not on the basis of my own experience with the lists I compiled; they worked well for me, for both my mail-order ventures and my seminars. What is perhaps true is that lists compiled wholesale from questionable sources, such as telephone directories, and without discrimination about their appropriateness are likely to prove low-grade ore. In compiling lists, bear in mind the qualifications you seek and discriminate accordingly in what you accept and what you reject as candidates for the list.

LIST MANAGEMENT

Part of the service list managers provide for their clients, the owners of lists of names, is entering the names into their computer systems to create files—lists—that can be manipulated and sorted in various ways. That is, with computer help, it is possible simply to code each name so that one can retrieve many different kinds of lists and yet have only one master list in the computer. The list broker's catalog describes and identifies many different kinds of lists, but these are not really separate lists; they are one or more master lists with each entry suitably coded. For example, if you order a list of engineers residing in area code 33000, the operator can have the computer sort through the master list and retrieve as many names as you wish that match these parameters.

As your own house lists (and your independence of rented lists) grow, you will begin building different house lists. For one, you will want to separate customer lists from prospect lists—that is, those who have bought from you in the past from those who have only inquired but so far have never bought anything. Later, you will begin to break these lists down into customers for various items and customers and prospects of various interests and other characteristics. Eventually, you will need such management of your house lists.

List management means compiling the main list and coding it suitably. It means, also, maintaining the list, adding names, and purging it as necessary by eliminating nixies and correcting errors as you discover them (often referred to as "cleaning" the list). Commercial list brokers do this for their clients, but you must do it for yourself, if you want to keep your lists clean and up to date.

Today, with a desktop computer in your own office, you can manage your lists for yourself, using any of many simple programs available for the purpose. You can use a simple database management (dbm) program or a special mailing list management program, which is actually a specialized dbm program. The general dbm program offers much greater flexibility, however, because it permits you to design your own mailing list program. It also provides facilities for printing out reports of various kinds (although most mailing list programs do so also).

There are several kinds of dbm programs: the simple *flat*

file, the *relational*, and the *spreadsheet*. You probably will find the flat file dbm, the simplest program, entirely adequate for your needs and easiest to use for a small business. Here is how a sample entry blank might appear:

Last Name_____ First Name_____

Company_____

Address 1_____

Address 2_____

City_____ State_____ Zip_____

Tel_____ FAX_____

Note 1_____

Note 2_____

You can sort your list by any of the items — last name, first name, company, zip code, or other. You can use the Note 1 and Note 2 items to enter special information, such as "book buyer," "customer," or "inquirer." The program would normally assign each entry a record number command in sequence as entered, and this identifies entries in a chronological sequence, although you can enter the dates of each entry, if you choose. (Chapter 18 will explore computer usage more thoroughly, and Appendix 1, a reference section, will suggest specific computer programs, some of them available at most modest costs.)

In summary, mail order does offer great business opportunities, but it also requires great attention to detail. Now let us have a look at another business arena: government markets.

Chapter Fifteen

Doing Business with Governments

Unfortunately, government markets, their size and availability to all, are almost invisible to most businesspeople. But it is not truly difficult to learn about and win your own share of this enormous market.

A FEW STARTLING STATISTICS

The federal government of the United States has many hundreds of agencies who must buy goods and services to carry out their missions, and they buy well over $200 billion worth each year—nearly a billion dollars every business day of the year. That procurement budget keeps about 130,000 procurement officials and aides busy. (It is not easy to spend that much money!) But even that figure is dwarfed by the spending of fifty state governments, 3,042 county governments, 18,862 municipalities, 16,822 townships, 15,174 local school districts, and 25,962 special districts, who spend about twice as much, collectively, as the federal government does. And if you are not impressed with the markets and money spent by the 79,913 "government entities" (the term used by the Census Bureau), you must understand also that the various governments each have multiple bureaus and agencies that swell the total number of customers in government into the millions. Capture only the tiniest fraction of this huge market—over $600 billion annually—and you have a prosperous business of your own.

WHAT DO GOVERNMENTS BUY?

You cannot find many goods or services that governments do not buy. The nature of what governments do today dictates a need for most of what our industry produces and makes available in both goods and services. The federal government classifies its needs into approximately 100 "supply groups" and subclassifies many items within those groups. There are two kinds of groups, however, for services and goods. And, predictably, each of these two groups has a "miscellaneous" subclassification. It hardly matters what you sell or do; it is a virtual certainty that somewhere among the vast assortment of goods and services the governments buy are specifications for what you sell and do for customers.

The state and local governments tend strongly to emulate the federal system, each producing its own catalog of the goods and services it buys with some regularity. In fact, the list of items the state of California buys is almost identical with that of the federal system, even down to a few kinds of military arms! There are, however, some marked differences, too, between purchasing by federal government agencies and state and local government agencies, which we shall discuss presently.

A FEW BASIC FACTS ABOUT
ALL GOVERNMENT PURCHASING

It is largely true that the most difficult part of doing business with government agencies is the market research, beginning with "finding the doors," or just discovering where the agencies and their purchasing offices are, to start with. But beyond that is the problem of discovering what the agencies want to buy and how to go about getting into the competition. Somehow, governments at all levels, federal, state, and local, have great difficulty in making their needs and opportunities widely known to business and industry; those who wish to do business with government agencies must seek those government agencies out and exercise a great deal of initiative to learn how to compete for this business.

The difficulty extends in both directions: Government executives who do not buy goods and services regularly or have a sudden unusual or unanticipated need often have difficulty in finding suppliers to bid or propose to them. Often they call people they know in other government offices to ask for help, or they borrow the bidders' lists of another agency. Sometimes they even turn to the private sector for help: I have had the experience more than once of getting telephone calls from government executives asking me to recommend someone for a given kind of service. An official in the Agency for International Development who was responsible for ordering printing services often had to call printers listed in the telephone yellow pages to invite them to bid. And on one occasion an executive in the U.S. Peace Corps also turned to the yellow pages to find a writer who would undertake a job for them. So it is not terribly difficult to win a share of government business, once you understand the systems, know how they operate, and know where to look. In fact, many government business opportunities are skewed to offer small businesses an advantage.

The Built-In Controls

Governments all spend public money—taxes—your money and mine. So they are not free to do whatever they please; their spending is controlled by public statutes, and there are a few common factors:

- All procurements must be announced or advertised in some manner to alert the public at large to the procurement.
- Everyone, the smallest and the largest business, is entitled to a fair opportunity to compete for and win a share

of government business. Favoritism in contract awards is immoral and illegal.

- Whenever possible, awards will be competed as sealed bids, opened publicly, with awards to the lowest bidders.

- When sealed bids with awards to low bidders are impractical (more and more the case today), negotiated procurement will be employed. Usually, this means that candidates for the contract must submit proposals and an objective, preannounced rating system will be used to evaluate the proposals to determine who will be entitled to negotiate.

- All systems provide for special situations and emergency conditions, when supplies or services are urgently needed and there is not enough time for the typical formal contracting procedure. "Sole source" or "selected source" procurements are justified in these circumstances. And similar justification is invoked legally when a supplier can provide a unique or proprietary product or service that is needed and not available elsewhere.

- All systems also provide for small purchases, which by their size alone do not justify the expense and time required to make purchases by formal means. Such purchases are thus permitted to be made by some expeditious means, usually by purchase order rather than formal contract. In the federal system, the law defines a small purchase as one less than $25,000. Most state and local jurisdictions set lower standards, usually from $500 to $5,000.

It would be foolish to pretend that there is never an effort, and frequently a successful one, to frustrate these laws; there are always those who place themselves above the law and try to seize special privileges for themselves or subvert the law for their personal convenience and profit. (At this moment, there is a serious investigation of irregularities in Department of Defense procurement and certain activities of the Department of Housing and Urban Development.) But by and large the American procurement systems have been quite clean and beyond reproach, far more than the procurement systems of some foreign governments and, in some cases, those of a few American cities and counties.

All government purchasing represents legitimate business opportunity, but for a number of reasons the greatest opportunities for most small businesses probably lie in pursuing federal government contracts. The federal government has a number of socioeconomic programs in place to support small businesses and minority-owned enterprises, including those owned by women. Most state governments also have such programs, but they are usually far less sweeping in scope than the federal programs are.

Overall, the federal government system is still a model for others, although it and others are all based largely on the Model Procurement Code developed and advocated by a special committee of the American Bar Association.

Finding Out about Requirements

The federal procurement system is unique in that it employs its own special publication, the *Commerce Business Daily*, to announce government needs and business opportunities, among other things. (The "other things" are announcements of contract awards, government surplus sales, foreign business opportunities, advance announcements of future procurements, and a few other special items of information.) The publisher of the periodical, which is normally a five-day-a-week publication but has occasionally published Saturday editions when there was an excess of information to be released, is the U.S. Department of Commerce. The actual printing is carried out by the Government Printing Office in Chicago, however, and the publication may be ordered from either the Department of Commerce or the Government Printing Office.

There are many government manuals explaining the procurement system; many of the major agencies publish their own manuals for suppliers. The Government Printing Office bookstores sell a number of these, but most of the agencies will send you a copy free of charge on your request for information about their purchasing and procurement systems. You will especially want to ask the General Services Administration for information. (See Part 5 for listings of the agencies and their names and addresses.)

Basic Procurement Methods

Contracting officers usually greatly prefer the uncomplicated sealed-bid procurements, where they simply award contracts to the lowest bidders in each case. More and more in this increasingly complex world, however, that is not practicable because of the increasing demand for custom developments. And that leads directly to a need to determine who is best qualified to turn out a reliable and effective product, not necessarily the cheapest product. (Who wants to fly an airplane made by the lowest bidder?) Consequently, candidates for award must frequently submit proposals; the best qualified rather than the lowest bidder is selected for negotiations and final decisions.

The majority of dollars spent by the federal government go to major contracts procured via proposals and negotiations, but the majority of contracts are relatively small and a large percentage goes to small businesses. In the federal system, however, there is relatively little centralized purchasing and procurement. The Federal Supply Service, the Defense Logistics Service, the new Department of Veterans Affairs, and the U.S. Postal Service each has its own centralized supply services, but these represent only a fraction of federal purchasing dollars. The bulk of federal purchasing is done independently by individual agencies out of their own budgets.

State and local governments tend to go the other way—to maintain central purchasing and supply organizations in the state capital, county seat, and city hall, reserving most purchasing authority to themselves and awarding annual supply contracts. (Many do, however, delegate purchasing authority to other agencies, as necessary, especially for specialized services.) Most urge suppliers to visit personally and meet with their various buyers. Most also have some kind of explanatory brochure, and some will supply a thick list of their supply groups on request.

Learning of Specific Requirements

Suppliers of the federal system are encouraged to fill out and file a Standard Form 129, Application for Bidders List. State and local governments have a similar form, but filing it as a form of registration is often a requirement and you cannot do business with that government until you have filed it. A few state and local governments charge a small fee also, but that is the exception rather than the rule.

Theoretically, having filled out such a form with the various governments, you should begin to get invitations to compete for contracts automatically, without further action on your part. Unfortunately, it does not usually work out that way, for several reasons. You must therefore make it a practice to visit contracting offices and review the bid opportunities of the moment, and it is almost mandatory to subscribe to the *Commerce Business Daily* (CBD) or the electronic version, the public database CBD ONLINE, if you are serious about pursuing government business consistently. (See Part 5 for instructions on how to do this.) Unfortunately, the CBD has become expensive, like most things; today it costs $208 for an annual subscription, and even that is by second-class mail (from Chicago). Subscription with first-class mail service is $268, but even that does not guarantee the quality of service the postal system once provided: Once, in the distant past, when the CBD cost $15 per year, the Monday edition arrived on Monday, the Tuesday edition on Tuesday, and all others on the day of their dateline. Today they rarely arrive on the date so optimistically printed on the masthead but usually several days later, and it is not unknown for them to arrive as much as a week late. Therefore, one of the major advantages of using the CBD ONLINE public database system is that you can get the Monday edition on Monday, the Tuesday edition on Tuesday, and all the others on the day of their datelines. (CBD ONLINE is available from several sources, listed in Part 5.)

State and local governments almost invariably advertise their requirements in the classified advertising columns of local newspapers under the heading BIDS AND PROPOSALS. (In most cases, the controlling statutes require this public advertising.) You can ask to be placed on appropriate bidders' lists, and you will be doing so when you file the registration form referred to earlier. But it is still necessary to monitor the classified advertising columns and stay in touch with the various purchasing offices. It is a good idea to visit them personally as often as possible and ask to see the current solicitations for bids and proposals. Public law usually requires that these be available for inspection at all times. In many cases, where the purchasing office is a busy one that buys goods and services regularly, there will be a bid room and a bid board on which will be posted copies of all current solicitations.

One way to gain an advantage in these markets is to position yourself for "sudden service." Government agencies of all kinds have the same problems other organizations do: Emergencies arise when they need things "yesterday." Under those circumstances, they can invoke one of the several rules that permit them to make purchases directly without the time-consuming process of bids, proposals, and formal contracting. If you make it clear to the contracting officials and buyers that you can handle such problems and you make it your business to remind them frequently of your availability via visits, telephone calls, brochures, and other means, eventually you will be called on for such a rescue mission. And once you have performed well in such circumstances, you will be remembered and regarded as a special supplier.

A Special Aid

The CBD lists the government's requirements in nineteen categories of services and seventy-eight categories of supplies and materials (supply groups, with subordinate listings); it also lists five miscellaneous categories of such things as sales of government surplus. Obviously, no one is interested in all the categories and so ignores at least two-thirds of the content of the CBD every day. But now a special marketing aid is available as an alternative to the CBD in either its paper or online version. That is the new periodical *Commerce Business Daily Weekly Release*, a weekly compendium of the previous week's CBD listings that are of interest to the subscriber. A subscription is, presently, $163 per year, and each subscription entitles the subscriber to select five categories. Along with each subscription, the publisher provides a book, *Guide to Winning Government Contracts and Subcontracts*, as a bonus. Information on this and CBD ONLINE is available from United Communications Group, listed in Part 5, along with many other resources.

Building Business Relationships

Doing business with government agencies is not much different from doing business with private-sector organizations, except for the regulations that control government agencies in purchasing. (And even that has its counterpart in the purchasing regulations and policies of many large corporations.) Personal relationships with the individuals in government offices are as helpful in marketing to those agencies as such relationships are in the private sector, and they should be carefully cultivated. Keep those relationships fresh and alive by your visits, calls, and occasional mailing of brochures and other reminder literature. You deal with individuals in government agencies as you do with private companies or individual customers, and you build a business over time based at least partially on those relationships with people in government agencies, as you do with private-sector customers. Customers are the same everywhere: They have their typical business problems and they need help, as we all do. When they find that you are a conscientious and dependable support element, they go out of their way to direct their business to you. It is in their own interest to do so, and nothing is more motivating than one's own interest. The cliché that you can get what you want by helping the other party get what he or she wants is as true here as it is elsewhere. All sound business relationships are based on *quid pro quo*, a fair exchange of something for something, in which each party is satisfied.

SUBCONTRACTING

No one, not even the largest of our supercorporations, does everything for itself. Companies who undertake and win substantial contracts with the government (and elsewhere, too, of course) invariably must "let" many subcontracts, some of them rather large, many of them quite small. RCA, in undertaking a billion-dollar radar/missile-detection program for the Department of Defense, let well over 300 subcontracts to support the program, for example. But even relatively small companies winning relatively small contracts often need help. They need things done for which they do not have the capability, or they are overloaded and need to get some outside help with typing, word processing, drafting, accounting, writing, or any of many possible tasks. And they often need this service on an impossible schedule, as noted earlier, which represents special opportunity.

Even government agencies contracting with other government agencies (a common practice) often subcontract part of their work. The U.S. Government Printing Office (GPO) operates the largest printing plants in the world (five of them) and contracts with other federal agencies for almost all government printing. (Federal law requires this, in fact, and only the GPO can normally authorize another federal agency to contract printing elsewhere.) The volume of printing done by the government is so great, however, that the GPO finds it necessary to subcontract out about 70 percent of its printing and typesetting. There are small print shops and even some not-so-small print shops that survive almost entirely on their contracts with and support of GPO.

SOCIOECONOMIC PROGRAMS

The federal government and the state and local governments (who are probably inspired primarily by the federal government's example) do a few things to encourage and aid small business generally, and minority- and women-owned businesses especially. That is the chief mission of the U.S. Small Business Administration (SBA), which offers a variety of services, including some assistance in winning contracts with the federal agencies. Among the chief programs of the SBA are these:

- Setasides, a program that sets aside some government procurements to limit competition to small business only. A small business representative in each government contracting office is responsible for finding contracts suitable for setting aside. (In the small contracting offices, the contracting officer may be required to wear a second hat as this functionary.)
- Loans and loan guarantees to aid small businesses in financing their ventures.
- Free consulting services, provided by firms contracting with the SBA to provide these third-party services.
- An assortment of special business publications, some free, others available at modest prices.
- A certification program to enable small businesses to overcome requirements to prove technical capability for contracts.
- The 8a program to help minority business owners win government contracts by underwriting them.

There are approximately ninety SBA District Offices, and they are listed for your convenience in Part 5. Visit the nearest one.

The Minority Business Development Agency (MBDA) in the Department of Commerce focuses entirely on that aspect, aiding minority-owned businesses. Their chief activity appears, however, to be help in financing, and they carry out their programs through contracts with firms in the private sector as a system of third-party services — that is, the MBDA pays the firm to provide services to a third party.

The Department of Defense is especially active in this field, operating its own offices responsible for protecting the interests of small and minority-owned businesses. Major defense programs have individuals assigned especially to see to it that minority firms and other small businesses are given a fair opportunity to pursue and win contracts and subcontracts.

The General Services Administration (GSA) is the federal government's housekeeper, with five subordinate divisions, including the Federal Supply Service. This agency operates thirteen Business Service Centers in major cities (all listed in Part 5), whose major function is to help orient you and help you in pursuing government contracts. Try to visit one of these, if at all possible. It will almost surely be worth the effort.

Most states have socioeconomic programs, too, necessarily less ambitious than those of the federal government but following the same philosophy. There are loan and loan guarantee programs, preference for small and locally based businesses, and other such aids.

PART FOUR

SOME PRACTICAL MATTERS
A Business Cookbook

The title chosen for this part was not intended to suggest that any of the foregoing material was not practical or was less practical than what appears here, but only that this part deals with the more prosaic and more mundane matters of physical business requirements, such as space, furniture, equipment, supplies, suppliers, and sundry other sources and specific details. So many books on the subject of conducting a small business, at home or elsewhere, deliver excellent lectures on marketing, accounting, inventory, management, and other important topics, but then fail to provide that necessary cookbook touch of specifying just *how* to go about doing things and just *where* to get things, including more information on highly specialized areas.

Without further ado, then, let us get on to a variety of practical matters and the cookbook treatment.

Chapter Sixteen

Physical Arrangements

*Making sensible analysis and
decisions when space is limited.*

SPACE AND FACILITY PROBLEMS

There are many practical problems other than those discussed earlier in Chapter 3 and elsewhere in earlier pages, and they are not always easy to solve. There are, in many cases, the problems of distracting noises of traffic, small children in your home or under your window outside, and other activity not under your control. It is unrealistic to expect children to understand your need for quiet, and certainly you can't stop trucks, buses, and automobiles from rumbling by, if you happen to live on or near a busy street or highway. That does not mean that you cannot do something about it however; you can.

Accept, first of all, that you can't really control the noise itself; even reprimanding your children rarely is very effective, as every parent knows, nor is it fair to the children. But if you can't do much about the source or cause of the noise, you can do something about the effects or results: You can deaden the noise in your office considerably. Use the heaviest carpeting possible. It does not have to be expensive carpeting, just heavy or, at least, with a thick pad. If you can, install a sound-insulated ceiling too. Hang heavy drapes. Again, they do not have to be costly; they can be made of an inexpensive material like burlap. The noises will still be there, but they will be much less evident when you have covered all those hard, echoing surfaces with sound-absorbing materials.

You may find that you would like to have more working space and more storage space. (Having incorporated your venture and given yourself the grand title of *President*, perhaps you think you ought to have an office worthy of that position.) But reality soon intercedes. You find yourself facing such practical constraints as those of available space and available cash, too. Your business needs as much capital as you can endow it with, and the more Spartan your physical arrangements are, the more capital you can make available for your venture.

Space and Facility Problems

The average home is not wired for industrial or business use, and the older homes are often not wired adequately for modern needs even as private homes. The many appliances and other devices that have come into common use over recent decades—television, videocassette recorders, automatic clothes washers, dishwashers, freezers, electric can openers, electric typewriters, home computers, and FAX machines, to name only a few—burden and overburden the wiring and electrical service of even recently built homes, in many cases. And in the case of some of these items, recent years have seen their proliferation in numbers, as well as in kind: Many people have multiple TV sets and VCRs, for example, adding further to the load placed on the systems.

If yours is a business requiring equipment that will add significantly to the load placed on your wiring system, you should consider the possibility that you will need your electrical service modernized or you will have to reduce the load in some manner. A competent electrical contractor can take a few measurements and make a suitable determination easily enough.

There is also the possible problem of space. Even when

you have enough space physically to accommodate your business needs, it may not be of a nature that works to your best interests in terms of allowable business deductions. For tax purposes—to maximize the tax writeoff you can take—you will do well to dedicate as much space as possible to business use. And it must be *dedicated* space to qualify. The IRS does not regard the cost of space shared for business and personal use as deductible for tax purposes, and unless you dedicate a complete room or closet for business use, the IRS is likely to challenge your declaration that some part of a room is used exclusively for business.

Some houses, especially older ones, have rather large rooms, rooms that are often larger than you need for personal use. If you are unable to dedicate a separate room or space, such as a garage or large closet, or if you can dedicate only one room but need more space, you may be able to satisfy the IRS requirement by installing some kind of room divider or partition and furnishing the partitioned-off portion in such a manner that it is clearly not suited to anything but business use.

In many cases, regardless of tax considerations or other matters, such as whether you are using partitioned-off space or a small room as an office, you simply do not have enough space to accommodate all your needs. The modern office usually includes at least these items:

Desk and chair, with side chair

Filing cabinet, at least two-drawer, preferably four-drawer

Book case or shelves

Telephone

Typewriter and stand

Computer and printer, with printer stand

FAX machine

Calculator

That can be quite a lot to get into a home office, and it is by no means all the furnishings, fixtures, and equipment you will need. In fact, it is probably only a starter list, and the number of items populating your office will grow rapidly. In my own case, there are, in addition to most of the items listed here, also two computer buffers, a modem, an external (3.5-inch) disk driver, a second printer, two surge suppressors and A-B switch, two ribbon-reinking machines, a parallel-to-serial converter, numerous plastic cases to house diskettes, and miscellaneous trays and contrivances used as in- and out-baskets and for storage of paper and items that fit nowhere else.

Sooner or later, you may have to resort to a number of space-saving devices, and you will benefit most by anticipating needs and considering the use of available expedients in advance. Here are a few suggestions that may relieve the burden a bit.

Desks are available in several sizes. Before you succumb to the temptation to buy a space-saving small one, consider the tradeoffs. If you do buy a small desk, you will almost surely need the filing cabinet. But if you do buy a larger desk, you can get one with a number of large drawers, at least one of which will accommodate a set of hanging files and perhaps eliminate the need for a filing cabinet. Too, if the desktop is of substantial size, you may be able to keep both your computer and printer on your desk and avoid the need for a printer stand and the space it requires. You may even find room on your desktop for a small FAX machine and some other of the devices you will almost surely accumulate as time marches on.

One mistake I made in buying my desk was to get one that did not have those two pull-out leaves that used to be standard and taken for granted in all desks. They are extremely useful when space is at a premium, especially when much of your desktop is permanently occupied by modern equipment and the inevitable stacks of paper (unless you are truly a clean-desk type, which is an increasingly difficult achievement to make a reality). I mourn my lack of foresight in this respect almost daily.

If you do not use your computer steadily all day, there are at least two or three things you can do to get maximum use out of the space it and its companion equipment occupy. You can get a swiveling arm and platform on which you can mount your computer monitor and swing it out of the way when not in use. And you can get a metal keyboard housing to serve as a base under your computer and furnish a receptacle to get your keyboard out of the way when not in use. Or, perhaps even better, you can mount your computer vertically on a little stand, and even keep it on the floor beside your desk.

In my own case, I no longer keep a typewriter in my office. I have found it possible to do all my writing, even of short notes and memoranda, via my computer and printer, using programs designed especially for that purpose. (Several such programs will be identified in Chapter 18.) If you must have a typewriter, perhaps you can mount it on a rollaway stand so that it can be stored elsewhere—perhaps in a closet—when not needed.

I have an abundance of books, not surprising for a writer, and I use tall bookcases, taking advantage of vertical space that is rarely used in the average room, although I keep several, frequently consulted books on my desk in front of me.

CUSTOMIZING YOUR OFFICE TO YOUR NEEDS

The needs that the physical arrangements of your office at home must satisfy will necessarily vary with the kind of business you are in and the kind of use you must therefore make of your office. In my own case, for example, the primary use I make of my office is to write manuscripts for publication by commercial publishers as books and articles, so my chief need is space for my computer, with my computer and paper files, and my library of books and journals, which are an important research facility for me. My office therefore has two focal points, the computer ensemble and the library. That is, of course, logically inescapable: The form must follow the function if the whole thing is to work.

I have chosen to have a conventional desk rather than one of those special computer desks so much in vogue today, and I have installed my computer and monitor on that desk, as shown in Figure 16-1. This decision is not by chance or whim; it is deliberate and logical (at least according to my logic). My reasoning is thus: Those special computer desks (see Figure 16-2) are designed for efficient use of space, but they are designed for those who use computers more or less sparingly and who cannot spare a great deal of space for their computers. That is not the case with me, of course; I am at the keyboard all day, almost every day. I have manuscript piling up on my desk steadily, and I am working with many kinds of paper—books, reports, articles, journals, and notes I have made while researching background data. I need desk space, much more desk space than those efficient little computer desks provide. In fact, I really do not have enough desk space even so. I wish there was room for a special computer desk in addition to my regular business desk (30 × 60 inches, laminated walnut, without a center drawer and without the slides, both of which would have been useful but which would have greatly increased the cost of this desk).

I really did not make the choice; it was made for me by circumstances, by the logic of my need, although within the constraints of available space and available cash or needs and

Figure 16-1 Computer and Regular Desk

possibilities. Those two factors—needs and possibilities—are or ought to be the sole factors controlling the decisions and choices. You start with needs and what you should have, ideally, for your needs. You then temper the ideal with what is possible or practicable and compromise accordingly. I would have liked to have a larger office, with more room for my books and papers, as well as a larger desk. I would have preferred a 72-inch desktop to the 60-inch desktop I have, but there was not enough room for that. I would have preferred a separate room, a study, for my library and files. But only one room, about 12 × 14 feet, is available for my use. I would have preferred several side chairs in my office. But there is room for only one side chair. I would like another file cabinet, or at least a larger one, but I settle for a small (two-drawer) one. I am a bit crowded with two printers. Most people settle for one. But I need two, so I do without some other things to enable me to have room for two printers.

Many people, perhaps most, keep their monitors placed atop the flat cabinet of the CPU (central processing unit, which is the computer proper). That is the arrangement you generally

Figure 16-2   *Special Computer Desk*

see in illustrations of computers. And perhaps its use of desk space is more efficient than the arrangement I have, in which I keep the monitor on the desk beside the CPU. But it is easier on me physically to have the monitor at eye level when I am seated at my desk, even when I am wearing reading glasses (as I must, when using the computer) instead of my usual trifocals. That is also a part of my need. You must consider your personal physical needs, your need to work in physical comfort, when you design and equip your office.

NOTHING IS PERMANENT

You will almost surely make changes in your physical arrangements after a while. Things rarely work out as you plan them. Initially, you will guess at your needs and the best arrangement. After a while you will begin to make adjustments, moving things around. You may even find it necessary to make drastic changes to the basic arrangement. That's quite normal; hardly anyone can predict how a given arrangement will work out over the long term. Your business needs will also change, as you gain experience and learn what works and does not work for you. You will be surprised, after a relatively short time, to find that you are not in quite the same business you planned and started.

I have made many changes over the years and have now achieved what I consider to be the best possible use of the space I have, now that I am reasonably settled and my writing and other activities are relatively stable: I have, within reach while I am seated at my desk, those two printers, several auxiliary devices for the computer (modem, surge resistors, buffer, A-B switch, and diskette storage cases), a telephone, a FAX machine, and my filing cabinet. I can turn my swivel chair and propel myself a couple feet across the room to my library of five bookcases. It is a relatively tight arrangement, but it is an efficient one, and it took some time to develop it and work out the details.

Still, I continue to make changes. I have been making changes recently that will enable me to make better use of my space. Those 5.25-inch floppy disks tend to proliferate wildly. (I think they breed like rabbits.) Soon they are everywhere. (By now, I am still struggling to find space to store over 500 of them.) But technology offers me at least a partial answer: First I added a 3.5-inch disk drive to my XT computer, but then I upgraded to an AT with a much larger hard disk. I am now converting most of my computer files to 3.5-inch disks because they are far more efficient and require much less physical space. (They are smaller physically and hold up to four times as much as the 5.25-inch disk.)

I also keep more stored on the big 65MB hard disk in my new AT computer. (Why did I ever think that the old 20MB hard disk was a big one or that the XT computer was fast?) My desk will be less crowded when the conversion is complete and I get rid of most of those larger disks and their cabinets.) My file cabinet will have more room available in it also. I have been slowly converting my paper files to computer disk files, gaining space there too. I have also been donating unused books to libraries. I hate to part with books, as most bibliophiles do, but I need the space. Necessity must rule. Working at home, even at a profession you love as I love writing, is a business with practical necessities. Attending faithfully to these necessities is what enables you to continue doing the work you love.

SOME SPACE-SAVING DEVICES FOR YOUR COMPUTER

You may not need to use a computer all day in your work, as I do, so perhaps you need to and can use your main desktop differently: If you will use a computer and printer only part of the time, perhaps only to keep your books and prepare invoices, you can turn to a space-conserving computer desk that enables you to store your computer and printer out of the way when you are not using them.

There are a number of space savers you can resort to (see Figure 16-3). One is mounting your CPU on end, rather than flat, and you do not have to have the CPU on your desk; it can be on the floor, alongside your desk. The CPU will operate as well on end as it will laid flat, and many people do operate their computers in that position. (In fact, some recent model computers, referred to as "towers," are specifically designed to be operated in that position as their normal mode.) If you find the CPU a bit unsteady so mounted, you can get a special stand designed to hold it in that position. Such stands, in plastic or metal, are readily available from suppliers.

You can also get a keyboard drawer that gives you a place to slide the keyboard away, freeing desktop space. Some models are designed to be fitted under your computer or monitor; others

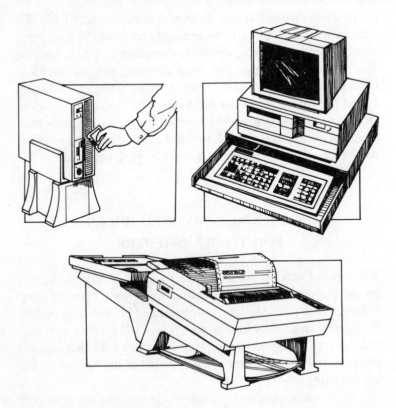

Figure 16-3   *Space-Saving Accessories*

are designed to be fitted on the underside of your desktop where some desks have a center drawer. And a pivoting shelf for your monitor is also available that enables you to swing your monitor out of the way when it is not in use. There are also space-saving printer stands, both table top and free standing, which enable you to store your printer paper under the printer. These are available in both plastic and metal models. I found it necessary to use such a stand for my second printer, if I were to have the printer positioned where I could reach it easily while seated at my desk doing my work.

Computers and their accessories—printers, modems, buffers, and other such items—almost always have their on-off switches on their back panels or on a side panel near the back of the item. That positioning is, presumably, a safeguard against your shutting down a unit accidentally and losing data. Unfortunately, it is also something of a nuisance: It makes the switches relatively inaccessible and forces you to reach around the units and fumble for the unseen switches when you want to turn the unit on. Many users overcome that problem, while accomplishing another necessary function, by installing a surge resistor, which is connected to the wall outlet, and into which are plugged all your units. There are several types of surge resistor available. Some of them have a master switch, and some have individual switches for each outlet.

All surge resistors provide the same main function of protecting the equipment against the occasional surges of current and voltage peaks that occur in any power system, especially during an electrical storm. Modern electronic chips are highly sensitive to overloads, and easily destroyed by electrical surges and short circuits that might do damage. When one of these occurs, overloading a circuit, the surge resistor triggers an overload protection device (a type of circuit breaker) shutting off the current entirely.

I use two different types of surge protectors (see Figure 16-4). One is a flat cabinet type with four outlets, three of which have their own switches on the front in addition to a master switch and indicator light, also in front. That gives me control switches for my computer, monitor, printer, and modem,

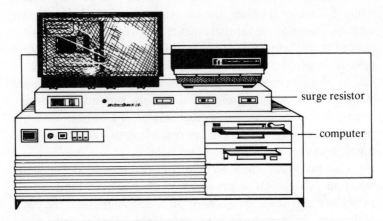

surge resistor

computer

Figure 16-4 *Surge Resistors with Power Controls*

conveniently located in front. When I ran out of outlets as I continued to add equipment, I turned to another type, an outlet strip with six outlets, a master switch, and an indicator lamp. I have a second printer and a buffer connected to this one, with three outlets remaining for other accessories I may buy in the future.

FAX MACHINES

FAX (facsimile) machines are not new, but there have been two new developments in the field of FAX machines: They have been greatly improved (the current Group 3 machines are superior in performance to the older Group 2 machines), and they have been greatly reduced in price. Or, perhaps more accurately, many more affordable (lower-priced) models are being produced today, and the popularity of FAX machines has suddenly assumed the proportions of a national fad. Whether this phenomenon is the cause or the result of the sudden public awareness of and demand for FAX machines is unclear, but probably the recent dramatic advances in computer and chip technology were a major factor in making better FAX machines available at lower costs than in the past—in other words, making

FAX machines practicable for small offices, as well as for large ones. Certainly, it is a logical development in this day of the demand for rapid communication, the steady decline in the efficiency and reliability of postal services, and the high cost of overnight express services.

FAX machines transmit over telephone lines. You must therefore have your FAX connected to a dial-up telephone line. If, however, you wish your FAX to be in AUTO mode at all times so that it is always ready to receive messages, you will have to have another line dedicated to it. The advantage of this feature is that most FAX machines can be programmed to send messages at night, when telephone rates are lowest.

FAX machines are rapidly becoming standard equipment in even the smallest offices as are typewriters, telephones, computers, and copiers. (FAX machines themselves provide a copying function, although of lesser capability than full-blown office copiers.) In Japan, it has been reported, the machines are so popular that people are installing them in their homes for private use. They may turn out to be popular as answering machines eventually.

You have two options in FAX machines today: You can get a standalone FAX machine, the most popular option by far. That is a completely self-contained unit that can correspond with (send to and receive from) any other FAX machine and can be installed and operated by anyone with instruction as simple as that needed for an office copier. Most of today's FAX machines are compatible with the older Group 2 FAX machines as well as with Group 3 machines, although it is not too likely that you will ever run into Group 2 machines: There were not that many of them in use, to begin with, and many who had those machines are changing over to the newer FAX technology by buying one of today's Group 3 machines. So the compatibility with Group 2 machines is probably of minor importance.

The quality of reproduction by FAX machines is not that of modern office copiers, although a somewhat improved quality, at the cost of slower transmission, is available. All except the most expensive models reproduce copy on thermal (specially treated) paper rather than ordinary paper. (You may recall that many office copiers of a few years ago used such paper.) Prices range widely, starting with list prices of $900 for the popular Murata M1200 model and running to well in excess of $3,000 for the most elaborate models.

FAX machines come with telephone handsets, which can be used as ordinary telephones. In most of the simplest and least expensive models, you must lift the handset and dial the number of the FAX machine you wish to send to. The more expensive machines provide a capability for dialing without lifting the handset and usually offer a means to store frequently called numbers for automatic dialing. They also provide automatic paper cutoff (most machines use paper in a continuous roll) and other convenience features. The quality of the copy is not affected by any of these features, however, although Group 4 machines, the FAX of the future, promise better quality of reproduction, using plain paper.

The more expensive FAX machines have sheet feeders that can handle five or more sheets of paper input automatically, whereas the less expensive machines must be fed sheets individually by hand.

Like so many high-tech products today, FAX machines are heavily discounted by many dealers. The Murata M1200, for example, is commonly offered at prices ranging from about $650 to $750 and has been advertised as low as $595. Most others are available at similar discounts of 10 to 30 percent below the listed price.

What you need in a FAX machine is determined primarily by how you will use it. If you use it only occasionally and usually to send only a sheet or two, it is hardly worth the extra cost of a sheet feeder and automatic dialing, for example. You must study all the available options and weigh them against your needs and projected probable usage.

THE FAX BOARD OPTION

It is possible to use your computer as a FAX machine by installing a FAX board in it. FAX boards are less costly than standalone FAX machines, starting at approximately $350. But there are some limitations. One is that you must have a modem, a device that enables you to transmit and receive computer signals to and from another computer or, in this case, to and from a FAX machine or FAX board in another computer. (Telephones are designed to send and respond to audible signals, and computer signals are not audible; the modem there converts computer signals to audible tones for telephone transmission, and audible tones to computer signals to receive transmissions.)

Another limitation of the FAX board is that you can send only what is in your computer and you receive the same way, so that you must print out a hard copy if you want a copy on paper. In some respects that is an advantage, for it improves the quality of reproduction to whatever quality your printer can turn out.

A possible drawback is that you must leave your computer on at all times (although some computer owners do so anyway, under the theory that the computer is less likely to develop trouble if never turned off—a theory with considerable technical and experiential justification) if you want it to automatically accept any message addressed to you at any time. Too, it is not nearly as simple to use as a standalone FAX machine: Sending information from your computer requires a little more skill (computer-using skill, that is) than using a standalone machine.

Whether a FAX board is more or less useful than a standalone FAX machine depends primarily on the uses you expect to make of FAX facilities. If what you send to others will almost invariably be composed by you on your computer, the FAX board is more convenient: You need not print the material out to send it, as you would if you were using a standalone FAX machine, of course. Likewise, if what is sent to you is always text, it is no great inconvenience to receive it via your computer. But there are two other options open to you, if you expect to require a FAX capability only rarely. One is a FAX service offered by CompuServe, but that is useful only for sending a FAX, not for receiving one, and requires that you be a CompuServe subscriber. The other is the use of a public FAX service, something that is springing up rapidly everywhere, in neighborhood copy shops, express shipping services, and other such convenience services. In fact,

252 THE COMPLETE WORK-AT-HOME COMPANION

coin-operated FAX machines have already been installed in public places where public pay telephones are in place, and they will probably proliferate widely in the near future.

HOME OFFICE FURNISHINGS AND SUPPLIES

The furniture you need will vary with the kind of business you conduct, of course. You may need a large work table, a drafting board, book cases, desks, filing cabinets, flat files, credenzas, or any of many other items. On the assumption that you are experienced in whatever work your business normally requires, I assume that you will know precisely what you need. Even so, some general advice that you may find helpful follows.

Buy Everything Conservatively

It is reasonable to assume that space and money are both limited for your start-up. Therefore, as I have stressed, buy the smallest number of each necessary item at first. Also, bear your space limitations in mind. If you need a work table, consider whether you will be working at it all day or only occasionally. Perhaps, for example, you should get a light folding table, one that can be stored away when not needed, rather than a heavy-duty table.

There are drafting tables and drafting tables: They vary widely in size and price. Perhaps a small, folding one will do you nicely.

Desks vary even more widely in size and cost. It's easy to spend a thousand dollars or more for a desk. But you can do the same work of the same quality for the same price and with the same comfort at a $150 or $200 desk. (We started with the most makeshift desks you can imagine!)

But do get a good chair, if you are going to spend a lot of time sitting in it. Try out chairs in showrooms and don't let anyone pressure you into buying a chair that is not completely comfortable for you. The human back is not well designed, the scientists tell us, so you must cater to it a bit. Save money on the desk, but don't save it on the chair at the cost of your back!

Filing cabinets are sized in two ways: by the number of drawers—from one to five, usually—and by the width of the drawers, which are "regular" size or "legal" size. The latter refers to drawers that accommodate 13- or 14-inch folders. But even the legal profession is turning to 11-inch paper and files today, so consider that question carefully: Try to get along with the regular size.

Apply the same conservatism to the purchase of all your equipment and supplies. Let's review some of the things you are likely to need, no matter what your business.

Equipment

You almost surely need a desktop computer today if you want to operate efficiently, but because Chapter 18 will address the use of the computer especially (in light of its importance), we won't dwell on it here, other than to note the need for a good one.

Of course, you need a telephone, and although you may prefer to get one from the telephone company, there are a great many models available commercially with desirable features at modest costs. You will probably find it useful to have a speaker phone, one that you can use for hands-free dialing and talking and for conference calls. It is especially useful when someone has you on "hold," because you can continue to work at something useful while waiting. A telephone with automatic dialing is a time saver, too.

You need telephone service, and there are a number of useful options you may or may not know about. There is *call waiting*, which beeps you to let you know someone else is trying to call you while your line is busy. You can take the call without losing the call you are on. There is *call forwarding*, which forwards your call to another number, if you wish. There is *three-way calling*, enabling you to carry on conversation with two people at the same time. (*Conference calls* enable you to talk to any number of people in a conference hookup.) These services may all be available in your area, or they may not be. You will have to check with your own telephone company.

You may need an answering machine of some sort, if your office is not attended consistently by someone all day. You can use an answering service, if you prefer, and have a live person take calls when you are out of the office, but it is more expensive and not necessarily more satisfactory. Besides, you may wish to encourage others to FAX messages to you, and to use the FAX to leave messages for them. In many ways, FAX is more economical than voice conversation, for at least two reasons: (1) The on-line time is usually quite brief when you send a FAX, and (2) you can program the FAX to be sent at night, when rates are lowest, so the other party can read it first thing in the morning. Actually, there is a third consideration: With FAX, you have fewer wasted calls because the message gets through whether the other party is in or not, and the message is in writing, not entrusted to a secretary's memory.

The FAX machine is an especially important piece of equipment today, for reasons already discussed at some length.

Copiers are probably one of the most frequently used and most indispensable office items in common use today. A FAX machine does provide some limited copying capability, but the copy is on specially treated thermal paper, unless you happen to have one of the expensive models that use plain paper. That means that the image may fade, with time, so the copies are not suitable for permanent records. Too, the copiers copy only single sheets, not bound books or other bound documents, and are not at all suitable for making multiple copies or long runs of copying. Bear all these needs and applications in mind when reviewing and evaluating copier models. You want to be as conservative as possible in buying a copier, but the copier that does not do the job you need done is no bargain at any price.

Supplies

Typical office supplies include paper, pens and pencils, stationery, envelopes, file folders, paper clips, typewriter ribbons, printer ribbons, computer disks, postage stamps (or a postage meter, if you do heavy mailing), memo pads, rulers, templates, and a miscellany of other such items. You can buy these locally in most cities and towns, but you can also usually save a great deal of money by buying from mail-order houses, if you use any of these in quantity.

Buy everything on the premise that your starting plan is tentative, that you are going to try out a lot of business ideas you have and find out which work as you hope and which do not. (Few businesses remain what they were at the start; the big question is not whether there will be changes, but what the changes will be and how soon they will take place.) In short, the nature of your business will probably change and with it, your needs will change. It is wise, therefore, to commit yourself to only those things you almost surely will need because every office needs them. Actually, if you have a good computer and printer, you can postpone buying any stationery but envelopes and business cards; it is quite easy to print your letterheads, as you go. Figure 16-5 is a sample of the simple letterhead I use most frequently, although not the only one I use. (It is simple, indeed, because I prefer it that way, but it is quite easy to make it more ornate, if you wish.) The ability to make and use more than one letterhead is one of the several advantages of this approach. And if your equipment is first class, the letterhead appears to have been formally printed by conventional printing methods.

Sources of Supply

As the popularity of the office at home has grown and spread, it has inspired many businesses to direct and dedicate their marketing efforts specifically to support of the home office market. More than a few of these have an orientation centered on the computer and its peripheral devices as the hub of the office at home. Crutchfield (1 Crutchfield Park, Charlottesville, VA 22906) is one of these, publishing the Crutchfield Personal Office catalog semiannually. The issue in front of me, Spring/ Summer 1989, is heavily illustrated, covers computers, printers, accessories, software, and dedicated word processors (machines that are more than automatic typewriters, and yet do not quite qualify as computers), plus FAX machines, copiers, calculators, and calculatorlike devices identified as "personal

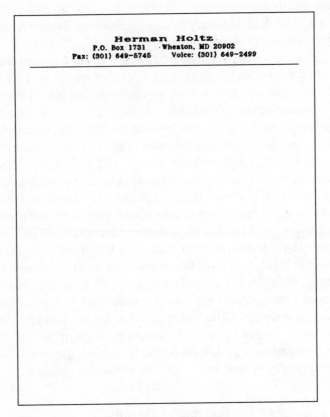

Figure 16-5   Example of Simple "Home-Made" Letterhead

organizers." Crutchfield, however, has a computer service department and devotes a generous portion of its 42-page catalog to explaining those services and providing some generally useful information about computers. It is a catalog worth having.

When it comes to catalogs and computers, however, the all-time champion in that department is a monthly magazine titled *Computer Shopper*, which contains so much advertising that it is more like a catalog with useful articles and news about computers than the computer magazine with advertising that it actually is. *Computer Shopper* is big in more than one way. For one thing, it is a large format, 10 × 13 inches. And it grows steadily. The issue I am looking at now contains 656 of those 10 × 13 pages, the majority of them offering mail-order sales of just about any computer-related product or service that might interest you.

In a large sense, this is an incredible success story, for the publishing experts (alleged experts, that is) sneered at the idea of this publication originally, predicting prompt failure for it. (Predictions are always hazardous to make and even more hazardous to accept blindly, no matter who makes them. True experts are well aware of that and are therefore usually slow to make absolute statements of that sort.) In fact, the early issues *were* pretty crude, with writing and editing that reflected the struggling start-up. Still, the idea was basically sound, so the magazine caught on and today is greatly improved editorially and cosmetically as well. Incidentally, the publishers are well aware that most of their advertisers are selling readers via mail order, so they have published guidelines for buying by mail.

The sources described here and others are listed in Part 5.

Chapter Seventeen

When You Need Help

No one in the business world,
not even the entrepreneur
or the freelancer, can be
entirely self-sufficient.

IS THERE SUCH A THING AS A ONE-PERSON ENTERPRISE?

I am a self-made man. I made whatever success I managed to achieve all alone, all by myself, against the odds, fighting upstream, etc., ad nauseam. Or so I like to believe. It is a human failing to dramatize our early struggles and persuade ourselves that we did it all on our own; it is probably a great boon to our egos to believe so. Anyone who struggled a bit more, or even a great deal more, than most people to find his or her niche in life, likes especially to indulge in that nonsense. And it is nonsense, of course. Even those who found life an exceptionally grim struggle to survive and succeed and who managed to do so did not do it without occasional help of some sort.

We tend to forget this fact, and we carry the fancy over. Like many others, I like to think that I "do it all" myself even today. In recent years I have become a freelance writer of books primarily, but I still find time to do some magazine writing, some consulting and custom writing, and occasional lecturing. It's a busy schedule, of course, and it means that I am not quite a one-man business; I need help frequently. I sometimes need an illustrator or a photographer, because I am no illustrator and I am of highly questionable merit as a photographer. Sometimes I need an expert to answer questions and provide information, or merely to offer me another opinion. Sometimes I need the services of a lawyer, an accountant, or a computer expert. And I always need the help of editors and other publishing experts to turn my clumsy manuscripts into handsomely bound books.

I need help also with things I am technically capable of doing but do not have the time to do myself. If I undertake a custom-writing task of great size, such as a large proposal effort, I need to call on others for help. I am fortunate that my wife handles the bookkeeping for me, or I would be forced to find someone to do that also.

It is a rare venture that you can truly run alone today. Almost certainly you will need help at least occasionally, as I do. It is a healthy state of mind to recognize and acknowledge that need, as it is a distinct hazard to your success to try to do everything yourself. Even then, you are likely to discover that it is not at all easy to find outside help with complete satisfaction. There is, however, some wisdom to be gleaned from others' experience, and we will explore that wisdom in this chapter. We will not discuss two people that you almost certainly need, a lawyer and an accountant, because we discussed those professionals and their services earlier.

TEMPORARIES

All kinds of temporary employees are available today, starting with office temporaries—for example, the famous "Kelly Girls"—but including all kinds of other services, which we will discuss.

Office Temporaries

Typists and clerical help are generally easy to get by calling any of the many "office temporaries" services you find listed in the yellow pages. The problem is, however, that you have no idea of how skilled an individual you will get until he or she arrives and starts to work. Most of those who use such help frequently always note the names of the best temporaries they get and ask for them by name after that. In time, you can develop a roster of office temporaries most acceptable to you and always request those workers if they are available.

Technical/Professional Temporaries

Many companies today provide a broad assortment of technical specialists for temporary assignments. These include engineers of all sorts—electronic, mechanical, stress, chemical, civil, aeronautical, and marine, among others—but also various kinds of scientists, technical writers, computer programmers, computer operators, maintenance technicians, system analysts, draftsmen and -women, illustrators, proposal writers, designers, photographers, and sundry other specialists of professional and subprofessional classes.

At least one firm supplies lawyers on a temporary basis and has no difficulty in finding lawyers interested in working on that basis. There are no precedents for this kind of temporary, but it is not out of keeping with what is happening generally.

There are services supplying nurses and nurses' aids as temporaries. This is a fairly common service, one that can be run by telephone from home.

The Working Arrangements

You can use temporaries for long or short periods—a few days or many months. Some large corporations have kept temporaries working on their premises for years at a time, as have some federal government agencies. Usually, both the provider of the service and the individual workers want to know the estimated length of the assignment.

It's a rather novel arrangement because, although the individual is nominally your temporary employee, directed by you, technically he or she is actually the employee of the service provider and is on the service provider's payroll. You do not pay the individual, therefore; you pay the individual's employer an hourly rate. You may also have to pay a subsistence or per diem allowance, if specialists have to be brought in from out of town, a not unusual situation.

If a temporary worker is not satisfactory, you are free to cut that person's employment short and request a replacement. Usually, however, you will have stated rather specifically what experience, capabilities, and other qualifications you require. Even in those categories I have named there are many specialties: Electronics engineers and electronics technical writers, for example, usually specialize in radar, communications, computers, other digital equipment, satellites, missiles, maintenance systems, or any of many other highly specialized fields. You will usually have requested and been given the resumes of applicants and may even interview them, if you wish to. (In the case of higher-level people, such as engineers and technical writers, this kind of screening is usually done.) You thus pick the people you want after verifying that they appear to have the qualifications you seek.

In terms of cost, you will pay the service provider an hourly rate that is substantially higher than the hourly rate you would pay a direct employee doing the same job. The differential will be, probably, as high as 40 or 50 percent, and even more in many cases. You have no significant overhead on such "employees," however, for you spend nothing to recruit them, you have no fringe benefits or taxes to pay, and you pay them no severance when you terminate their services, so you are not really paying any more than if they were direct, and possibly even saving money. The service provider is also paying the individual more than he or she might earn as a direct employee but furnishing only rudimentary fringe benefits and carrying an overhead of about 32 to 35 percent. This policy gives the provider a modest profit.

The providers of such temporary technical/professional labor are commonly referred to as *job shops*, and the people they provide to their clients as temporaries then become *job shoppers*. These terms, it must be noted, are used somewhat derisively in the industry, very much in the manner of soldiers jeering at themselves and at what they do. Understandably, the service providers themselves don't use the terms, at least not on the record. They tend much more to company names designating *technical services*, *designers*, *engineers*, and *consultants* or derivatives therefrom. And, in fact, *consultants* is not at all inappropriate as a descriptor.

INDEPENDENT CONSULTANTS

Independent consultants often work as technical/professional temporaries, but they serve as their own service providers, contracting directly with you for their services on whatever basis you both find acceptable. But there are some background circumstances you ought to understand here.

A great many job shoppers enter that field only temporarily because they are between jobs and need temporary employment. They stay for a few months, perhaps a year or two, but leave the market when the opportunity arises to join a company with an acceptable permanent position.

On the other hand, many job shoppers like the life. It's a gypsy life because a job shopper never really knows how long a job will last or where the next job will be. The "professional job shopper," that person who prefers temporary and would never "go direct" (become someone's permanent employee, which he or she regards as heresy), travels the country and even the world, for many foreign assignments are available. Most of these people work for the various job shops as the occasions and needs arise. (Job shopping for less than two years, I was the employee of three different job shops, assigned to three different major high-tech corporations and projects.) As soon as they settle into an assignment, they update their rèsumés and get copies out to all the job shops so that the shops know where to reach them with offers of new assignments.

A few of these worldly travelers strike out as independents after they have worked as job shoppers long enough to understand the entire business and know and become well known to many regular users of job shoppers. They start making direct deals with client companies, contracting directly for their own services. And they tend to continue in the mold of the job shop industry, quoting their rates on an hourly basis, with overtime (time and a half and double time) rates specified, and payment on a weekly basis requested or, at least, preferred. Those are norms in that industry.

Other independent consultants, in contrast, who have never job-shopped and don't even know the industry exists. They are usually technical or professional experts in some field who are not positioned to work on site but are quite willing, nevertheless, to work on either the client's premises or their own. By the nature of what they do, however, they are often called on to work on the client's premises. And so they are doing essentially the same thing the job shopper is doing, augmenting the client's staff temporarily. They have become, at least for the moment, independent job shoppers, even if unknowingly!

The difference is, primarily, that frequently this consultant has no notion of the concept of job shopping and probably sets entirely different terms for his or her services. He or she may be willing to work by the assignment—on a flat fee for the job—or by the week or month, rather than by the hour, and he or she may want to sign some kind of agreement with you and may want a retainer or substantial deposit in advance, a common practice.

What Should You Expect?

The advantages of using such help for work overload relief and other temporary needs go beyond those already enumerated. The new regular employee is normally expected to require some time (perhaps a week or two, at least) to become oriented to his or her new job and become a full contributor to the work of the organization. Most employers accept this break-in period as a necessity. But the true consultant or job shopper is expected to be an experienced specialist who can launch full scale into the work and become productive immediately. That is the kind of capability for which you are being charged, and you have the right to expect it. You need settle for no less, and you should not settle for less.

Moonlighters and Other Part-Timers

There have always been *moonlighters*, usually people with full-time jobs, housewives, or students who work evenings and weekends to earn some extra money. Some work at the same kind of things they do in their regular jobs; others work at different kinds of tasks. Sometimes a daytime sales clerk is an excellent night-time artist, or a full-time engineer is a good part-time writer.

There have also always been *part-timers*, such as workers who are not available on a full-time basis and retired persons who do not want to work full time but are available during normal business hours.

As usual, there are tradeoffs in using moonlight and part-time help. The pros are that you may save money, for one thing. Because moonlighters do not ordinarily depend on their moonlight work for their main income, they often work for lower rates of pay than they earn in their regular jobs. Part-timers, too, often tend to ask for rather modest rates of pay. For some, the money is secondary in any case because they are moonlighting for special reasons, such as gaining experience to help them break into another field on a full-time basis. Sometimes it is much more convenient for you to have people working at night, over weekends, and on holidays. In fact, perhaps that is the only time you can provide them with space and facilities to do the work. And, of course, perhaps your business cannot afford full-time help as yet.

There are also cons in using these kinds of workers. People who do not depend on their jobs for survival find it easy to decide, on the spur of a sudden desire, to watch TV or go out to a show and therefore not show up for work. And they may or may not call and tell you that they will not be there. This, the questionable dependability of some moonlight and part-time workers, is a most definite hazard, and it is a serious one when you are depending on the help to meet an important commitment.

Another hazard concerns capability and competence: You may find these traits less than optimum in help you hire casually—if, indeed, you hire moonlighters and part-timers any more casually than you would hire a permanent full-time employee. There is a distinct tendency, perhaps an unconscious one, for most of us to do just this because we know that we are not making a major commitment. But you must guard against it, for hiring inept help may have disastrous consequences.

Consultant Versus Job Shopper

There is a potential problem for you in hiring any extra help, whether moonlight, part-time, job shoppers, or consultants. Because you are working in an office in your home, it will probably be highly impractical for you to provide work space for temporary employees, even on a moonlight basis. Most independent consultants who are not professional job shoppers have their own offices and facilities, often in their own homes, in fact, and so it is usually not absolutely necessary to provide them with office facilities. On the other hand, job shoppers, moonlighters, and part-timers rarely have suitable working facilities of their own. That alone may be a major consideration for you in seeking help. Usually, the independent consultant will charge you the same rates without regard to whether or not he or she works on your premises, for the consultant's overhead is not really affected by the location of the work. (In fact, it may be higher when working on your premises because daily travel is required.)

Another Alternative

One more option is available to you. Depending on need and circumstances, it may be more practical or more efficient to send the work out to be done than to bring someone in to do it. The telephone yellow pages list thousands of individuals and organizations who satisfy thousands of kinds of needs. If you have the idea that you need someone to design a cover for a training manual, you can turn that notion around and send the cover out to be designed at some local graphic arts establishment. If you need to have someone make up a direct-mail package or draft a campaign plan, those things can be done by outside specialists as well as by on-site consultants. And they do not even have to be local firms. You can have work done via mail, telephone, and FAX communication easily enough.

SUGGESTED PROTECTIVE PRACTICES

There are hazards in all business dealings. The graphic arts shop with its luxurious offices and beautiful brochures may not do as good a job as the amateur illustrator you hire. Or they may do a good job but hand you a staggering bill for it. No matter how or where you get help, you need to protect yourself against incompetence, chicanery, and plain dishonesty, for all exist in superabundance and you can protect yourself against them only with positive preventive measures.

Defining the Need

The first step is always defining the need. Otherwise you probably will lay yourself open to a commitment to pay someone an undefined amount for undefined work and undefined results. That is not as ridiculous as it may sound, for it does happen. If you are not absolutely clear in your own mind about just what it is that you need and want, you are likely to charge someone with doing something so vaguely specified that the other winds up doing what he or she prefers to do. The result is almost inevitably a dispute. (In large projects, where this occurs, too, the result often is to wind up in court, fighting a lawsuit.)

Admittedly, it is not always easy to define your need with any greatly detailed specificity. Part of your need may well be for help in defining your end need. But if that is the case, you must recognize that you need help in defining just what it is that you must have. (Experienced consultants know that quite often their first task in any assignment is to help the client identify and define his or her need.) Suppose, for example, you need illustrations drawn for a manual. You can leave it entirely to the illustrator to decide how to illustrate the manual, but there is an excellent chance that you will not be happy with the results. You must specify what is to be illustrated and suggest how you want it done. This will probably require that you have made some notes in advance and that you and the illustrator go over the manual and your notes, refining the notes until you have at least a brief word description of each illustration and a decision on whether it is to be a cartoon, a line sketch, a wash drawing, or other type of drawing. The illustrator must help you with definitions and suggestions, of course, but the final decisions will always be yours. (It need not necessarily be the illustrator who advises and helps you in this area, either; it may well be a publications expert or consultant in that field.)

You would probably be well advised to ask the illustrator to make up two or three rough sketches first, so that you can choose one. In fact, many illustrators will do that without being prompted to. But it is a good idea to make sure to ask for the sketches explicitly.

All this ought to be without a final commitment, if you do not know the illustrator and his or her work. You need to first see a sample or two *prepared especially for you*. General samples are meaningless; you know nothing about how they came into existence. You can judge properly only by seeing samples of work prepared for you to your specifications.

The matter of costs can be a trap for the unwary. I have a built-in reluctance to charging and being charged by the hour. If you hire someone by the hour to do a job and he or she happens to be a very slow worker, you pay more than the job is worth. You should not suffer because a worker is excessively slow or because he or she is not properly equipped and therefore uses archaic tools and methods. Moreover, agreeing to a fixed hourly rate tends to result in almost a blank check for the worker. And if the work is to be done on the worker's premises and not on yours, it is even more difficult to be sure that your interests are properly protected. On the other hand, I have no desire to pay a well-equipped, good worker less than the job is worth.

To resolve this dilemma and avoid these problems—and because so many consultants and others are conditioned to think in hourly rates—I recommend that you first discuss with the individual how long it ought to take a competent person to do the job defined and negotiate the time required until you are both satisfied that it is a reasonable standard. Once you are agreed on the time required, you can negotiate the schedule and the rate. If the schedule is a difficult one, requiring a crash effort, that may affect the rate, and so the schedule needs to be agreed on also.

When you have reached an agreement on both time and rate, you can easily calculate the price for the job. You can then make a fixed-price agreement. That protects both of you. If the illustrator, who has agreed to the time and rates, refuses to do the job on the basis of that fixed price, you should seek another illustrator.

I negotiated a contract in this manner once with a house-wife who was a part-time artist, and we agreed on $400 for the job in this manner. The work, when she delivered it—much behind schedule—was acceptable, but barely so. I did not consider it to be of true professional quality, but it would serve my need. She launched into an explanation of how difficult the work was and told me that her husband had ordered her to ask for more money, $700, because the work took longer than estimated. I refused to pay any more, of course. It was precisely to avoid this situation that I had negotiated the original contract. The problem was that she was not yet fully proficient, but that was her problem, not mine.

Estimates seem always to have a way of escalating, if a ceiling is not established. In my own consulting, I use the same method. I state a day rate and an estimated number of days required, and I then sign a contract guaranteeing not to exceed that amount, unless the conditions specified originally change. In that event, I renegotiate with the client. I have never had a problem over price with a client, which leads me to believe that it is a proper system.

When the Need Is Difficult to Define

There are situations where it is extremely difficult or perhaps actually impossible to estimate the hours required with any accuracy or even to define a need absolutely until a great deal of preliminary work has been done. This is the kind of situation that inspires the cost-plus and other such open-ended contracts let by government agencies and sometimes by corporations. And even they often install safeguards to avoid handing the contractor a blank check via a vague and carelessly written contract. The small, home-based business can even less afford that hazard.

There are two ways of coping successfully with this kind of situation. One is to let a preliminary contract, the chief purpose of which is to identify and define the need precisely. Such a study or "front-end analysis" is not an uncommon measure taken to cope with this kind of situation. Governments and other organizations often have studies performed before attempting to issue contracts, and contracting organizations in certain kinds of custom work, such as the development of training plans and materials, often perform what they commonly call a *task analysis*. The end product of this analysis is a detailed report and plan, including specific objectives and an outline of the product to be developed. The client may then use the report/plan as the basis for a project to be carried out in house or to be let to a contractor—not necessarily the same one.

The alternative approach is similar, except that the commitment to the follow-up work and the contractor to do the work is fixed in advance, so the analysis is authorized as the first phase and the second phase can begin only when the client has reviewed the first-phase results and authorized the remaining work to begin.

There are pros and cons to each approach. The first approach is more costly because a completely separate procurement must be made for the follow-up or final work. It also gives the contractor for the analysis a motive to shade the work and report in his or her own favor. But it allows the client (you) a maximum of freedom, and in some cases you may not wish to decide about the second phase until you have seen the results of the analysis. And it may be in your interest to split the phases into two distinctly separate contracts and disqualify the first-phase contractor from bidding for the second phase, as government agencies often do. That not only helps keep the first-phase contractor more objective, it is also more fair to those bidding for the second contract because the first contractor would almost inevitably have an advantage over others.

NEGOTIATIONS AND CONTRACTS

Negotiating successfully is a fine art, requiring many skills, not the least of which is good judgment. But before discussing what negotiating is, let's note two things that, probably contrary to popular opinion, it is *not*:

- It is not a battle of wits, although one should have his or her wits about him- or herself.
- It is not a struggle to mislead, distract, take advantage of, defraud, or otherwise exploit the other party unmercifully.

A platitude about negotiation has it that a successful negotiation is one in which each party is satisfied that he or she got what he or she wanted. The fact that this is a platitude does not make it less true or less wise an observation. Incidentally, you may substitute the word *contract* for the word *negotiation* and the statement will be equally true. Try that substitution in other statements about negotiation that follow.

The inverse of that platitude is also true: A negotiation that leaves one party unhappy and feeling that he or she was bludgeoned into agreement spells almost certain trouble for the future of anything that results from that negotiation. It will prove to have been a bad bargain for both parties, in all probability, as the aggrieved party makes efforts to "get well," recovering in some manner from a bad bargain.

The most astute negotiator I have ever known and negotiated with personally was a government contracting officer who firmly believed these principles. He was also acutely aware that as the customer he was in a position to dominate the negotiation and force disagreeable terms on the contractor. He was determined to refrain from doing that. Rather, he probed constantly to see what conditions the contractor would yield on most readily. That gave him a clue about what the contractor's throwaway items were. (Most experienced contractors do include such items in their proposals, to be used as bargaining chips.) He also noted what items were most important to the contractor. And it was where he encountered steely resistance but felt he could not himself yield much that the most serious negotiations took place. In those areas he tried hard to engineer a fair trade, one that would satisfy the contractor. Finally, at the conclusion of the negotiation, he asked the important question: "Are you satisfied to conclude this now and settle on this agreement, or are you still hurting badly somewhere?" In a display of complete fairness, he was ready to discuss any remaining sore points. And it was probably his image of open and fair trading, as much as anything else, that helped keep contractors satisfied that they had received fair treatment and had a "good" contract.

One objective of negotiation is to test the validity of the other party's terms. If you are negotiating with someone who has provided you with a proposal, you have a beginning set of terms; otherwise, he or she has or will state them verbally. But you need to test those terms for their technical validity and for the validity of how accurately they reflect the proposer's sincere intent and desire.

You will probably begin with those items of greatest concern to you or those about which you are somewhat skeptical. The need for the various steps, functions, materials, or other expenses listed is always a matter for discussion and verification. Maybe there can be a good bit of cost cutting in some areas without losing anything important. (Or perhaps the contractor is "fattening his part," as they say in show business.) The schedule is a matter of concern: Does the contractor guarantee the schedule? And so the negotiation normally reviews anything about which you question the need, the scope, and the importance to the contractor.

Costs are usually the last item to be discussed, except as they come up incidentally in discussion of other items. As a negotiator, you want to be sure that the costs are fully justified, and you want to minimize as much as possible without jeopardizing the work.

(Of course, it is useful to bear all this in mind when you are the proposer, as you may well be.)

Chapter Eighteen

The Role of the Computer

*We all start in a state of
ignorance; how could it be
otherwise? But ignorance is
always curable, and now is
always the right time to begin.*

WHAT HATH DIGITAL TECHNOLOGY WROUGHT?

A great many people believe that the desktop computer, also originally known as the personal computer, was the chief inspiration for the enormous surge in popularity of home-based businesses. Sarah Edwards, coauthor (with her husband Paul) of the popular *Working from Home* (Los Angeles: Jeremy P. Tarcher, 1987), estimates that 26 million people work from home.* The two Edwardses, acknowledged experts in the home office field, host the *Home Office Show* on the public database, CompuServe, and write a regular column each month for *Home Office Computing* magazine, among other related activities. They were among the early advocates of the use of the new computers for home-based business activities.

"Tips and Ideas," *Sharing Ideas*, June/July 1989.

Whether the new computers were or were not the sole or main inspiration for the great surge in setting up home offices, they were certainly a substantial contributor and remain a pervasive influence. This newcomer, the desktop computer, has become a ubiquitous element: Millions of small home offices boast at least one computer, many more than one. But there are many more millions of small home offices that do not yet benefit from this now almost indispensable asset. Nor is cost the bar to its ownership and use that it was a few years ago; it is now possible to have a serviceable entry-level computer for what amounts to little more than a week's wages for many middle-class workers. Fear is more an inhibiting factor than cost: The high-tech image that computers carry as part of their baggage is far more intimidating to many than is their cost. People are intimidated by technology itself and by the reputation of the computer as a "smart" machine. And yet, though properly in awe of cousin Amy's ability to use her own home computer with ease, most people do not admit to being less bright than cousin Amy. Irrational? Yes, but that's the way we humans are.

There is even a secondary fear. Observe the average adult at the computer keyboard for the first time, gingerly pressing on the keys, in obvious fear that a wrong move will result in a grinding noise and a puff of smoke emanating from the machine.

That ought to be a fear easily overcome. It is virtually impossible to do harm to a computer by pressing the wrong keys. Computers are "trained" to come to a halt and usually to issue a message to the user that operations are suspended for the moment. But aside from that, if you are one of those who dread a confrontation with this awesome creature, pay close attention: These machines are becoming more and more tractable. (Happily, no one uses that awful term "user friendly" any more.) But the real problem—that is, the real cause of so many people's fear and trembling at the mere thought of confronting these blinking beasts—is ignorance, which is primarily the result of the technogentsia's almost total inability to communicate with the rest of humanity. Indeed, they have difficulty in communicating among themselves with their cabalistic jargon and overblown technical treatises. Do not be awed or dismayed by those terms. You will learn, soon enough, what RAM means—you can't avoid it—but you don't really need to know what ROM, BIOS, or many other strange acronyms and jargon terms mean.

The primary purpose of this chapter is to attempt to overcome part of that problem by relieving at least some of the ignorance and fear that you may feel. As the mathematician quoted in Chapter 6 said, what one fool has learned another fool can learn. It was that message that helped embolden me to buy my first computer (a Morrow MD3 CP/M model) and apply myself to learning how to use it. And here I am six years later, working easily every day with my third computer, a machine many times more complex and more capable than that first machine of six years ago, but perfectly relaxed with it and still learning the new and greater features built into it. As in the case of automobiles, almost every year brings new and more convenient features as computers get smarter and smarter.

How Smart Is a Smart Computer?

Smart, a term used to describe computers and related equipment (modems, printers, terminals, etc.), refers to the degree of automation built into a given model, usually as a result of built-in programming. The "smartness" of a computer is actually the smartness of the people who designed and wrote the programs as well as those who designed and built the machines. The programs attempt to anticipate all possibilities and provide a suitable action for each. When your screen displays a message such as "Bad command" or "Non-DOS disk," it is simply doing what it was *programmed* to do when it could not execute a command you gave it or read a disk you inserted in a drive. Actually, the method by which the computer "decides" what to do and what to display on the screen is so laborious that the dullest human mind is far superior by comparison. The real secret of the computer's alleged brilliance is its speed. You and I might be able to multiple 17 by 9 mentally, but the computer must add 17 to itself nine times to reach the same answer. It can, however, do this so quickly that it appears to be instantaneous to our human perception.

One trend in computer development is toward ever-greater speeds of operation. Another is to greater memory—RAM, for *random access memory*. This capability is not unrelated to other features, for the amount of memory has a great deal to do with how sophisticated the computer's programs can be. All operations take place in that area of the computer known as RAM or memory. Data are moved from storage on a disk or entered from the keyboard into memory, the operations you call for are performed, and the data are sent to wherever you order them sent—to the printer, back to storage, to an external disk, or to all. If the RAM is not big enough to hold an entire file or entire program, the computer may transfer data from and return them to storage piecemeal; many programs are smart enough to do that. If that is not possible, you will get the message "Not enough memory to run," or something similar.

You may wish to know the technical details of how a computer does all this, and there is nothing wrong with pursuing such knowledge, of course. But having the knowledge is certainly not necessary to mastering the use of a computer. (It does, however, have the useful result that it tends to overcome any awe of computers that you might have had originally.)

What Can a Computer Do for You?

By far the most popular use of a computer is word processing. Many computers on secretaries' and typists' desks are used for word processing alone. But desktop computers can do everything that their big brothers, the mainframe computers, can do, even if not on the same scale. Probably everyone knows that computers can be and are used widely for accounting, to keep the books and prepare the payroll and tax records. But those are only most basic and general functions; there are many other functions, perhaps less well known, that computers can help you with. Let's look a bit more closely at some of these.

Word Processing

Word processing is often used as a kind of automated typing. This is almost a tragic underuse: A computer and its word-processing software (a word processor is a program, not a computer) are far too costly to be merely a more sophisticated typewriter. It can actually aid the user in becoming a *better* writer because it encourages reorganization and revision of first-draft material. But for now, let's look at the many possible uses of word processing in the typical office (assuming a modern, sophisticated word processor) and consider a number of other kinds and classes of software.

One complicating factor may confuse you if it is not explained here. More and more, modern software programs, especially word processors, are really sets of programs with multiple capabilities. The modern word processor, for example, is likely to include an outlining program, a mailing-list management program, a graphics program, and a telecommunication program, among others. And many of the other programs include at least some word-processing capabilities. That is one of the factors that will result in apparent redundancies in some of the following lists.

> General writing—letters, outlines, proposals, reports, manuals, articles, memoranda, manuscripts, camera-ready copy
>
> Swipe files and boilerplate for proposals, bids, and quotations
>
> Personalized—individually addressed—sales letters, other form letters, and envelopes (using mail-merge feature)
>
> Presentation materials—handouts, transparencies, other copy
>
> Schedules and appointments
>
> Lists, telephone and other—establish, maintain, sort, print out

Outlining

Outlining programs are sometimes called *idea processors* because they are intended to help the user come up with, think out, and develop ideas. They are often especially prized by inexperienced writers who need help in planning their writing. They are also helpful in guiding users not familiar with outlining techniques and formats who may be required to produce a detailed outline.

> Prepare multilevel outline
>
> Provide for expansion of any item at any level
>
> Permit display of outline at any level
>
> Facilitate reorganization or revision

Accounting

Accounting programs are available at a great many levels of size and sophistication, from the computer version of the Dome book (a simple system in a single book that you can buy in any office supplies store) to a complete system suitable for a large corporation.

> Day journals
>
> General ledgers and books
>
> Payroll records
>
> Check printing
>
> Invoicing
>
> Accounting records—e.g., payables and receivables
>
> Tax information
>
> Cash flow and other reports
>
> Keep, monitor expense accounts

INVENTORY

> Inventory records
>
> Status reports
>
> Usage reports

PURCHASING

Purchasing ledger

lists of suppliers

Ordering lead times required

Purchasing records

GRAPHICS

Presentations (addition to or vice word processors), including copy for slides, transparencies, posters, flip charts, handouts

Typesetting newsletters, catalogs, specification sheets, other sales and promotional literature (with or without importing word processor files)

Clip art, for use in manuscripts, presentations, sales literature

TELECOMMUNICATIONS

Researching public databases

Communicating with – getting information to and from – customers, suppliers, and others

Facsimile transmissions, using FAX board

DATABASE MANAGERS

Database management (dbm) programs are highly versatile and can be used to do many of the things already listed for other kinds of software. You can get mailing-list management programs, for example, but using a database manager for mailing-list management gives you greater flexibility and freedom. There are two broad classes of dbm software: *relational* and *flat file*. The flat file is simpler and thus the easier one to use.

Organize data – notes, lists, other – store and retrieve

Build, maintain, sort mailing lists

Print out mailing lists, selectively or totally, on labels, envelopes

Print reports of or based on mailing lists

Print reports of or based on any file stored by program

Inventory management functions

Manage, track time or other charges

Maintain reminder list (with or without aural or visual alarms)

Spreadsheets

Spreadsheet programs can be used to do everything a database manager can be used for, but it is overkill to use a spreadsheet program for something as simple as mailing-list management. Spreadsheet software has its own special and unique capabilities for which it is intended to be used. It is a powerful tool for planning and testing various configurations of all kinds, such as the following few examples:

Modeling—making what-if projections and trial fits

Planning budgets, taxes, cash flow

Scheduling

Designing complex charts and presentations

Miscellaneous and Specialized Programs

There are a great many highly specialized programs, most of them variants of the types already listed but oriented and adapted to specialized use. Here are just a few, as a representative sample:

Rèsumé writing assistance

Standard business forms

Money management

Collection letters (for delinquent accounts follow up)

Stock market charting/portfolio management

Foreign language tutoring

Calendar drafting (any month for many years past and future)

Business plan outlines and guidance

Translation software (translates text between otherwise incompatible machines, such as Macintosh and DOS)

A SPECIAL KIND OF "COMPUTER CRIME"

In the eyes of a purist, it is a virtual crime to sacrifice a sophisticated and expensive computer by relegating it to such "scut work" as mere automated typing, but this crime is committed by many who appear not to understand the deeper significance of word processing and other basic computer operations. The army had trouble persuading old cavalry officers to dismount from horses, take off their spurs, and "mount" armored cars and tanks for World War II. And the cavalry-turned-armored officers of World War II had to be virtually bludgeoned into embracing their new mounts in Vietnam, the helicopter gun ships.

The cast of characters in the business world is different, but the scenario is the same: Professionals and executives will not easily surrender their sharpened pencils and lined yellow pads in exchange for computer keyboards and monitor screens. Hoping still to cling to those familiar writing tools of the past, they have a secretary, typist, or "word processor operator" translate their holographic manuscript into computer-disk files and neatly printed draft, as they once did with IBM Executive (later Selectric) typewriters.

Were the inefficiency of this sadly outdated method the sole problem, it would be deplorable enough. But far more serious is the fact that the writer is losing the advantage of working with a word processor, a facility that almost forces reorganization and rewriting, with inevitable benefits in improved quality of the final product. It is not a waste or inefficient use of an executive's time to work at a keyboard. Quite the contrary, it is a boon to overall efficiency, for it produces far better first drafts, and immeasurably better final drafts. Editors and reviewers ought to work at the keyboard also, and learn to review, edit, and revise on screen. Many editors and writers resist it, insisting that they can't properly appreciate, scan, and work on copy unless it is on paper. That is nonsense, for writing, rewriting, reviewing, and editing on screen can be learned, just like anything else can be learned, and it is a far more efficient way of working.

Precisely the same thing may be said for accounting work. It is equally inane and "criminal" to do accounting by more archaic methods and then assign the results to someone trained to enter the results into the computer. Today's accountant ought to be able to work directly at the keyboard, entering the raw data and using the computer to do the necessary manipulations – and today's bookkeeper should be as skilled at the keyboard as he or she is at the adding machine or calculator.

TYPES OF COMPUTERS

IBM has long been dominant in the mainframe computer world, but that dominance has not transferred to the desktop computer world. And yet it has, in a strange way. IBM desktop computers have a substantial, but not dominant, share of the market, but IBM clone computers – computers fashioned on, closely resembling, and compatible with IBM computers – do dominate the market, counting or not counting those bearing the true IBM label.

Before IBM entered this market, it was thoroughly fragmented with dozens of computers that were almost entirely incompatible with each other. That lack of standardization was a serious barrier to the development and growth of the industry. No matter what computer you owned, only a relatively small share of the software offered would run on your computer. Almost every desktop computer therefore suffered from a lack of suitable software.

The entrance of IBM into the market brought change in the form of de facto standardization. The power of the IBM name caused a surge to IBM computer standards and computers that were compatible with IBM's computers. Because it was easy to build clones of the IBM computers, clone manufacturers sprang up, many of them existing manufacturers who abandoned their old models and turned to clone designs. (Most of those who refused to do so or who delayed too long in making the change soon perished and disappeared from the market.) Sales of the new generation of desktop computers began to soar, and the desktop computer world became an IBM-compatible or MS-DOS world.

A few other, non-IBM type computers survived, despite the DOS avalanche: Commodore with its Amiga; Atari; Heathkit-Zenith; and Apple, principally. Of these, however, only Apple with its Macintosh computers has a truly significant share of the market. The Macintosh pioneered computer graphics and is reputed still to be preeminent in graphics applications; at least until now, however, it has not been able to achieve a serious penetration of the business market for other than graphics applications. For most practical applications, therefore, the choice is between a Macintosh computer and an IBM-compatible or MS-DOS computer. But even there you have a limited choice, for the sheer numbers of MS-DOS computers all but compel you to settle on an MS-DOS computer for yourself because it is an MS-DOS world, and there is no way to change that, at least for now. The established base of millions of DOS computers is a giant barrier to change on any sizable scale in the near term. But that insurance of longevity is a great comfort to those of us who have made a substantial investment in our DOS hardware and software. And the dominance of the DOS standard also assures us of a superabundance of suitable software and accessories.

You can put a Macintosh to work to do everything a DOS computer can do, and you can find suitable software also. But in light of the conditions just described—essentially, the far greater resources available for DOS systems—I can only encourage the acquisition and use of a DOS-type computer for major business functions. (Of course, you may find the Macintosh a better choice for publications and graphics. Many firms, small and large, use both kinds of machines, the DOS for most general business applications and the Mac for those applications where it excels.)

Configurations

You have a broad array of options in hardware, as you do in software. The major functional elements every computer must have are these:

- *Memory*, that theater of the computer (known technically as RAM) in which data are operated upon.
- *Input*, one or more devices through which you gain access to RAM and enter programs, commands, and other data.
- *Output*, one or more devices through which the computer presents or displays data.
- *Storage*, one or more devices in which data are stored on permanent or long-term basis, even when the computer is turned off.

To provide you with a more detailed understanding, brief discussions of each of these elements follow.

MEMORY   RAM or memory is volatile. Turning the computer off or any interruption that has that effect, such as a break in the electrical supply during a storm, erases whatever is in memory at the moment, and the data are thus lost. It is good practice to send newly generated data to storage frequently (i.e., to "save" them) to minimize the loss, should one occur.

Memory is rated in size, in thousands of bytes. A *byte* is a string of eight digital ones and/or zeros, which can be arranged in 128 different combinations. There is a defined combination for each letter of the alphabet, upper and lower case, for each numeral, for each common mathematical symbol, and for a few other special symbols or characters. Through these combinations the computer recognizes the meaning of data and displays information on the screen.

Most DOS computers today have a basic RAM of 640,000 bytes, expressed in kilobytes or KB (i.e., 640KB). Although many recent models have extended memories, 640KB is the maximum basic memory of most of the DOS machines of recent years. In text, that would be the equivalent of approximately 160 single-spaced, typed pages or twice that number of double-spaced pages. This was considered to be a momentous breakthrough in RAM size because the earlier machines had RAM that peaked at 64KB, but modern programs need a lot of memory and many of them are a bit too large for 640KB memories.

INPUT   Most desktop computers have two means for input of programs and other data: the keyboard and the disk drives. The *keyboard* is based on the typical typewriter keyboard, with many additional keys. There are a number of different keyboard styles and models in use, with the principal difference the placement of certain keys, especially the special function and cursor keys.

The *disk drives* are of several types. Most common is the 5.25-inch floppy disk drive, accepting a flexible disk. This is the kind of disk on which, until recently, almost all available programs were delivered. The 3.5-inch disk, which holds much more data than the 5.25-inch floppy, has been becoming more and more popular, and most programs are being made available in that format today.

Most computers being used for "serious" purposes today (e.g., for business and career purposes) have fixed or hard disks. These are not removable, as floppy disks are, but are sealed units and have much higher capacity. Where most floppy disks are in the range 360KB to 1.44MB (megabytes, or millions of bytes), most hard disks in use are of 20, 30, or even more MB. (Hard disks of 60MB and more are becoming common in the latest desktop computers.)

OUTPUT   There are three avenues of output for the typical computer system: Data may be displayed on the monitor screen, printed out on paper, and/or transferred to storage on any of the disks. An alternative is tape, although that is used generally for hard disk backup, which will be discussed further in connection with storage.

Most desktop computers come with a 12-inch (diagonal measurement) monitor. The favorite phosphor color today appears to be amber, although most special-purpose computers found in such places as hospitals and industrial establishments appear to use bright green phosphor. The standard is generally monochrome, but many users prefer color monitors. This adds considerable expense to the system, for not only is the color monitor far more expensive than the monochrome monitor, it also requires extra circuitry—a "card"—installed in the computer.

It is also possible to use larger monitors, if you prefer. (I use a 14-inch monitor with a pale green phosphor.) A monitor installed in the opposite orientation, like a typical page—the shorter dimension being the horizontal one—and displaying a full page, rather than the typical 23 to 25 lines, is possible but adds some $2,000 in cost to the system.

Today a wide array of printers is available for your choice. The daisywheel printers, using the same printing device that many typewriters use, was once highly popular as the only printer that produced "letter-quality" printing. But as dot matrix printing technology advanced, producing "near-letter-quality" (nlq) results with 9-pin printers, the popularity of the daisywheel machines began to decline. Today, most of the 24-pin printers produce true letter quality and daisywheel printers are not much in evidence anymore.

The best printed quality is produced by the laser printers, which use the technologies of the office copier and the laser to produce high-quality copy at excellent speeds of about eight copies per minute. A camera copies the image of the original and transfers an electrical analog of that image to a drum in the copier. A laser beam is modulated by the computer data stream, and the laser "paints" the electrical analog of the data on the drum, in the laser printer. From that point on the process is the same, with toner clinging to the charged areas, transferred to the paper, and fused by heat.

Costs are in proportion. Good 9-pin dot matrix printers can be purchased for well under $200, 24-pin printers for approximately $350 up, and laser printers for prices starting, usually, well above $1,000 and easily up to several thousand dollars. (High-speed dot matrix printers, however, can cost as much as laser printers.)

STORAGE Data storage is entirely on disks, disks of any description, with one exception. Data and programs you use only rarely are best stored on removable disks. Data and programs you use and need access to frequently are best stored internally on the hard disk. Because there is always the hazard of damage to that disk with subsequent loss of data stored on it, however, everything on your hard disk should be backed up with duplicate copies stored elsewhere. One of the backup systems used most commonly, especially for the larger hard disks, is tape storage. The tape is of the cassette type, hence can be removed from the recording device and stored elsewhere, so that it can become, in effect, an alternate storage device as well as a backup device.

Auxiliary Hardware Items

A computer is actually a system, not a single machine. Many of the elements that form the system are peripheral to the central unit that makes up the computer proper. Those features we just reviewed are peripheral units essential to the basic functioning of the computer as a computer, and they may be either internal units, housed in the same case as the computer proper, or external units, housed in their own cases. (Electrically, it makes no difference where they are housed.)

There are other peripheral units, devices that add capabilities to the computer system. Brief discussions of several of these follow.

MODEMS The most commonly used and perhaps most useful ancillary device is the *modem*, whose name is a contraction of the first few letters of the longer descriptive term *modulator-demodulator*. It is a device used to enable a computer to communicate with another computer via telephone, as you may recall from earlier discussions, by converting the computer's signals to audible tones for transmission and back to computer signals at the other end of the line.

The rate at which modems transmit information is expressed in *baud*, an old telegraphy term that is translated today as equivalent to bits-per-second. Early modems operated at 300 baud and were soon replaced by 1,200 baud modems, which have been steadily yielding to 2,400 baud modems, with 9,600 baud modems on the horizon and beginning to come into use.

Modems can be internal, a card installed in your computer's housing, or external, a standalone device in its own housing. Internal 2,400 baud modems can be bought as cheaply as about $125, and external models for about 20 percent more. These, however, are at the low end of the price range, which runs to more than twice these figures and even higher, for some models, such as the Hayes, long the standard for modems.

BUFFERS Except for some rather advanced models, the computer cannot do two things at once. If you are printing a file, for example, the computer cannot work on other things until the printing is done. To overcome this problem, many people use buffers. A *buffer* is a hardware device for temporary storage or isolation of data. In this context, however, a buffer is a device that takes over the responsibility for printing and thus frees the computer to do other things. That is, you can work on another file while the computer is printing, if you have a buffer.

Strictly speaking, a buffer is a hardware device, usually an external device with several controls and indicator lights. The function of taking over the printing control, however, can also be accomplished by software, a program that was originally known as a *spooler* but is now often called a buffer.

Many of the later computers and the later programs include buffers or spoolers integrally, but hardware buffers are also used by many because they do not require the use of the computer's internal memory or storage.

SWITCHBOXES Every computer has *ports*. These are output jacks to which are connected printers, modems, or other devices. Ports are *parallel* or *serial*, meaning they accept data presented in parallel or serial fashion, and there are generally at least one of each description, although some computers have two or more of each.

In many uses, it is desirable to have more than one output unit of a kind. For example, you might easily wish to have two or even three printers. (I use two, one loaded with paper and the other loaded with labels.) If you do not have enough ports for all your output devices, you can use a switch box. Then, with a flick of the appropriate switch, you can connect or disconnect various devices to suit your needs.

ADDITIONAL DRIVES   Drives are normally internal devices, with provision for inserting and removing disks, in the case of floppy drives. It is possible, however, to add external standalone drives, mounted in separate housings and connected to one of the computer ports. Today many computers are sold with a hard disk, a 3.5-inch drive, and a 5.25-inch drive. This means that there is no provision to copy one 3.5-inch disk directly to another 3.5-inch disk, and the same is true for the 5.25-inch disks. If your computer use involves such copying on other than an occasional basis, an additional drive, internal or external, is a great convenience.

TAPE UNITS   The tape units normally used to back up the hard drive can also be internal or external units, like the drives are. The tape cassettes are available in 20, 40, even 60MB lengths.

PUBLIC DATABASES AND ELECTRONIC BULLETIN BOARDS

One of the many great benefits available to computer owners is that a computer together with a modem provides a window on the world, communication with many other computers and the contents of their memories and storage systems. Here we are going to consider, briefly, two such assets, public databases and electronic bulletin boards.

Public Databases

Your computer, modem, and telephone line provide you with access to an enormous wealth of information contained in public databases. The concept of databases stems from the maturation of computers, but only the owners and operators of the mainframes knew about, cared very much about, or benefited from those databases before the advent of the desktop computer. The latter changed the picture considerably.

The term requires some explanation: A *public database* consists of a bank of information stored by a computer in its peripheral devices (one or more large hard disks), and made available to the public generally, via computer-to-computer exchange, using modems and dial-up telephone connections. The user generally pays a subscription fee, which may include an initiation charge (often a monthly minimum charge), and generally is also charged for "connect time" for each use.

Two broad types of public databases are available. There is the database/information service designed to be of interest to the general public by providing such information as airline schedules, stock market reports, news headlines, movie reviews, electronic mail and message centers, and other such items. There is also the specialized service offering information of special interest to businesspeople and professionals.

For example, let us suppose that you are a lawyer and you want to look up precedents in a certain type of legal proceeding. There are public databases that can do a suitable search for you—that is, you can make the search, via one of these services, without leaving your desk! You will have to be a subscriber to the system, and you will be charged for the time required—for the time you are connected to the system and it is searching for you, that is. But it will probably be a matter of a few minutes only, and the charges will usually be by the minute. You may have to also pay toll costs for a long-distance connection. But the compensation is that it takes virtually none of your time to make the search. Using a law clerk to make the search would almost surely be more expensive, no matter how little you paid the clerk! For example, it cost me about $100 and perhaps 10 minutes of my time to do a search of certain federal procurements for a client, using a public database that stores such information. When the system produced the information I wanted, I "downloaded" it. That means I transferred it to my own hard disk and printed it out later, when I had disconnected. Printing is relatively slow, compared with copy to a disk, and copying the data to your disk is therefore the fastest way to obtain the information and get off the line, which is costing money for every second. You print the data out later, at your convenience.

It took about 15 minutes to edit the printout of the data I got from the service and convert it to a report for the client. I could hardly have been as efficient in any other manner!

There are such public databases of all kinds of information—medical, legal, scientific, environmental, demographic, financial, industrial, political, social, psychological, geographic, meteorological, and many others. In some cases, a single service deals in a single kind of information, a single database; in others, the service has many different kinds of information and many different databases. There are also electronic newsletters issued at regular intervals, most of them electronic versions of printed newsletters but sometimes condensed versions of or abstracts from printed periodicals. But there is still a third situation, in which the service is interconnected to other, specialized databases, and acts as agent or broker, offering you a *gateway* or connection to those others.

In any case, the wealth of information available and—at least equally important—the facility in doing the research quickly, comfortably, and most efficiently are an enormous asset to many businesses. The public database is, in fact, one of the factors that makes the home-based business feasible: It provides you an enormous library on your desk and at the end of your telephone-modem-computer system. (In Part 5 you will find a representative listing of these public databases, with descriptions of what they offer.)

Electronic Bulletin Boards

Public databases existed before desktop computers did. The National Library of Medicine operates MEDLARS, a main-frame-computer–based information service for the medical profession, and the Department of Education operates ERIC, a similar service for educators. And there are many others based on the mainframe computers that have been available for a number of years. Electronic bulletin boards, however, are a more recent phenomenon, a product of the desktop computer age, and have proliferated swiftly: There are many thousands of them in the United States alone. The current issue of the *Computer Shopper*, for example, lists over 500, and that is admittedly far from a full count.

BBS, for "bulletin board system," is a popular abbreviation for electronic bulletin boards. By far the overwhelming majority are available free of charge to everyone. (A few make a one-time annual charge that is nominal, partly to discourage a certain type of caller and partly to help defray a bit of the expense; a few others ask for voluntary contributions.) They are run by individuals as a hobby, by computer clubs as a service to members, by government agencies as a public service, and by business organizations as a service to customers and as a PR and marketing tool. NEC, a well-known Japanese manufacturer of computers and many other products, operates a BBS in Boston, for example, and the computer magazine *PC Resource* operates one in New Hampshire for the benefit of readers and prospective readers.

The two major services provided by most BBSs are an electronic mail/message center and a vast library of shareware programs. Regular callers carry on regular correspondence on a daily basis that amounts to virtual conversation. Many boards permit callers to make some of their messages private, so that only the party addressed and the operator of the system (the *sysop*, in the jargon) can read it. Many create various *conferences*, open forums on one subject or another, with everyone invited to join in and express opinions. Such conferences are on many subjects, such as word processing, database management, computer programming, current events, writing, education, equipment, sources of supply, and many other topics. Conferees exchange ideas, experiences, information, advice, and jests. Some of the callers are tyros at running a computer, others are quite expert, and many are professionals in the computer field. Callers often ask for advice about technical problems, recommendations on good suppliers, reports on bad experiences, and sundry other questions. That alone is a most valuable service—a free consulting service, in fact, the result of a certain comradeship that grows up. Most of us who call these boards have been helped by others more than once.

Like the public databases, many of the BBSs are specialized. I know of one for real estate people that specializes in news and information in that field. Another specializes in tax information, a third in the banking business. Several agencies of the U.S. Department of Commerce sponsor BBSs, as do the Navy, NASA, the General Services Administration, and other federal government organizations.

Most of these BBSs, especially those run by individuals, carry large assortments of public-domain computer software and a special variety of computer software known as shareware.

SHAREWARE

Shareware is something you must learn about. It is a special variety of software, and it has its origins in the desktop computer era.

In the early days of the desktop computer, primarily in the time of the CP/M operating system that preceded the PC-DOS and MS-DOS systems of today, there was something of a shortage of software. Many gifted individuals, some of them professional computer programmers, others dedicated and talented hobbyists, wrote programs that they placed in the public domain—donated to anyone who wanted to use them.

Many of these were tiny programs written to do special but simple tasks, such as counting the words in a manuscript or doing a better job of presenting a directory on screen than the DOS command does. But many others, such as the Modem 7 programs for communications, were sophisticated and complex programs, and many were equal or even superior to commercial programs selling for hundreds of dollars.

A bit later the idea of shareware occurred and quickly caught on among individuals who wrote programs and decided to adopt this novel way of distributing their products. There are still a few pd—public domain—programs contributed by individuals, but by far the majority of software produced outside the regular commercial channels is what we know today as shareware.

Shareware is software made available to users on a try-before-you-buy basis, with payment voluntary and on the honor system. The author copyrights the program and grants license freely to everyone to distribute the program at no charge and in its entirety. Initially, these programs were distributed mainly by listing on bulletin boards, with callers invited to download what they wanted, and that is still a major channel of distribution. (In fact, gaining access to shareware is the chief reason for many of the calls to a BBS.) There are at least two other important avenues of distribution, however. One is the computer clubs, of which there are many hundreds. Members may get shareware programs at club meetings for a few dollars—usually $3 to $5—per disk. The charge is not for the software, because that is forbidden by the copyright owner, who wants to be paid for the software. The charge is for the disk and the service. The other distribution channel is the small business that specializes in offering just this service, usually charging from a low of about $1.50 to a high of $5 per disk, the price varying, as a rule, with the quantity purchased. This latter venture has become a popular business and is profitable enough to enable many of the operators to take out full-page advertisements in many computer magazines. Some others advertise via direct mail.

When you buy a commercial program, you generally get a set of printed instructions, even an entire manual when the program merits a full, bound manual. That is impracticable in shareware. Most shareware authors, however, include "read.me" files offering some basic explanation of the program and instructions for using it. In some cases, these are full manuals organized to be printed out on your own printer. In many, probably most, cases, the author offers a full, commercially printed manual to everyone who pays for the program. Usually the author suggests a price, one that is usually far below that for an equivalent commercial program. As a further inducement to pay for using the program, the author is likely to offer free updates and notes, as they are issued, to anyone who "registers" (pays for) the program.

Understandably, by far the majority of users probably do not register the programs, but that is not always because the user wants to take advantage of the author. Many people download and try out hundreds of programs but use only a few regularly. It is only those few that they use more or less regularly that they are expected to pay for. Even so, most shareware authors do not make very much money from their creations, although there are a few exceptions.

Some listings of, and guidelines to, a number of the most popular shareware will be offered in the final part.

PART FIVE

SOURCES AND REFERENCES

Albert Einstein and Henry Ford both rejected the idea of memorizing reference data, information that can be looked up. The important thing is not to know by heart a wealth of facts, but to know how and where to find them when needed.

This part is offered as an easy reference convenience. To some degree, a portion of the material here will overlap information presented earlier. The earlier presentations, however, were deliberately tutorial how-to, whereas this section is strictly informational: where/how to find what you need.

Over the years I have taken great pains to compile many lists and directories of various kinds. Some are in the form of source books on my shelves, others are archive files on my computer disks, still others are files of my database management program. These are among my most valuable and most treasured business resources. They include listings of books, magazines, newsletters, and other periodicals;

book publishers; software and software publishers; hardware and hardware manufacturers; and federal and state government agencies of interest. They also include outlines, notes, and models for various kinds of projects.

In this final part I share some of this treasure with you. You will find a number of appendices presenting a selection of those references and resources I believe most valuable for your needs and purposes generally. These are certainly not the complete list of such items; you will undoubtedly add to the lists yourself. But they are a good starter and worth studying as an information resource and guide.

Also included here are the details of some how-to instructions, such as a detailed outline for writing a business plan or financial proposal (a necessity in seeking funding), and guidelines for writing technical and cost proposals in pursuit of contracts.

Books, Periodicals, Associations, Software, and Online Public Databases

RELEVANT BOOKS

Consultant's Guide to Proposal Writing, Herman Holtz, John Wiley & Sons, New York, NY 10158, 1986.

Direct Mail Copy That Sells, Herschell Gordon Lewis, Prentice-Hall, Englewood Cliffs, NJ, 1984.

Electronic Cottage Handbook, Lis Fleming, P.O. Box 1738, Davis, CA 95617, 1978.

Great Promo Pieces, Herman Holtz, John Wiley & Sons, New York, NY 10158.

Homemade Money, 3rd ed., Barbara Brabec, Betterway Publications, Crozet, VA 22932, 1989.

Home Offices and Workspaces, Editors of Sunset Books and Sunset Magazine, Lane Publishing Co., Menlo Park, CA 94025, 1986.

Home-Office Tax Deductions, Thomas Vickman, Enterprise Publishing, Wilmington, DE 19801, 1988.

How to Get Free Software, Alfred Glossbrenner, St. Martin's Press, 1984.

How to Make Money with Your Micro, Herman Holtz, John Wiley & Sons, New York, NY 10158, 1984.

How to Make Your Home-Based Business Grow, Valerie Bohigian, New American Library, New York, NY 10019, 1984.

How to Succeed as an Independent Consultant, 2nd ed., Herman Holtz, John Wiley & Sons, New York, NY 10158, 1988.

Ideas That Work: Ten of Today's Most Exciting and Profitable Self-Employment Opportunities, Live Oak Publications, Boulder, CO 80306, 1985.

Information U.S.A., Matthew Lesko, Viking Penguin, New York, NY 10010, 1986.

Instant Information, Joel Makower and Alan Green, Prentice-Hall, New York, NY 10023, 1987.

Proposal Preparation Manual, U.S. Department of Transportation, Research and Special Programs Administration, Office of University Research, Washington, DC 20590, 1981.

Small Business Guide to Federal R&D, National Science Foundation, Office of Small Business R&D, 1800 G Street, NW, Washington, DC 20550, 1979.

The Winning Proposal, How to Write It, Herman Holtz and Terry Schmidt, New York, McGraw-Hill, 1981.

Word Processing Profits at Home, Peggy Glenn, Aames-Allen Publishing Co., Huntington Beach, CA 92648, 1983.

Work-at-Home Sourcebook, Lynie Arden, Live Oak Publications, Boulder, CO 80306, 1988.

Working from Home, Paul and Sarah Edwards, Jeremy P. Tarcher, Los Angeles, CA 90069, 1987.

RELEVANT PERIODICALS

Better Business, 235 E. 42nd Street, New York, NY 10017.

Business Age Magazine, 135 W. Wells Street, 7th Flr, Milwaukee, WI 53203-1800.

Business Marketing, 220 E. 42nd Street, New York, NY 10017.

Business Opportunities Digest, 301 Plymouth Drive, NE, Dalton, GA 30721.

Business Today, P.O. Box 10010, 1720 Washington Blvd, Ogden, UT 84409.

Business View, P.O. Box 9859, Naples, FL 33941.

Challenges, P.O. Box 22432, Kansas City, MO 64113.

Communications Briefings, Encoders, Inc., 806 Westminster Blvd, Blackwood, NJ 08012.

Computer Product Selling, Lebhar-Friedman, 425 Park Avenue, New York, NY 10022.

Direct Response Specialist, P.O. Box 1075, Tarpon Springs, FL 34286.

DM News, 19 West 21st Street, New York, NY 10010.

Entrepreneur, 2392 Morse Avenue, Irvine, CA 92714-6234.

High-Tech Marketing, 1460 Post Road East, Westport, CT 06880.

Home Business News, 12221 Beaver Pike, Jackson, OH 45640.

Home Office Computing, 730 Broadway, New York, NY 10003.

In Business, POB 323, 10 S. 7th Street, Emmaus, PA 18049.

Inc., 38 Commercial Wharf, Boston, MA 02110.

Income Opportunities, 380 Lexington Avenue, New York, NY 10017.

Memphis Business Journal, 88 Union, Suite 102, Memphis, TN 38103.

National Home-Business Report, P.O. Box 2137, Naperville, IL 60566.

New Business Opportunities, Entrepreneur Group, Inc., 2392 Morse Avenue, Irvine, CA 92714.

New Career Ways Newsletter, 67 Melrose Avenue, Haverhill, MA 01830.

Opportunity Magazine, 6 N. Michigan Avenue, Chicago, IL 60602.

Personal Computing, Hayden Publishing, 10 Holland Drive, Hasbrouck Heights, NJ 07604.

Sharing Ideas! 18825 Hicrest Road, Glendora, CA 91740.

Small Business Opportunities, Harris Publications, Inc., 1115 Broadway, New York, NY 10010.

Today's Office, 645 Stewart Avenue, Garden City, NY 11530.

Training Magazine, 50 S. Ninth Street, Minneapolis, MN 55402.

Woman's Enterprise, Paisano Publications, Inc., 28210 Dorothy Drive, Agoura Hills, CA 91301.

Worksteader News, 2396 Coolidge Way, Rancho Cordova, CA 95670.

Venture Magazine, 521 5th Avenue, New York, NY 10175.

ASSOCIATIONS

American Home Business Association, 397 Post Road, Darien, CT 06820.

Mother's Home Business Network, P.O. Box 423, East Meadow, NY 11554.

National Alliance of Homebased Businesswomen, P.O. Box 95, Norwood, NJ 07648.

National Association for the Cottage Industry, P.O. Box 14460, Chicago, IL 60614.

National Association for the Self-Employed, 2316 Gravel Road, Fort Worth, TX 76118.

New Families Work Options Network, P.O. Box 41108, Fayetteville, NC 28309.

SOFTWARE

There are a great many software publishers, both commercial and the shareware variety described in the previous chapter.

There is thus a great abundance of software of both genres. In fact, the abundance is so great that I can only touch on some of the more popular programs here, which makes this only a starter list.

Word Processors

WordPerfect	Reported to be by far the most popular today
Word	In widespread use
XyWrite	Favored by many professional writers and publishers
WordStar	A pioneer and my personal choice
PC Write (shareware)	Excellent quality
Galaxy (shareware)	Thoroughly professional in quality

General comment: Be sure that the word processor you choose has a good spelling checker and other modern features that are important to you. Here are some of the many other features and capabilities available, both as separate programs and as elements of word processors:

Thesaurus	Page preview (WSYIWYG)
Footnoting	File manager
Shell-to-command line	Key redefiners
ASCII/conversion to ASCII	Windows
Communications	Indexing
Outliner	Graphics
Table of contents	Global search

Database Managers

File Express	A shareware program that has had many favorable reviews; easy to learn and use

PC-File	Another well-regarded shareware program, somewhat more elaborate than File Express
D Base III	A popular, very well-known commercial program

Spreadsheet Programs

Lotus 1-2-3	The pioneer and leading spreadsheet program
Symphony	Integrated software, with ancillary capabilities
Quattro	Another successful commercial spreadsheet program
Qubecalc	A shareware spreadsheet program, offering three-dimensional modeling
PC-Calc	A popular shareware spreadsheet program
As Easy	Shareware, similar to Lotus 1-2-3

Accounting

Quicken	Popular, easy to use program for small business
Medlin Accounting	Shareware, thoroughly professional quality

Communications

QModem	Popular shareware
Procomm	Also popular shareware
Telix	Again, popular shareware

There are so many excellent shareware communications programs that I am hard put to find commercial programs to list here.

Key Redefiners

SmartKey   I have used SmartKey from the begin-
                    ning, although I have tried a few
                    others. I am well satisfied with it.

ProKey   Well known, well rated

Desktop Publishing

Ventura   Popular product of Xerox Corpo-
                    ration

PageMaker   Very successful product

FormWorx   Not exactly a desktop publisher, but a
                    useful graphics program

Readability Measurement

Maxi-Read 2.0   Shareware, excellently done

PC-Read 2.5   Shareware, simple program

Read 2.1   Shareware; a program to calculate
                    Flesch readability scores

Grammar Correction

Grammatik   Well-known program, a pioneer in
                    the field

ONLINE SUBSCRIBER SERVICES AND PUBLIC DATABASES

Following are a few of the many online subscription services
available. In all cases it is best to make inquiry of the organiza-

tion listed for rates, services, and types of databases. Information listed is that reported at time of writing, but may have changed. In any case, written or telephone inquiry is necessary to gain full information.

BRS/Bibliographic Retrieval Services, BRS/After Dark, 1200 Route 7, Latham, NY 12110, (518) 783-1161 and (800) 833-4707. Two services, offering over 80 databases on science, medicine, education, business, other subjects.

CBD ONLINE. The CBD Online database may be found on a number of public database systems, including the following:

United Communications Group, 4550 Montgomery Avenue, Bethesda, MD 20814, (301) 656-6666

Data Resources, Inc., 2400 Hartwell Avenue, Lexington, MA 02173, (617) 863-5100

Softshare/MCR Technology, Inc., 55 Depot Road, Goleta, CA 93117, (805) 963-3841.

CompuServe (H&R Block), 5000 Arlington Centre Blvd, POB 20212, Columbus, OH 43220, (614) 457-8600 and (800) 848-8990. Electronic banking, word processing, travel service, business news, airlines schedules, other general information and services.

Customer Service Bureau, Business Computer Network (BCN), POB 36, Riverton, WY 82501, (800) 446-6255 and (800) 442-0982. This is a special service that offers subscribers access to other database subscription services, including Data Resources, Inc., 2400 Hartwell Avenue, Lexington, MA 02173, (617) 863-5100, *Commerce Business Daily* online, and other business databases, including Value Line.

Dialog Information Services, Inc., Dialog Information Retrieval Service, and Knowledge Index, 3460 Hillview Avenue, Palo Alto, CA 94304, (800) 227-1927 and (800) 982-5838. Wide range of business databases, including the *Commerce Business Daily* online, agricultural data, data on computer and electronics industries, general news. Can be accessed via Tymnet, Uninet, or Telenet.

ITT Dialcom, 1109 Spring Street, Silver Spring, MD 20910: An electronic mail system with access to airlines' flight information, news, and other databases.

Dun & Bradstreet, 299 Park Avenue, New York, NY 10171, (212) 593-6800. Various business information services, especially credit reports on businesses, but other data on businesses and general business information as well.

Innerline, American Banker and Bank Administration Institute, 95 W. Algonquin Road, Arlington Heights, IL 60005, (800) 323-1321. Primarily financial data pertaining to banking (e.g., money markets) and banking information/news generally.

LEXIS, LEXPAT, and NEXIS, Mead Data Central, POB 933, Dayton, OH 45401, (513) 865-6800. LEXIS is a legal research service, LEXPAT a patent search service, and NEXIS a news service, offering several business magazines and the AP and UPI National and Business wires online.

National Library of Medicine, 8600 Rockville Pike, Bethesda, MD 20209: MEDLINE and MEDLARS databases, medical information provided to physicians and hospitals (but available to and subscribed to by others), including diagnostic assistance.

Nielsen Business Services, A. C. Nielsen Co., Nielsen Plaza, Northbrook, IL 60062, (312) 498-6300. Offers its Neilsen Retail Index, database pertaining to inventories and other information about retail trade in food, drug, health, alcohol, cosmetics, and related lines.

TRW Information Services Div., Business Credit Services and Credit Data Service, 500 City Pkwy West, Orange, CA 92668, (714) 937-2000. This is a consumer credit reporting service, reputed to be the largest one. It is operated in association with Standard & Poor and the National Association of Credit Management (NACM).

The Source, Source Telecomputing Corp., 1616 Anderson Road, McLean, VA 22102, (800) 336-3366. General and business news, including stock reports, data storage service, airline schedules, other such information.

United Information Services, Inc., 20 N. Clark Street, Chicago, IL 60602, (312) 782-2000. This is a service to programmers to sell their software online through an Authors Program. The service includes related information shared among subscribers.

Westlaw, West Publishing Co., 50 W. Kellog Blvd, POB 43526, St. Paul, MN 55164, (800) 328-9352. This is an information service for law offices, searching citations, other legal information, and news services.

Sources of Supply

"Buying right" is no small part of business success. The term is used casually to refer to buying at bargain prices, but that isn't all that "buying right" means: It means also buying useful items, items that contribute to your business success. It means buying items that you can resell at a profit, if you are in the business of selling goods, but it also means buying the right equipment, fixtures, and supplies you need to conduct your business efficiently. Unless you are already quite expert, you must do some comparison shopping to help you make the right judgments and decisions. Professional purchasing agents rely on catalogs to do much of their comparison shopping.

COMPUTERS AND OTHER OFFICE NECESSITIES

Computers and everything related to them are widely advertised, so it is not at all difficult to "shop" without leaving your desk. The *Washington Post,* the capital's most prominent daily newspaper, offers readers a special thick tabloid business section every Monday morning, and at least half of its pages are heavy with computer advertising. The following are some of the catalogs that are likely to be most appropriate to keep on hand for price comparisons and general references.

CATALOGS

Crutchfield *Personal Office*, Crutchfield Corporation, 1 Crutchfield Park, Charlottesville, VA 22906, (800) 521-4050. Computers, other electronics and office machines, computer service department.

Computer Direct, Inc., 22292 N. Pepper Road, Barrington, IL 60010, (800) 289-9473. Discount catalog lists many bargains in computers and other office equipment and related supplies.

Computer Discount Warehouse catalog (quarterly), 2840 Maria Avenue, Northbrook, IL 60065-3048, (800) 233-4426, FAX (312) 291-1737. Primarily computers and directly related items.

Computer Shopper, Coastal Associates Publishing, 5211 S. Washington Avenue, Titusville, FL 32780, (800) 274-6384. Actually a magazine but carries more information and offers than most catalogs, and from a wide variety of suppliers. A must for general references and, especially, to find sources of supply (if it exists, it is probably listed in here somewhere) and to save money by using mail order. (Virtually all advertisers in this publication are geared for mail-order sales.)

Global Computer Supplies, 1050 Northbrook Pkwy, Suwanee, GA 30174, (800) 845-6225, FAX (404) 339-0033. General catalog of computer hardware and related accessories and supplies.

Inmac, 2465 Augustine Drive, Santa Clara, CA 95054, (800) 547-5444. Issues catalog of computer and extensive array of related items.

Misco, P.O. Box 399, Holmdel, NJ 07733, (800) 876-4726, FAX (201) 264-5955. Catalog lists wide variety of computers, related supplies, and general office furniture.

Quill Corporation, P.O. Box 4700, Lincolnshire, IL 60197-4700, (312) 634-4800. Semiannual complete catalog, monthly sales catalog, periodic special mailings. Handles wide variety of office and other general business supplies, some computer items. Discounts.

Sears, (800) 255-3000. Produces catalog *Office Essentials for Your Home or Business,* lists discount office equipment and furniture.

MAILING LISTS AND OTHER DIRECT-MAIL NEEDS

The following is a representative listing of active mailing list brokers, but only a small portion. There are many, many more.

Alvin B. Zeller, 475 Park Avenue S., New York, NY 10016, (212) 223-0814.

American Bar Association, 750 N. Lake Shore Drive, Chicago, IL 60611, (312) 988-5435.

American Church Lists, 1939 Stadium Oaks, No. 110, Arlington, TX 76004, (817) 261-6233.

American Institute of Physics, 335 E. 45th Street, New York, NY 10017, (212) 661-9404.

American List Counsel, 88 Orchard Road, Princeton, NJ 08540, (201) 874-4300, (800) 822-5478, FAX (201) 874-4433.

American Management Systems, 9255 Sunset Blvd, Los Angeles, CA 90069, (213) 858-1520.

Best Mailing Lists, Inc., 34 W. 32nd Street, New York, NY 10001, (212) 868-1080, (800) 692-2378, FAX (212) 947-0136.

CBS Magazines, 1515 Broadway, New York, NY 10036, (212) 719-6677.

Donnelley Mktg. Information Services, 1351 Washington Blvd, Stamford, CT 06902, (203) 965-5400.

Dun & Bradstreet International, 99 Church Street, New York, NY 10007, (212) 265-7525.

Ed Burnett Consultants, 99 W. Sheffield Avenue, Englewood, NJ 07631, (201) 871-1100, (800) 223-7777.

Jammi Direct Marketing Services, 2 Executive Drive, Fort Lee, NJ 07024, (201) 461-8868.

List Services Corporation, 890 Ethan Allen Highway, Ridgefield, CT 06877, (203) 438-0327.

Qualified Lists Corporation, 135 Bedford Road, Armonk, NY 10504, (914) 273-6606.

R. L. Polk & Co., 6400 Monroe Blvd, Taylor, MI 48180, (313) 292-3200.

Roman Managed Lists, Inc., 101 West 31st Street, New York, NY 10001, (212) 695-3838.

Standard Rate & Data Service, 3004 Glenview Road, Wilmette, IL 60091, (312) 441-2153, (800) 323-4601.

Woodruff-Stevens & Associates, 345 Park Avenue S., New York, NY 10010, (212) 685-4600.

W. S. Ponton, 5149 Butler Street, Pittsburgh, PA 15201, (412) 782-2360.

THE SURPLUS/DISCOUNT/CLOSEOUT MARKETS

America is a land of plenty. We have enormous surpluses of many things, especially manufactured goods. When a new product appears—transistor radios, pocket calculators, video-cassette recorders, and many other items—it is often an immediate sellout at high prices. (Small transistor calculators sold for $300 and more when they first appeared, and many people paid up to $2,000 for the first videocassette recorders.) Mass production and subsequent market saturation, plus competition from cheaper models (somebody will always find a way to make it cheaper) drive the prices down, and suddenly manufacturers and dealers are holding huge, slow-moving inventories. Or it may be style changes, bankruptcies, miscalculations, "dumping" by foreign manufacturers, or other misfortunes and chance occurrences that produce such great surpluses of inventory. Whatever the cause, the result is usually the same: The goods become *closeouts*, items offered far below their normal prices, even below their actual cost frequently.

These are all opportunities for dealers, brokers, agents, finders (who don't even have to buy and sell or even see the merchandise to make thousands of dollars as a special kind of middleperson or broker) and other alert and astute individuals.

Some of these entrepreneurs buy the items for resale – in bulk, individually, at wholesale, at retail, by mail, to foreign countries, and perhaps even in other places and by other means. Sometimes these entrepreneurs buy closeout and surplus goods for their scrap or salvage value. (Some products contain valuable metals, such as copper, iron, and gold, for example.)

Some finders work entirely in closeouts, tracking down both buyers with needs for sources and sellers with needs for buyers, matching them up and collecting a finder's fee from one party or the other. Or a finder may act as the agent or broker, buying up only what he or she knows can be resold immediately – usually with a buyer already lined up and waiting to consummate the deal – thus earning more than simply the finder's fee.

Dealing in closeouts is a dynamic and competitive business. Good buys are snapped up quickly. Even a little hesitation may cost you a good opportunity. On the other hand, it can be hazardous to buy closeouts if you do not know your markets and your merchandise. You could get stuck with 20,000 Nehru jackets or maxicoats, or even with a load of defective merchandise, such as telephone answering machines that do not work. You must know what you are doing, but if you do not know your merchandise, it is much safer to be a finder – for then the buyer, not you, takes the risks.

Closeouts can be in virtually anything – clothing, canned goods, machinery, tools, jewelry, raw materials, farm products, or anything else sold in the marketplace. Even the federal government has many closeout sales, getting rid of government surplus, some of it used and not in the best of shape, some nearly new, and some new and never used – even in original packing. Some who deal in closeouts specialize in certain kinds of goods or certain kinds of sources; others wheel and deal freely, ranging widely.

THE OPPORTUNITIES: CASHING IN ON THEM

You can deal in closeouts and surplus in many ways. Here are just a few:

Buying and selling large lots: To do this successfully, you must know both the merchandise and the markets, and it is most helpful to have a "want list." That is a list of buyers and items they are looking for, either at the moment or on a continuing basis, with some data on prices they are willing to pay, terms, and other important information. And when you find some item on your list, be sure to check with your buyer and make sure he or she is still in the market for the item before you commit yourself; it is possible to get stuck with something your intended buyer no longer wants. Of course, if you are going to do the actual buying and selling yourself, you need to have a supply of cash or an established line of credit you can draw on.

You don't have to actually handle the goods, if you have a good, up-to-date want list. You can get on the phone immediately, make your deal with your buyer (actually, your client), have the goods shipped directly to the buyer, although billed to you. You then bill your customer and take your profit.

You can do this as a finder: You'll make a little less profit this way, but you take no risks and need no capital. Buyers and sellers use finders because it's often cheaper and faster than hiring salespeople and purchasing agents, and often a more reliable way to find goods or buyers; it is therefore worth paying 1 to 3 percent (and sometimes even more) to a finder.

Buying for resale at retail: There are several ways to go about this. You can sell through your own surplus or closeout "outlet" store in an established business neighborhood or shopping center. (Some cities today have malls and shopping centers made up completely of such stores.) You can retail your goods at flea markets, country auctions, fairs, roadside stands, or from a van or truck. Or you can sell by mail, as many do.

Buying for resale at wholesale: Again, there are several ways to do this. You can sell to retail stores, surplus/closeout outlets, flea markets, wagon jobbers, and the like. You can warehouse and drop-ship for mail-order/catalog dealers. You can be a wagon-jobber yourself, carrying your merchandise in a van and making sales to retailers, with immediate delivery. And you can use mail order and other methods to recruit dealers, setting them up to sell by mail and either stocking your merchandise as inventory or filling all their orders by drop-shipping.

There are many variants of all these ideas and methods. Any of them will work if you buy wisely and market aggressively.

WHERE/HOW TO FIND CLOSEOUTS/SURPLUS AND FINDER'S-FEE OPPORTUNITIES

First, a note of caution: There are many sources of information on closeouts, surplus, and finder's-fee offers. But this is a dynamic, ever-changing industry and markets change, so some of the listings may be out of date by the time you read this. Moreover, most entrepreneurs in this field have built up their own exclusive lists, which they guard jealously and reveal to no one. Therefore, treat the listing here as a mere starter and build your own exclusive list; it will be your most valuable property.

CLOSEOUT/SURPLUS PUBLICATIONS

To keep up with current markets, you must read all information you can find. Here are some general sources that often prove helpful:

- *The Business Opportunities Digest,* 301 Plymouth Drive, NE, Dalton, GA 30721 (listed earlier) is a particularly rich source of information. Publisher J. F. (Jim) Straw also offers a large number of reports and books of interest.
- Administrative Brokers, 3463 Crowell, Riverside, CA 92504.
- The Auction Block, Box 2412, Chicago, IL 60690.
- *Closeout Report*, 15 W. 38th Street, New York, NY 10018.
- *Army-Navy Store & Outdoor Merchandiser Magazine,* 225 W. 34th Street, New York, NY 10001.

- Institute of Surplus Dealers, 520 Broadway, New York, NY 10012.
- The back pages of the financial section of the *New York Times* Sunday edition usually lists many closeouts and surplus sales. The *Wall Street Journal* also furnishes useful tips.
- Newspaper classified advertisements often list bankruptcy sales, estate states, sales for unpaid taxes, and closeouts. It pays to keep an eye on these, too.

A MORE DIRECT WAY TO FIND CLOSEOUTS AND SURPLUS

Everyone who deals in large quantities of merchandise runs into problems of overinventory, slow-moving items that never catch on with the customers, and similar problems. And every manufacturer has a certain number of *factory seconds* or *irregulars*—merchandise with slight flaws, not perfect enough to qualify as first-class merchandise, yet perfectly useful.

Sometimes the owner of such merchandise will advertise its existence, holding "warehouse sales" to get rid of the surplus inventory. But quite often the goods lie in the warehouse for long periods; no one has had the time or taken the initiative to do something about getting rid of the surplus. If you approach the owners of such merchandise, you will be invited to make an offer. Of course, you must negotiate and buy the merchandise at the right price. But if you are a good negotiator, you can often make an advantageous deal.

Many active and astute closeout dealers make regular buying trips to manufacturers, chain stores, jobbers, and distributors in quest of such inventories. Here is a general approach for doing this: Call on the executive who is most likely to be in charge of unloading excess inventory. He or she will probably be the buyer or marketing manager, depending on the kind of organization, but you can also simply ask who is in charge of disposing of closeouts or surplus inventory. Explain that you are a dealer in such goods.

Often enough, you will find that your prospect has an over-supply of last year's model or even a slow-moving current model, "seconds," clothing in odd sizes, or other items he or she is eager to get rid of. (You may get a somewhat cagey response at first because it is a poor bargaining tactic for the prospect to admit to great distress and great eagerness to unload the inventory. Don't be misled by this.) At this point, you will have to negotiate a price. Don't jump at the first price quoted, no matter how great a bargain it appears to be; you can almost always do a great deal better with a bit of bargaining – offering a far-too-low initial price and negotiating your way up to the best price you can get.

HOW TO ESTIMATE WHAT TO PAY

It's easy to get selling prices. You know what the goods cost you, what your related costs are, and what your profit margin ought to be. It's not so easy to know what to pay, maximum. You have to make an accurate estimate of how much you can get for the goods in resale. But there are some guidelines:

First, you must know the wholesale value. Often a call to a regular jobber/distributor/manufacturer of the goods will get you that figure. If not, calculate the retail price less 40 percent for a maximum wholesale price. Of course, that is far too much for you to pay. You probably have to get the goods for not more than half that wholesale figure, and you probably should start by offering about one-quarter of that figure, no matter what the seller quotes initially. If you pay anywhere close to wholesale prices, you will probably be stuck with goods you can't get your money out of, let alone take a profit. So don't hesitate to offer $1 or $2 (opening price) for items that sell for $10 or $12; you'll be surprised at how often you will get the lot at that price! But don't hesitate to walk away when you can't make a deal for the right price.

FINDER OPPORTUNITIES

Seeking out closeouts and surplus lots is time consuming. And even if dealers did not have to actually go out and spend time to find such lots but were being besieged with offers, they would still have to go look the stuff over and then negotiate a price. That's why a busy dealer will pay finder's fees to others for finding suitable lots. The finder's fee is worth the time saved by the dealer: the finder has *earned* his or her fee.

In short, you can do all the things described here without spending or committing a dime of your own simply by knowing which dealers are willing to pay finder's fees. Then go out and find suitable lots, using the methods described here, do the bargaining and negotiating, reach agreements, and then get back to your client to either close the deal in the client's name or have the client close it, if he or she prefers that. Of course, you should be protected by having a signed agreement with the client.

Proposal Notes and Guidelines

SINK OR SWIM ISSUES

For many kinds of businesses, the proposal is an absolute requisite for success, and it is a valuable asset even when it is not mandatory. In fact, and probably contrary to popular notion, proposals are not used solely to win sales. Far from it—proposals are valuable business tools generally, useful in many situations other than those that involve competing for sales contracts. Wherever there is conflict or controversy, the written proposal serves the useful purpose of helping you think out and reason out your arguments and compromises carefully and in advance, with a far better chance, therefore, of reaching agreement. Here are just a few general examples of the possible needs and uses for a proposal, other than the most common one of responding to a specific request for proposals from a customer:

- Making an offer for goods, real estate, or other property (bid proposals).
- Following up a meeting, casual or formal, with a prospective client, to make a reasoned, thought-out sales presentation.
- Making an appeal for backing—debt financing—from a lending institution of any kind (financial proposals or "loan packages").

- Trying to win equity financing from venture capitalists, private investors, or even prospective full working partners (the business plan).
- Trying to settle any controversial issue with another party or organization, no matter what the issue or the relationship.

GENERAL NATURE OF THE PROPOSAL

All proposals are sales presentations, efforts to win the reader to your views and persuade him or her to the action you want—award you the contract, invest in your company, lend you the money, agree to your offer of settlement, or otherwise come to terms with you. The broad rationale of a proposal, any proposal, is therefore easy enough to define:

1. Identify the issue generally and the concerned parties.
2. Identify the *critical* issue—the *essence* of the true issue—and discuss it.
3. Explore all directly and closely related issues and parties and discuss the alternatives to solve the problem, indicating your own choice and explaining your reasons, as persuasively as you can, for your choice.
4. Identify precisely what you propose be done—usually, what *you* propose to do yourself, explaining your specific plans and rationales for what you propose and for your predictions of success.
5. Tell the reader what your plan will cost and/or what it will produce (if it is an appeal for funds).

Two specific proposal approaches are offered here, one for the pursuit of contracts, the other for the pursuit of financing. If you study these, you will see that the elements listed here inhere in both kinds of proposals, the contract proposal and the business plan, although the latter is far more detailed and extended because it is a generalized model that must be modified and adapted to many different situations. But the basic methodology and rationale are appropriate to, and can be applied to, all proposal situations.

PROPOSAL CONTENT AND FORMAT
(PROJECT PROPOSAL)

I: Introduction

A. Brief statement of who/what you are, general qualifications, and brief précis or abstract of your approach to solving the problem or providing the required service. (Details to be offered in later sections of the proposal.)

B. Concise statement of understanding, to demonstrate that you truly understand the need/problem. (Must be stated in your own words and not as an echo of client's words.)

II: Discussion

Extended discussions of the requirement, analyzing all aspects, identifying problems, exploring and reviewing alternatives, giving pros and cons of each. (This is a key section in which you explain the [alleged] benefits and superiority of your proposed program, and demonstrate the validity of your grasp of the problem, of how to solve it, of how to organize the resources, and otherwise *sell* the idea. Should culminate in a clear explanation of the approach selected and lead logically into the next main topic.)

III: Proposed Project

This is where the specifics should appear:

A. Staffing and organization, resumes of key people, identification of tasks and assignments, quantification of main tasks and labor. (Must demonstrate mastery of requirement by showing ability to plan effectively and in detail.)

B. Project management: procedures, philosophy, methods, controls, anything else relevant to management. (For large projects, this section may have to be subdivided into technical management and administrative/contract management.)

C. Deliverable items: Specify, describe, quantify, as

explained. (These items should be totally compatible, in both quality and quantity, with demonstrated understanding of your requirement and the proposer's theories of methods to satisfy your need.)

D. Schedules: Specify with precision and clarity. (Same rationale as for previous item.)

E. Résumés: Résumés of key staff. (Again, same rationale as for previous items.)

IV: Proposer's Qualifications

Description of proposer, past/recent/current projects, especially those similar to one under discussion, resources, history, organization, key staff, other résumés, testimonial letters, special awards, other pertinent facts.

THE FINANCIAL PROPOSAL OR BUSINESS PLAN

Where aspiring entrepreneurs fail most often is in the tricky business of raising money, whether it is debt financing (borrowing, usually from banks) or equity financing (selling shares in your company). The problem is that bankers, other money lenders, venture capitalists, and other investors do not part with their money casually. They want some kind of assurance that they will get their money back and that it will earn something in the meanwhile.

Your enthusiasm is encouraging, but it is not enough, not nearly enough; lenders and investors want more solid evidence. They want to see a business plan with all the details. Somehow the details, even if they are only your estimates, lend confidence that you know what you are doing; lack of details has the reverse effect.

Although developed with high-technology ventures in mind, the plan described here is readily adaptable to other kinds of ventures. In fact, every business plan must be adapted to the characteristics and circumstances of the business in question, so that any plan may be used as a model, but only in general terms. Moreover, even the carefully tailored business plan may have to be changed spontaneously to suit or adapt to changed conditions. (Venture capitalists and other lenders or investors are well aware of this likelihood and do not expect you to produce a plan graven in granite.) Therefore, the following is a *general guide* for preparing a business plan, offering suggestions in outline form. This plan may must therefore be tailored and adapted to your needs in more than one way:

1. Study each element of the outline carefully and be sure that it is appropriate and fits the business you plan. Make whatever changes are necessary to ensure that fit.
2. Consider business conditions of the moment and make any changes necessary to make your plan a sensible one vis-à-vis market and financial conditions. Be prepared also to review the plan periodically to revise, update, and/or otherwise modify the plan to meet sudden or unexpected changes in business conditions.
3. The model represented here would be adequate for launching a relatively large venture. To adapt it to describing and seeking capitalization for a small venture, you must merely reduce the scope of the coverage, eliminate irrelevant/unneeded items, and so on.

SOME OBSERVATIONS ABOUT BUSINESS PLANS IN GENERAL

- The *executive summary* is critically important. This is a brief summary—two to three pages, in most cases—of the plan. For most prospective investors, the executive summary constitutes that important first impression, because they usually read this first. (It is, in fact, designed to be read first.)
- The plan must be highly *specific*. It must specify products and/or services to be developed and marketed, and where and how these things will be done.(Will you manufacture? Have products manufactured under contract? To whom will you sell? Identify markets. How will you reach your markets?) Avoid vague generalizations here.

- Shun *hyperbole*. Facts are much more impressive and much more convincing. Use nouns and verbs, not adjectives. Avoid superlatives and sweeping claims. They smack of Madison Avenue and arouse immediate suspicions about your sincerity and honesty.
- Trim your language. Verbose plans are a liability, not an asset. Write it all out in your draft—as many pages as you wish. But then edit thoroughly, and that means get it down to 25–40 pages (for most cases).
- Make sure your document looks thoroughly professional, that it shows clear evidence of care with careful proofreading, checking all mathematical data, complete accuracy, and good organization. A plan that is poorly organized and has grammatical and spelling errors and columns of figures with errors to boot does not arouse the prospect's confidence in you!
- Don't go to the other extreme and make it too slick; an overdone, ostentatious document (one with fancy printing, costly paper and binders, overly elaborate and unnecessary illustrations, and other such frills) is likely to arouse misgivings in lenders and investors. Prospects are quite likely to regard this as evidence of poor judgment and financial irresponsibility, at best, and possibly even of an attempt to "snow" or "con" them.
- Use positive language. Avoid vague disclaimers, such as "might," "probably," "maybe," "perhaps," and similar terms. They reflect doubts and so stifle the prospect's enthusiasm for your plan.

AN OUTLINE

I. Nondisclosure Agreement

A nondisclosure agreement should appear in the front matter of the plan. It states that the information in the plan is proprietary and is not to be shared, copied, disclosed, or otherwise compromised. It calls for the reader to agree to respect those conditions. The actual agreement can be verbal or can take the form of signed documentation. It may, in fact, have a line for the reader's signature. Investors, however, are often hesitant to sign such an agreement, believing that it ties their hands too much, and you may have to negotiate on that matter.

II. Control Numbering

It is a good idea to number each copy of the plan and keep a record of each copy—to whom issued and when. Much of the information in the plan is proprietary, whether the prospective investor has signed an agreement or not, and it is a good idea to keep track of all copies.

III. The Executive Summary

In a way this is the most important part of the plan, as mentioned earlier, because it is what investors read first. It should be the "hook" that will capture the investor's interest and persuade him or her to study the entire plan.

In practice, the executive summary will be the last thing you write because you do not have anything to summarize until you have drawn up the plan! Moreover, the executive summary must include the most important and most persuasive elements of your plan, and you can't be sure in advance what these will be. This outline, however, presents the order in which the elements of the plan will appear and so will be discussed here.

Keep the executive summary as short as possible: one to three pages. It should summarize the main points but focus on the heaviest assets, for although its ostensible purpose is to give the investor a brief overview, its hidden agenda is to generate immediate interest and enthusiasm. It should, however, include the following specific information, albeit in summary style:

- *The Company*
  When formed (or when to be formed)?
  For what purpose?
    design a new product
    manufacture
    market
    other

- *The Product(s)/Service(s)*
  What are you selling?
  What makes it better/unique?
  Is it a proprietary product?
  At what stage is its development?
  Comparison with competition
    pricing
    quality
    other

- *The Market*
  Current/estimated size (basis for figures)
  Domestic/international
  Recent growth (cite sources)
  Projected growth (cite sources)
  Estimated company market share

- *Financial*
  Financing sought
    for what purposes?
    will carry company how far?
  Five-year revenue and net income projections
  Projection of when profits will begin (2-4 years?)

- *Management*
  How complete is the team?
  Brief past experience
  Highlight strengths

IV. Other Front Matter

The principal other front matter (in addition to the nondisclosure statement and the executive summary) are the title page and the table of contents. The title page is usually a replica of the cover, with the addition of a date and a control number. The table of contents lists chapters or sections, by title, and usually includes also a list of tables and a list of illustrations. The latter would include graphs and charts, in most cases, but might also contain drawings and photographs, if they are relevant or necessary to help the investor understand the venture and develop faith in it and in the founders.

The chapters or sections normally found include most, sometimes all, of the following:

The Organization

The Market(s)

Marketing Strategy/Plans

The Product(s)/Service(s)

The Development Plan

The Operations/Manufacturing Plan

Management Plans

Financial Needs, Plans, and Projections

V. The Organization

In this section a more detailed description of the company is made, but it is essentially the full details that were reviewed briefly in the executive summary, including most or all of the following items:

- When the organization was (or is to be) founded and by whom? Who are the principals and main executives?
- What is the organization structure to be? (Charts?)
- What markets will be pursued?
- Is the company creating/planning to create new demand, anticipating new demand, or responding to existing demand? (Cite sources/bases for conclusions.)
- What will the products do for buyers? Reduce costs; improve efficiency; other.
- Who are the buyers (not specifically, but in general, i.e., disk drive manufacturers, appliance retailers, other)?
- How many people in the company now; how many expected in the future?
- What technologies being used in production?

Generally, this section will run two to five pages in length and will serve to highlight details covered in greater depth in later sections.

VI. The Market

This is for many by far the most difficult section to write because it is almost always most difficult to foresee marketing developments — opportunities, changes, and problems in the markets. Consequently, this section may require the greatest effort, for it must be specific and detailed, too. Moreover, it is most important to cite sources and explain the basis for estimates.

- *Market size*
  Recent
  Current
  Projected (five to ten years)

- *Market trends*
  Where is the market going and why?
  What are the relevant trends?
  Maturity of market — growth stage or level?

- *Products in the market*
  What is available?
  How many suppliers?

- *Market players*
  Who is buying? OEMS, wholesalers, end users, others?
  Why are they buying?
  What are they looking for?
  On what factors are buy decisions made?

- *Market segments*
  Natural splits — geographic, industries, volume vs. unit buyers, etc.
  Growth prospects within each segment

- *Market distribution*
  How are products delivered to buyers?
    direct sales
    manufacturers' representatives
    distributors

- *Competition*
  Who are they?

Strengths?
Weaknesses?
Markets addressed (segments)?
Reputation?

- *Marketing/financial projections*
  Retained earnings (loss)
  Total liabilities and equity

As supporting documentation to the financial projections, notes should be included detailing assumptions, payment policies, receivable policies, and the like.

The better you know your competition, the better you'll be able to plan around them (and the more you'll impress potential investors). Good information about competitors adds a great deal of strength to the plan. Here are just a few of the many possible sources for gathering intelligence about the market and the other players (competitors) in it:

- *Existing manufacturers*: (competitors) write for their product brochures.

- *Interviews*: ask marketing people (which requires a degree of brashness, but don't be timid in asking a potential competitor to lunch to pick his or her brain). You can succeed at this surprisingly often.

- *Trade publications*: if you don't know what's available, ask someone who does; call editors for further suggestions on sources. Visit your public library; there are many directories of trade publications.

- *Analysts' reports and annual reports*: available from many securities brokers (Merrill Lynch; Hambrecht & Quist, others).

- *Users of existing products*: such as purchasing directors and manufacturing directors.

- *Potential customers*: it is an absolute must that you have as many discussions as possible with users before, during, and after formation of the company. Their feedback should be incorporated into both your products and plans.

VII. Marketing/Sales Strategy

After describing the market, explain here how you plan to reach prospective buyers and sell them.

- *Target market by segment*
  Geographic
  Industry
  Type of buyer

Identify the market niche you will pursue and explain your rationale for the decision. What is it about the segment that makes it right for your company? Is it a niche ignored by competitors or ill served by competitors? If you go into it and make a profit, why won't a larger competitor enter it, also? (Furnish reasons for your conclusions.) Cover the following topics also in presenting the rationale for your marketing decisions and plans:

- *Credibility:* company and product, why should customers buy a new product or buy from a new and unproven company?

- *Pricing strategy:* high, medium, or low relative to market? Why?

- *Warranty policies:* standard or nonstandard?

- *Image targets:* quality, reliability, service, response time — all are key components in imaging and should fit neatly with other strategies. Be especially careful to explain and justify apparent anomalies, such as the promise of highest quality at lowest prices.

- *Advertising and public relations:* again, these strategies should match with other strategies and tactics. For example, are you choosing the most appropriate media for advertising and other marketing activity?

- *Distribution channels (getting the product/service to the customer)*
  Factory distribution
  Company-owned regional distribution
  Independent remote distribution
  Order long-lead items

- *Servicing (servicing of products – how, where?)*
  Factory-only service
  Company field service engineers
  Contracted service
  Service contracts
    profit centers
    loss leaders

- *Sales*
  Direct sales
  Reps
  Distributors
  Hybrid

How are you going to actually sell the product? If you use manufacturers' representatives, rather than house salespeople, what kind of incentives will you use to get them to handle, learn, and promote your products? Is special skill (e.g., engineering or computer knowledge) required to sell it? At what level in the buyers' organizations will sales be made? Should senior management in your company participate directly in the sales effort to establish company and product credibility? How will you compensate sales – Commissions? Bonus? Salary? Other?

VIII. Products

Provide a detailed description of existing products and plans for future products. Are products market-ready and, if not, how long until they will be? Provide a description (illustration, if appropriate) and the following:

Bill of materials (major components, not too detailed)

Potential component supply problems

Proprietary protection (trademark, copyright, patent)

Advantages/disadvantages to competing products

Price and cost

Differentiation from competition: Here, a high-level matrix comparing your product's capabilities, strengths, and characteristics to your competitors' is useful. (Be sure your product is more easily visible in the matrix—bold face print at top of matrix is appropriate.)

You may want to include a section on future products describing:

Innovations to existing line
New products
Development time lines

IX. Manufacturing/Research & Development

Depending on the nature of your company, these two areas might more appropriately be separated. Elaborate on the following:

- *Financial resources to be committed to R&D*
  How much?
  With what goals?

- *Facilities requirements*
  Leased
  Purchased

- *Labor requirements*
  Local labor pool
  Skilled
  Unskilled
  Full time/part time

- *Subcontracted production*
  Sole or multisourced
  Quality control
  Supply problems

- *Capital needs*
  Equipment list
  Financial requirements

- *Quality control*

- *Critical processes*

- *Seasonality*

- *Inventory control*

X. Management

This is as important as any other subject, even marketing, for investors must have confidence in management before they will risk their money. Highlight the past experiences of the management team that will combine to reduce the risk typically associated with a startup venture. Remember the venture capital axiom that a mediocre product with great management is always a better gamble that the reverse — a great product with mediocre or poor management. Investors are well aware of that truism. Include the following:

Résumés of top people. Avoid excessive detail, but do hit on important past accomplishments and experience; include references with phone numbers.

Functional responsibilities. Who will handle what?

Important management vacancies. Important functional areas are not currently filled; what steps are being taken to fill them?

XI. Financial

Although underlying detail should be available for further discussion, financial projections should include high-level figures, not line item detail, department by department. Present five-year projections, monthly for at least the first year (but not more than two) and quarterly or annually for the remaining years.

- *Profit and loss statement*
  Units sold
  Reserves
  Costs of goods sold
  Operating expenses
  Net income (loss)

- *Cash budgets*
  Beginning cash
  Cash from operations
    sales
    interest
  Cash from other sources
    investors
    lenders
  Cash uses
    capital expenditures
    cash operating expenses
    cash interest expense
  Ending cash

- *Balance sheet*
  Current assets
    cash, investments
    receivables
    inventory
    other
  Fixed assets
    machinery and equipment
    accumulated depreciation
  Total assets
  Current liabilities
    accounts payable
    notes payable
    other
  Long-term liabilities
    notes to officers

term debt
    other
Equity
    paid in capital
    retained earnings (loss)
Total liabilities and equity

As supporting documentation to the financial projections, notes should be included detailing assumptions, payment policies, receivable policies, depreciation utilized, and any other information used in generating the figures.

Government Markets

GOVERNMENT MARKETS

Government is not a single market. It is a whole population of markets. Not only are there hundreds of agencies — departments, commissions, administrations, and other organizations — but many of these entities contain multiple markets. Monolithic though the government may appear, it is remarkably unstandardized and diverse in many ways. Therefore, although you should make all efforts to learn the official procurement regulations in general, it is also necessary to understand that each agency has its own policies. For example, although the law permits the federal agencies to spend up to $25,000 via government purchase order, the agency's contracting officer or other top official may restrict that to some lesser amount as the maximum that can be spent without an official and formal contract.

In general, the best government prospects are the organizations that have their own in-house departments or special offices for whatever it is that you do. That sounds like a strange idea to those not familiar with how large organizations do things, but the explanation is quite simple: The existence of a separate organization for such functions, as distinct from burying these functions in another office, demonstrates that the agency has regular or at least frequent need for such work. Such organizations are characteristically often overloaded and need help. In practice you will therefore usually find many more sales opportunities in this type of governmental agency.

Sometimes an organization does not by its nature furnish any definitive clues to its probable opportunities as a market. I once found the Value Management offices of the General Services Administration, an engineering office, a rich lode of contracts for writing for several years. And the Wind Energy Office of the then Energy Research and Development Administration was another totally unexpected and unsuspected opportunity. You must be alert for such windfalls, too.

Over recent decades, the governments in the United States have become increasingly large and important as a set of markets. The U.S. Census Bureau identifies 38,777 federal, state, and local (county, city, and municipality) governments. But the bureau includes with these 41,136 school and special districts, thus identifying 79,913 "governmental units," each with its own purchasing power. With federal government purchasing at over $200 billion and purchasing by state and local governments in excess of twice that figure, government represents a set of markets difficult for aggressive businesses to ignore. And where the bulk of purchasing by governments was once earmarked for public works — buildings, bridges, highways, and similar facilities — today governments at all levels purchase a broad variety of goods and services, virtually all that are offered anywhere to anyone.

A few insights are offered here. However, you can get a great deal of useful information directly from the government's own Federal Procurement Data Center (FPDC), which is part of the Office of Federal Procurement Policy (OFPP), of the Office of Management and Budget (OMB). The General Services Administration prepares and issues a number of reports gathered by the FPDC and available on request from the following office:

Federal Procurement Data Center
4040 N. Fairfax Drive, Suite 900
Arlington, VA 22203
(703) 235-1326

THE FEDERAL SYSTEM

In the federal system, the big spender by far is the Department of Defense, accounting for at least 80 percent of all federal spending. That fact by no means diminishes the importance of other federal agencies, however.

Government Decentralization

Organizationally, the first level below the president in the executive branch of government are the departments, each of which is represented by a head who is a member of the president's cabinet. Thus, the Department of Defense (DOD) is headed by a cabinet officer. Within DOD, however, there are three military agencies, the Army, the Navy, and the Air Force, each of which is also called "Department of" (the Army, the Navy, and the Air Force), although none of these rates a cabinet officer at its head. (The U.S. Marine Corps is part of the Navy, of course, and the U.S. Coast Guard is part of the Department of Transportation [DOT], although it reverts to the Navy in time of war.)

The DOD procurement expenditures reported by the Federal Procurement Data System and cited in part here are for all military procurement, but only a small fraction of that procurement is made in Washington and/or by DOD itself. By far the bulk of the purchasing is done by the military units, and not entirely at department levels, either, but often directly by the individual military organizations at the various bases.

Each of the services has some centralized procurement. The Navy, for example, maintains extensive centralized headquarters offices in the Virginia suburbs of Washington and does much of its major procurement there, although the Navy maintains busy purchasing offices in California and other states. The other two military departments do their procurement on a far more decentralized basis, with relatively little of it in Washington. And DOD has its own centralized procurement activities in the Defense Logistics Agency and other DOD support agencies.

What is true for the military is equally true for other federal departments and agencies, virtually all of whom have a number of offices and installations scattered throughout the United States and even in foreign countries.

Whether all of this is the most efficient way to organize a government bureaucracy and/or to procure needed goods and services is a moot point, but this is the way it is done. It offers the advantages of diversity and, probably, far greater opportunities for small businesses, consultants, and other entrepreneurs.

The Basic Structure

The federal government today includes these departments:

Department of Agriculture

Department of Commerce

Department of Defense
  Department of the Air Force
  Department of the Army
  Department of the Navy

Department of Education

Department of Energy

Department of Health and Human Services

Department of the Interior

Department of Labor

Department of Transportation

Department of Veterans' Affairs

All of these departments have regional offices, and most have numerous subordinate "offices of," "administrations," and other organizations in their infrastructure. In turn, some of these have their own regional offices and field offices, laboratories, bases, and other physical facilities. The result is that many of these departments actually represent large and complex networks of organizations and facilities. But they still represent only part of the federal establishment, which also supports some sixty "independent agencies" of the federal government, some of them as large as the larger departments, others rather small. Some of these are also large complexes of subordinate organizations, offices, and facilities, every bit as imposing as the departments. The following are the most significant, in size and purchasing power, as potential markets (although this is not to say that some of those small agencies not listed here may not be occasional customers, too):

> Agency for International Development
>
> Environmental Protection Agency
>
> Equal Employment Opportunity Commission
>
> Federal Communications Commission
>
> Federal Emergency Management Agency
>
> Federal Trade Commission
>
> General Services Administration
>
> National Aeronautical and Space Administration
>
> National Science Foundation
>
> Nuclear Regulatory Commission
>
> Office of Personnel Management
>
> Peace Corps
>
> Tennessee Valley Authority
>
> U.S.Information Agency

Wheels Within Wheels

Many well-known and busy agencies are not on this list because they are part of some department and therefore not independent. In fact, often the subordinate agency is better known than is the department to which it belongs. The Occupational Safety and Health Administration (OSHA) is probably one of those. Relatively few people not concerned directly with OSHA in some manner are aware that it is part of the Labor Department.

The following are some of the more well-known and important (from the marketing viewpoint) agencies within departments and major independent agencies (note, however, that in most cases these are not all the agencies within the departments and other major agencies):

- *Department of Agriculture:* Forest Service, Soil Conservation Services, Farmers Home Administration
- *Department of Commerce:* Maritime Administration, Minority Business Development Agency, National Bureau of Standards, National Oceanic and Atmospheric Administration, National Technical Information Services, Bureau of the Census, Office of Telecommunications, United States Travel Service
- *Department of Defense:* Defense Advanced Research Projects Agency, Defense Communications Agency, Defense Intelligence Agency, Defense Logistics Agency, Defense Contract Administrative Services, National Security Agency, Department of the Air Force, Department of the Army, Department of the Navy. (Note: Each military department has a number of commands, generally for training, systems development and management, electronics, materiel, supply services, personnel, communications, and whatever major weapons systems—aircraft, tanks, ships, etc.—are peculiar to that military service.)
- *Department of Health and Human Services:* Public Health Service; Alcohol, Drug Abuse, and Mental Health Administration; Food and Drug Administration; National Institutes of Health
- *Department of the Interior:* National Park Service, Bureau of Geological Survey, Bureau of Indian Affairs, Bureau of Land Management
- *Department of Labor:* Employment and Training Administration, Employment Standards Administration, Occupational Safety and Health Administration
- *Department of Transportation:* Coast Guard, Federal Aviation Administration, Federal Highway Administration, Federal Railroad Administration, National Highway Traffic Safety Administration, Urban Mass Transportation Administration
- *General Services Administration:* Automated Data and Telecommunications Service, Federal Supply Service, Public Buildings Service, National Archives and Records Service

STATE AND LOCAL GOVERNMENTS

The state and local government markets are not exactly microcosms of the federal government, but there are many parallels and similarities nevertheless, with size one measure.

The fifty states of the United States vary widely in size, of course, in terms of both geography and population. The largest geographically is Alaska, a huge land mass, more than twice the size of the formerly largest state, Texas. Ironically enough, Alaska is also the smallest in population, having a smaller population than even such sparsely populated states as Wyoming, Montana, New Mexico, and Nevada, and even smaller than those of such tiny states as Rhode Island and Delaware. On the other hand, California is our most populous state, although New York State is not far behind California in population count.

Taking the state governments together as a set of markets, some are better prospects than others simply because they are bigger markets: They buy more, in terms of both total procurement dollars and diversity of needs. One index to market size is the size of the state in terms of population, because the population is an index to the tax base, and the sizes of procurement budgets bear a direct relationship to the tax base. Here are the fifty states, in descending order of approximate population:

STATE	POPULATION (millions)	STATE	POPULATION (millions)
California	20.0	Indiana	5.2
New York	18.2	North Carolina	5.1
Pennsylvania	11.8	Missouri	4.7
Texas	11.2	Virginia	4.7
Illinois	11.1	Georgia	4.6
Ohio	10.7	Wisconsin	4.4
Michigan	8.9	Maryland	3.9
New Jersey	7.2	Tennessee	3.9
Montana	7.0	Minnesota	3.8
Florida	6.8	Louisiana	3.6
South Dakota	6.7	Alabama	3.4
Massachusetts	5.7	Washington	3.4

STATE	POPULATION (millions)	STATE	POPULATION (millions)
Kentucky	3.2	Utah	1.1
Connecticut	3.1	New Mexico	1.0
Iowa	2.8	Maine	1.0
South Carolina	2.6	Rhode Island	1.0
Oklahoma	2.6	Hawaii	0.8
Kansas	2.2	Idaho	0.7
Colorado	2.2	New Hampshire	0.7
Mississippi	2.2	North Dakota	0.6
Oregon	2.1	Delaware	0.5
Arkansas	1.9	Nevada	0.5
Arizona	1.8	Vermont	0.4
West Virginia	1.7	Wyoming	0.3
Nebraska	1.5	Alaska	0.3

Industrialization Is a Factor

California and New York State are among our most highly industrialized states, in dollar volume and diversity of industry, as well as in numbers of industrial workers. So it is no great mystery that these two and several other states rival the federal government in the diversity and activity of procurement, if not in total dollar volumes of purchasing. In fact, if we compare the lists of goods and services normally purchased by each—the purchasing of the federal government versus that of California, for example—we find a remarkable similarity. (Even the supply classification numbers are almost identical.)

Purchasing by State and Local Governments

Where federal government procurement is largely decentralized, procurement by state and local governments has the opposite orientation. It tends strongly to be centralized in a purchasing and supply organization in the state capitol, county seat, city hall, and town hall. Even those central organizations, however, do delegate certain purchases to various agencies within the state or local government. (And these are surprisingly numerous in even states of modest size.) For example,

California's Office of Procurement (Department of General Services, Sacramento) buys no services but delegates to each state agency its own purchasing authority to buy engineering, programming, consulting, and other services, as necessary. Figures on California's total annual procurement are not readily ascertainable because of the decentralization of many classes of procurement, especially of procurement of services, but they are obviously in the multibillion-dollar range.

New York State also reports a highly diversified list of goods and services purchased regularly. The central Standards and Purchase Group (Office of General Services in Albany) alone accounts for nearly $1 billion annually. Like California and many other jurisdictions, New York State authorizes its many state agencies to negotiate separately for services they require. This again makes it difficult to determine with any accuracy the total state-government spending for all goods and services. However, New York State's commodity lists, as an example, list the typical broad diversity of goods bought more or less regularly, which ensures that related services must also be required. And there is no doubt that procurement and purchasing by New York State rival those of the purchasing divisions of other major state governments.

California, New York, and many other states and even local governments also rival the federal establishment in the diversity and number of state agencies, bureaus, and institutions scattered across their states. Each state government is articulated with many kinds of official support organizations, and many of these have a number of offices throughout their respective states. So the fifty states actually represent upward of 10,000 or more potential customers—for, as in the case of the federal and commercial markets, many of the commodities and services respond to a horizontal market rather than a vertical one.

A Typical State Purchasing Organization

North Carolina, with a population of approximately 5 million, is both agricultural and industrial, has a fair share of high-tech industries, and is fairly representative of the most states in its purchasing policies and methods. Its Division of Purchase and Contract is similar to many other such organizations: It includes seven procurement teams, a purchasing consulting group, a data processing group, and a staff group that reports to a purchasing official in charge of the entire operation.

Major Cities

There are about 125 major metropolitan areas in the United States. These are 125 of the country's approximately 18,000 incorporated communities (cities, towns, and townships), taken together with their suburban environs and including over 125 of the nation's 3,000-odd counties. Some of these coincide with major centers of federal procurement activity, but all are important elements in terms of local government markets—in terms, that is, of their own purchasing power. All have their own government structures, which include a purchasing office and staff in the city hall or county executive building. In some cases, city boundaries and county boundaries coincide (as in the case of Philadelphia, for example), and in some cases city and county purchasing are merged, wholly or in part.

I conducted a broad survey of local government purchasing, of which the following appear to be typical of the pattern generally:

The Central Purchasing Department of the City of San Diego reported about $45 million in purchasing generally, excluding certain kinds of purchases and including, primarily, purchases of items for central stock in its own supply department, listing a staff of nine, including six buyers.

The City of Milwaukee operates a Central Board of Purchases, headed by a city purchasing agent.

The City of Memphis includes a purchasing agent in its Division of Finance and Administration and says,

> This department purchases all goods and services required by all City Divisions including the Park Commission. Exclusions are: the School System, Memphis Light, Gas and Water Division, City of Memphis Hospitals, and all

Shelby County Government agencies such as the Sheriff's Department, the City/County Health Department, and the Library System.

The City of Oakland Purchasing Department operates with a staff of several buyers, has a thoroughly structured set of procedures and policies, and specifically excludes about a dozen city/county agencies for which it does not buy, such as the school district, the local housing authority, and the local utility companies.

Some Major Counties

For purposes of illustration only, here are a few of the larger counties in the United States (1 million or more population) along with their population figures. (There is no particular significance to the order in which the counties are listed because the list is exemplary only. Not surprisingly, however, the larger ones generally include a major city and even a major metropolitan area.)

COUNTY	POPULATION (millions)	COUNTY	POPULATION (millions)
Los Angeles, CA	7.032	Nassau, NY	1.429
Orange, CA	1.420	New York, NY	1.539
Alameda, CA	1.073	Queens, NY	1.987
Santa Clara, CA	1.065	Suffolk, NY	1.127
Dade, FL	1.268	Allegheny, PA	1.605
Cook, IL	5.492	Philadelphia, PA	1.949
Middlesex, MA	1.398	Dallas, TX	1.327
Wayne, MI	2.667	Harris, TX	1.742
Bronx, NY	1.472	King, WA	1.157
Erie, NY	1.114	Milwaukee, WI	1.054
Kings, NY	2.602		

In most cases the county has its own purchasing office, especially if it is a county of some size. (Despite the relatively small number of counties of over 1 million population, there are many counties of several hundred thousand population, as well as a few of only a scant thousand or two.)

State and local governments advertise their requirements in the daily newspaper classified columns under *Bids and Proposals*. Be sure to keep an eye on those listings, and visit procurement offices in your state capital, county seat, and city or town hall.

INDEX